Harpur, T.
Born again.

PRICE: $32.95

MAR 2011

Books of Merit

Born Again

TOM HARPUR

BORN AGAIN

My Journey From Fundamentalism to Freedom

Thomas Allen Publishers
Toronto

Library and Archives Canada Cataloguing in Publication

Harpur, Tom
Born again : my journey from fundamentalism to freedom / Tom Harpur.

ISBN 978-0-88762-738-5

1. Harpur, Tom.   2. Harpur, Tom—Religion.
3. Spiritual biography.   4. Newspaper editors—Canada—
Biography.   5. Journalists—Canada—Biography.   I. Title.

PN4913.H36A3 2011   070.92   C2010-907344-4

Editor: Patrick Crean
Jacket and text design: Gordon Robertson
Jacket image: Andy & Michelle Kerry / Trevillion Images

Published by Thomas Allen Publishers,
a division of Thomas Allen & Son Limited,
390 Steelcase Road East,
Markham, Ontario L3R 1G2 Canada

www.thomasallen.ca

ONTARIO ARTS COUNCIL
CONSEIL DES ARTS DE L'ONTARIO

Canada Council
for the Arts

The publisher gratefully acknowledges the support of
The Ontario Arts Council for its publishing program.

We acknowledge the support of the Canada Council for the Arts, which
last year invested $20.1 million in writing and publishing throughout Canada.

We acknowledge the Government of Ontario through the
Ontario Media Development Corporation's Ontario Book Initiative.

We acknowledge the financial support of the Government of Canada
through the Canada Book Fund for our publishing activities.

1 2 3 4 5   15 14 13 12 11

Printed and bound in Canada by Transcontinental Printing.
Text Printed on a 100% PCW recycled stock.

For Susan
She always will know why

But we cannot live the afternoon of life according to the program of life's morning—for what was great in the morning will be little at evening, and what in the morning was true will at evening have become a lie.

— C.G. JUNG, Modern Man in Search of a Soul

Contents

Wanderlust

The wanderlust is calling, is calling, is calling,
the wanderlust is calling
from lands across the sea;
the wanderlust is calling
and I know it's calling me.

From Inca ruins in Peru
all wrapped in silent wonder;
from castle walls whose towers once knew
the roar of cannon thunder;
there comes a small voice beckoning me
in clear persistent tones,
to seek adventure and romance in
new terrestrial zones.

The wanderlust is calling, is calling, is calling,
the wanderlust is calling
and the tide is on the race.
I'll port my helm, unfurl my sails,
and paths of heroes trace.

— Written by Tom Harpur, aged sixteen,
for the 1945 edition of the Malvern High
School yearbook, *The Malvern Muse*

1

SURPRISED
BY GOD

MANY READERS of this book will be aware that in the spring of 2004, just before Easter and within days of my seventy-fifth birthday, my world was rocked by the publication of *The Pagan Christ*. I was thrown suddenly into the centre of a whirling vortex of controversy, praise, criticism and media attention such as I had never experienced before. Already a bestseller even before its official "pub date," the book remained at the top of several Canadian bestseller lists for many months, and the *Toronto Star* and the *Globe and Mail* later judged it to be the number-one bestseller of the year. The book and its author were attacked with vitriol by conservative critics in all camps, while emails of gratitude and congratulation began to flow in by the hundreds from an ever-widening circle of avid readers whose primary emotions seemed those of joy at release from old, religion-induced fears and of renewed spiritual energy at now being freed to get on with a rational trust in God. My publisher and chief editor, forty-year publishing veteran Patrick Crean at Thomas Allen Publishers, said publicly that *The Pagan Christ* "is the most radical and important book I have ever worked on." We could scarcely keep up with media requests for interviews, while simultaneously several TV producers were vying for the film rights. Eventually, CBC and an independent producer, David Brady Productions, won out. There was also a behind-the-scenes tug-of-war for foreign rights. The book went on to sell in the United States, Australia and New Zealand, and in translation in France, Holland, Germany, Japan and Brazil.

Put in its simplest form, the message of *The Pagan Christ* is that the Christian story, taken literally as it has been for centuries, is a misunderstanding of astounding proportions. Sublime myth has been wrongly understood as history, and centuries of book burnings, persecutions and other horrors too great to be numbered were the result. The light crying out to be rediscovered is that every human being born into the world has the seed or spark of the Divine within; it's what we do with that reality that matters. Building upon the work of earlier scholars, I set out my reasons for being unable to accept the flimsy putative "evidence" for Jesus's historicity. In its stead I made the case for the Isis–Osiris–Horus myth of ancient Egypt as the prototype of a much later Jewish version of the same narrative. The media jumped on that as their leading theme. The message of my follow-up book *Water into Wine* leads on from there. Its thesis is that the "old old story" is indeed the oldest story in human history, and it focuses upon us. The story of the Christ is the story of every man, woman and child on the face of the earth. The miracles, rather than being snipped out of the text with scissors à la Thomas Jefferson (who did it to solve the problem of their otherwise seeming to contradict the very laws of physics said to be God's own creation), are shown to be allegories of the power of the divine within us all. Read as historical, they border on the ludicrous. Read as allegory and metaphor, they shine with contemporary potency for one's daily life.

Obviously, for a theologian who had become a freelance journalist with the express objective of reaching the greatest possible number of people with a genuine message of faith and hope in terms they could readily comprehend, it was an exciting, even thrilling moment in which to be alive. Everything before that took on the aura of a guided preparation for this peak adventure. But it was a very stressful time as well. I had challenged traditional religious doctrines and taboos in a wholly radical way and the guardians of orthodoxy were not about to take that without a fight. While there were many clergy of all denominations among the enthusiastic readers of *The Pagan Christ*, and subsequently of *Water into Wine*, there were also those who felt it their duty to attack these books vigorously in print, on TV, in the lecture hall or from the pulpit. A few former clerical friends disappeared into the woodwork altogether, while many admitted they had no intention of upsetting their beliefs by exposing themselves to "heresy." In other words, they were afraid to have to rethink in any way what they have chosen always to preserve "as it was in the beginning, is now and evermore shall be, Amen."

Looking back to even my earliest memories, I realize how deeply rooted was the impulse to search for and know God—and at the same time to possess a reasoned, reasonable faith open to everyone and not just to holy huddles of specially chosen ones. This is far from saying that I held reason alone to be the sole path to that ultimate mystery. As the familiar words of Blaise Pascal in his *Pensées* remind us, "The heart has its reasons which reason knows nothing of." However, our greatest gift as human beings is our faculty of self-reflective consciousness (our ability to think about what it is we are thinking and feeling)—in other words, our ability to think rationally. What we hold to be true about God must never contradict or oppose reason. Thus, for example, while I believe the current mushrooming crop of atheists, however vocal or eloquent they may be, to be very mistaken, I have a great deal of sympathy for their sense of exasperation or even disgust at much of the pious, popular religion of our time that has little use for reason at all.

This morning I received a letter from a young New Zealand woman who has just written her first novel. Speaking of *The Pagan Christ* and *Water into Wine* in particular, she wrote: "Your work gave

me the courage to journey where I felt my soul had always been."
Interestingly, that has been the overwhelming message carried by
the response to both volumes. I say this with the greatest sense of
humility because of my commitment to the belief that the Holy
Spirit of God does indeed guide and inspire us all the days of our
lives no matter how often we stumble or fall. Indeed, one of the
things I believe the discerning reader will find in the narrative that
follows here—and may well recognize from a similar phenomenon
in his or her own life—is that events or insights which initially
seem isolated and perhaps unconnected to anything else often can
suddenly become pregnant with meaning, linked together, illumin-
ing a far larger landscape than was anticipated at first.

Reflection since the momentous happenings of Easter 2004 and
then Easter 2007, when *Water into Wine* first appeared, has shown
me very dramatically that neither of these books dropped from the
sky. As what follows illustrates, they came as the product of many
years of study, travel and experiences of many kinds. Yes, there was
much immediate, painstaking research in the laborious months
before publication, but all the major themes were already there,
percolating throughout the length of an eventful life. My editors
encouraged me to digest the research but above all to use my own
"voice" in the light of a lifetime of experience, and that is eventually
what happened. I had finally found a way to make sense of the traditional Christianity in which I had been reared and professionally
trained and to which I owed so much in a way that resonated with
my heart as well as my intellect.

To my mind, the process I'm describing is somewhat like that of
the prospector of an earlier era who spent his entire lifetime search-
ing for an elusive treasure. There were moments when his journey
up winding creek beds and over mountain trails seemed bleak and
void of purpose. But from time to time he would catch amidst all
the debris and seeming chaos around him a tiny gleam of gold, the

promise that the reality was there somewhere to be found. Then one day, perhaps when and where he least expected it, the true mother-lode was revealed to him and he rushed to share the good news. Using this as an analogy, I now see that the creation of *The Pagan Christ* and *Water into Wine* was a kind of spiritual alchemy. The dross of weary-making traditionalism and the emptiness of outworn and in some cases enslaving dogmas had in spite of themselves been car-riers of a buried wisdom. There truly was some spiritual gold to be found buried and hidden in "them there tired ecclesiastical hills."

When I was preparing for my final examinations in Classics at Oxford, my tutor in philosophy, Richard Robinson, called me to his study for a brief chat. He was a man who made a habit of taking long pauses for thought before he ever spoke a word. At times it was almost alarming, as if he'd forgotten what he was going to say. But he definitely had not. It's a habit many of us could well emulate, to everyone's profit! On this somewhat solemn occasion he said to me: "Harpur, let me give you a word of advice. When you get the exam-ination paper, study it well for a few moments. If you see a question you can write something intelligent about, do so. If you don't see such a question, then pick out a question that is itself questionable. Examiners are not infallible. They can be wrong. In any case, you have nothing to lose by taking the question itself apart. Dissect it. Parse it. Put it under scrutiny and show its innate contradictions—if any—or demonstrate how it could have been improved upon or otherwise directed. That will save you from the risk of either writ-ing nothing at all or demonstrating your ignorance in some other fashion. Sometimes challenging the questions themselves is the best path to knowledge I know."

Clearly I have never forgotten those few words of a warm, gen-tle afternoon in the spring of 1954. They are deeply connected with the events of spring 2004, a half century later. From the very begin-ning it's as though I already knew the wisdom of Robinson's insight somewhere deep in my own unconscious mind. Though all through my childhood, youth and years of training for the ordained ministry of the Anglican Church I was a model of conformity, at the same time I was quietly questioning the major questions themselves. The tradition assumed a hubristic superiority over all other faiths. As I matured, I was silently asking myself, was it right that a white man's saviour was the only mediator or redeemer of the many billions here on earth today? And what of the far greater number of billions making up "the majority," as the Romans referred to them, those who have died over the entire span of *Homo sapiens sapiens*' presence on the planet? Why did it take the Church five centuries—not to mention so much bloodshed—to work out its understanding of how Jesus could be wholly God and wholly man without rupturing the basic concept of a truly human humanity entirely? The struggle to make sense of this conundrum is clear in the words of the Athanasian Creed from the Anglican Book of Common Prayer, which says Jesus Christ is "God, of the Substance of the Father, begotten before the worlds: and Man, of the Substance of his Mother, born in the world; Perfect God, and perfect Man: of a reasonable soul and human flesh subsisting; Equal to the Father, as touching his Godhead: and inferior to the Father, as touching his Manhood. Who although he be God and Man: yet he is not two, but one Christ . . ." Based upon Greek philosophy, this makes little or no sense to the average person today.

What kind of religion, I later asked myself, would burn at the stake three of its own bishops in the city of Oxford (a short distance from my own college of Oriel) simply because they could not accept the dogma of transubstantiation, that is, that the symbols of bread and wine actually become Jesus's body and blood in the Mass? Latimer and Ridley, the latter of whom was the Bishop of London, were burned alive in Oxford on October 16, 1555. Cranmer, the Archbishop of Canterbury, was killed on March 21, 1556, for the same offence. The travesty is that, whatever its meaning, Holy

Communion or Mass was meant to bring people together, to enhance life. It certainly has nothing to do with murder. Once again, mistaking symbols for facts had cost—and continues to cost—the Church dearly.

The following narrative tells of a quest for truth. Its goal is hopefully to bring more light. For me, it has been the spiritual journey of a lifetime.

2
BIRTHMARKS ARE FOREVER

IN 1969, I did something that in my teens I'd never expected to do—reach my fortieth birthday. In a Byronic, Romantic mode, I had earlier seen myself as destined for a premature, no doubt spectacular demise in the midst of some high adventure. Reflecting on this development, I was aware that all of the major goals my parents, their friends and various clergy had set before me from the beginning had been reached. I was an ordained priest of the Anglican Church of Canada, a former Rhodes Scholar and hence a graduate of Oxford University as well as the University of Toronto, where I had graduated in 1951 with the gold medal in Classics. I was also a graduate of Wycliffe College, Canada's evangelical Anglican seminary, and had been the class president and valedictorian in my graduating year. Furthermore, I had had a highly successful parish ministry for eight years, highlighted by the building of a beautiful new church to accommodate a large and growing congregation. I had left there in 1964, after another year of graduate studies at Oxford, to become an assistant and then a full professor of New Testament and Greek back at Wycliffe. I was in good health. So too were my then wife and three much-loved daughters. There was every reason for me to be happy with these successes.

"They"—the proverbial and in part shadowy influences that too often one can attempt to live one's life by—were happy. But I was not.

The truth is, I was profoundly miserable. At times I had a feeling of having arrived successfully at a defined destination after having taken the wrong boat. It seemed that I was reaching a major turning point. Deep inside I felt I was bursting with repressed creative energy, but at the same time I was baffled and uncertain about where to go with it. Although it was far from clear at the time, a process was beginning that would utterly transform me at every possible level. I was about to experience a radical series of changes that I now realize was a kind of second birth. It would lead eventually to a total transformation of my understanding of God, of the Christian religion, of human evolution, and of myself. What ensues is the story of how that came to be and of what it led to. Like all births, it happened in stages. Like most, it wasn't always neat.

What follows, then, is not a memoir in the usual sense. It is a spiritual odyssey, the story of one individual's escape from the narrow grip of a rigid, wrong-headed religion. Many who grew up in similar backgrounds have escaped as well, by abandoning their spirituality altogether. In my case the struggle was to hammer out a believable faith in God. Of course, by the traditional term *God*, I mean that transcendent, ever-present "presence" whose offspring, as the ancient Pagans also saw, we truly are. This is the great *mysterium tremendum et fascinosum* of Rudolph Otto—the Mystery that kindles in us both an overwhelming sense of awe and a heart-yearning desire that can never be satisfied with anything less.

The question most often posed in the many hundreds of letters that have poured in over the past few years is this: "How did you come to the radical conclusions set out in 2004 in *The Pagan Christ*? You were once an evangelical preacher, weren't you?" A partial answer is given at the beginning of that book. But the real answer, like most truths worth knowing, can only be fully told in a more detailed narrative. I invite you to come with me on this adventure.

While we all are born as genetic composites of previous generations, our ideas and outlook must of course grow and adapt to our ever-changing surroundings and intellectual development. Over the last fifty years and in the span of only two generations, beliefs and ideas in my own family have changed radically. Few could have predicted the extent of the change in the understanding of God and religion that I am about to describe. But I am fully aware in saying this of the truth of an aphorism attributed to Muhammad Ali: "The person who views the world at fifty the same as he did at twenty has wasted thirty years of his life."

Both my parents were born and raised in Northern Ireland and came from fairly large families, with each of them having six siblings. My maternal grandfather, who always wore a wing collar and a black bowler hat for going to church and other dress occasions, served as an ambulance driver in World War I, and I vividly remember him telling how their convoy was attacked one night by bombs from a German dirigible or blimp and they all had to scramble for cover into a ditch, where they lay for several hours in the cold. He could be very kindly, but his basic demeanour was stern and forbidding. I first met him at the age of nine in 1938 on a visit to Belfast, and soon shared my cousins' view that he was dangerous when provoked. Grandpa Hoey, as he was called, was definitely of the old school where discipline of children was concerned. Following the end of the war he was hired as chauffeur and gentleman's gentleman by a wealthy Belfast industrialist. My grandmother's family name was Cooper and they were from farming stock near Portadown on the coast. She was a jolly, comfortable-looking woman who loved nothing better than being up to her elbows making Irish soda bread.

My mother's family had been Presbyterian for generations, and she too was raised in that somewhat unbending, rigorous mould. She grew up in Belfast when the Troubles were just beginning. She remembered swinging on the lamppost at the corner of her street with two or three other little girls while soldiers nearby crouched behind sandbags with an eye out for snipers. Tragically, one child on her street was killed when a soldier accidentally dropped his rifle and it fired. This incident made quite an impression on me when I first heard about it at the age of six or seven. It was at about the same age that I heard my father, who joined the Ulster special police at sixteen by lying about his age, describe some of the violence of that period, including an account of one night while on duty near a cinema in downtown Belfast when he was set upon and attacked by three Fenians (IRA sympathizers) who immobilized him by suddenly winding his rain cloak about his arms and then proceeded to beat him up.

My father was born in a tiny village in the heart of County Tyrone about sixty miles west of Belfast. When my siblings and I were young, he talked incessantly of Tullyhogue (it means "the hill of the young men" and at one time the kings of Ulster, the O'Neills, were crowned there), and when I first visited it as a child I saw why. It's even today a kind of storybook place. The hill, called Fort Hill by the locals because of the ancient earthworks of a fortification going back to prehistoric days, affords a view of lush green countryside for miles around, and the gleaming waters of Lough Neigh off to the east. At the edge of the village the Tullywiggan River descends swiftly to join the larger Balinderry River, a prime trout and salmon stream flowing into Lough Neigh and from there on to the North Sea. Where the two join, at the foot of Fort Hill, there is a small castle with crenellated towers called Killymoon. In a nearby estate there still stands the rural retreat of Dean Jonathan Swift of *Gulliver's Travels* fame, who used it on his summer vacations when writing. It overlooks the rapids of the Tullywiggan, and the sound of the falling water never ends. I couldn't know on that first brief visit what a part Tullyhogue would play in my later life and how I would grow to love it almost as much as my father did.

My paternal grandfather, Thomas William Harpur, whose full name I was given, was a blacksmith and postmaster by vocation. But his avocation was leading and teaching flute bands throughout the towns and villages of the county and beyond. He was a great reader, though it's difficult to fathom how he found time for it. Books were scarce, but he made great friends with the local Church of Ireland minister and often disappeared up the lane behind his house to call on the rectory and borrow items from the library there. I still remember him in his smithy, hammering at a glowing horseshoe on a huge anvil, plunging it with fierce hissing into the water, and then allowing me to ply the bellows for him as he thrust the shoe back into the fire. He gave me a wonderful penknife and then taught me how to make a passable pocket flute with it from a willow branch.

When I next visited Tullyhogue as a young man of twenty-two, he and Grandma Harpur had both gone to join their forebears in the walled, circular cemetery in a field beyond the village and close to the ancient church. The burial ground is called Donnarisk and whenever I recall it I remember the priory well a few yards outside its perimeter. It has iron caging around it to keep out the cattle, and when you stoop and look into it you can see the grains of white sand at the bottom boiling as the spring bubbles up. That sight fascinated me as a small boy and has somehow reassured me ever since whenever I have had the privilege of going back. It has always been an archetypal image for me of "living water" and of the life of the Spirit in each of us.

Both my parents left school early. My father joined the police in Belfast and my mother worked as a sales clerk in a downtown millinery store. Just before they met—at a fair, near a ride called the roundabouts—a pivotal event occurred that was to have a great

impact not just on their lives but later on those of myself and my
brother and two sisters. A then-famous British evangelist by the
name of Billy Nicholson came to Belfast for a week-long crusade.
He was a somewhat rough, plainspoken man—more like Billy Sunday, another well-known preacher of the period, than Billy Graham
in our own day. The meetings were packed and Nicholson was able
to evoke such a "conviction of sin" and other emotions that local
papers reported how Belfast's main employer, the great shipbuild-
ing works of Harland and Wolff (who crafted the *Titanic*), didn't
know what to do with all the stolen tools that workers who had
been "saved" were returning!

My parents attended the mass rallies independently, and though
both had been raised in a church context from childhood, they went
forward at the altar call to "give their hearts and lives to the Lord."
It was a commitment to an all-embracing, fervent evangelicalism
that was to last a lifetime. But more of that later.

Both were very young to be dating, given the mores of the time
in Ireland, and when my father appeared on a motorcycle to whisk
his youngest daughter away on what seemed like a "casual pinion,"
Grandpa David Hoey was less than pleased, to put it mildly. There
were the usual rows common to this atavistic struggle between love
on the one hand and parental caution and control on the other.
When my father finally wrote him a formal note asking permission
to marry Betty, Grandpa Hoey relaxed a little and gave cautious
consent in a letter that my sisters still cherish.

My father, having grown disillusioned by police work, soon afterwards announced that he was going to emigrate to Canada in
search of a better future than strife-torn Northern Ireland seemed
likely to offer. He already had an older brother who was living and
working in Toronto, and the plan was that my father would live with
him, get a job and then be joined by my mother a year later. A few
days after his arrival, although work was scarce in Toronto in the
late 1920s, he was hired by a prominent wholesale paper firm,

Buntin and Reid (today a part of the Domtar empire), to sweep floors. With an energy and determination that marked him all his life, he made a rapid advancement, and it was not long before he became foreman over the entire warehouse on Peter Street, not far from where the SkyDome (Rogers Centre) and CN Tower now stand, and where he would work through the Great Depression and eventually become a traveller for the company.

Though it saddened her family, my mother, a shy and somewhat anxious person by nature, kept to her resolve to join Billy, as she called him, in Canada. Her father feared—or perhaps even hoped— she would change her mind when she met her husband-to-be after the long absence. Accordingly, he insisted on sewing the money for her return passage into the lining of one of her dresses (it eventually helped pay for some furniture). The ship, the Cunarder SS *Athenia*, left Belfast Lough on April 14, 1928. The ocean voyage, which in those days took from nine or ten days to a fortnight, was not pleasant. My mother, who all her life could grow queasy at the mere mention of boat travel or even a swing, was wretchedly seasick for most of the time.

My father met the boat in Montreal and on April 25, 1928, a day after arriving in Toronto, they were married in historic St. Peter's Anglican Church at the corner of Bleecker and Carlton streets. It was and remained for many years one of the bastions of Low Church, evangelical Anglicanism in the city. Only two witnesses were present and there was no honeymoon in any modern sense of the term. I was born the next year, the year the stock market crash echoed around the world. My sister Elizabeth arrived seventeen months after my birth, my brother George was born a full ten years later, in 1939, just after World War II had begun, and my sister Jane was born in 1943. Another baby brother, Robert, was born in 1950 but lived only a few days.

My parents lived for a couple of years in the flat my father had at his brother's home at 13 Badgerow Avenue, not far from the old

Don Jail and Riverdale Zoo. I was born shortly after midnight on Sunday, April 14, 1929, in a small private clinic a few blocks away, on Victor Avenue. The next year, expecting another child, my parents moved to a rented house just south of Queen Street and east of Broadview Avenue. My mother used to push me in a large, old-style pram along Queen Street to meet "Billy" when he came home from work by streetcar every night. There was very little money, but in 1930 anybody with a steady job was among the truly fortunate. One night a short time later, while out for a walk after supper, again with the pram, they met a man they recognized from "over home." They talked and it turned out he had a house for sale on Lawlor Avenue, which was a little farther east, running north off Kingston Road in a district known today as the Upper Beaches. A deal was struck, my parents came up with $200 for the down payment, and they moved once more. The full price of the house at 164 Lawlor Avenue was $4,000. In all, we lived in three different houses on the same street over a span of more than twenty years. In 1949, I left home to live in residence at the University of Toronto, and finally for good in 1951, on my way to Oxford.

Looking back, I realize what an extraordinarily rich experience it was growing up in Toronto's old east end in what was essentially a working-class neighbourhood before, during and after World War II. The public school, of institutional brick, with a cinder playing ground, was named after Sir Adam Beck, the original architect of the Ontario hydroelectricity system. It lay at midpoint on Lawlor between Kingston Road to the south and Gerrard Street to the north. On Kingston Road there were innumerable small shops, much like an English village, a cinema or "show"—which my sister and I were forbidden to enter—and a large United church. At one end of our normal range there was a tavern and at the other a Roman Catholic church where God alone knew what strange rites were performed! As children, we saw this church as a mysterious and possibly dangerous place. In the years since then I have had Roman Catholic adults tell me they were led to feel much the same way about non-Catholic churches in their childhood.

Few people we knew had a car before the war. When we finally got one in 1941, gasoline was rationed and so it didn't really do us much good. Travel downtown normally took place by streetcar, the old kind where the seats were all made of wood and the conductor sat in a little station halfway down the car. There was a small stove beside him and in winter it paid to sit as close to its blazing warmth as possible.

The streets themselves were alive with every kind of horse-drawn vehicle imaginable: the milkman, the bread man and vendors of every type, including a bearded Jewish junk man who cried his rendition of "rags and bones" as he drove his nag and cart past the door. My mother enjoyed haggling with him over the worth of her surplus odds and ends. To our embarrassment, if we were anywhere nearby when one of the horses happened to relieve itself in a serious manner, we were instantly dispatched with a garbage can lid or other container to sweep up the manure for her precious rose bed. On many a hot summer day there would be a horse, still in harness, standing on our front lawn trying to reach the leaves of the maple tree. The wagon behind would lurch precariously until the driver got back from his delivery.

Since everybody had iceboxes instead of refrigerators, ice deliveries in the peak of summer were almost daily. The ice, hauled from Lake Simcoe in the winter and stored in deep sawdust in sheds until the hot season, was delivered by truck. All the kids from near and far would gather at the back as blocks were chipped out of the larger slabs and grab slivers of ice to suck on. You'd have thought it was something truly special and not just frozen water! Milkshakes at the corner parlour sold for five cents. The pie man, who rode a bicycle with a cart bearing the slogan *Man shall not live by bread alone*, also charged five cents for small pies. My favourite was pumpkin, although raisin came a close second.

Perhaps because the city limits were just five blocks away—Victoria Park Avenue marked the eastern boundary then—there were regular deliveries of fresh eggs, fruit and vegetables from the Mennonite farms to the northeast of the city, near the villages of Markham, Stouffville and Uxbridge. I vividly remember old trucks laden with crates of fresh strawberries appearing first, and then, later in the summer, the same farmers would be back with boxes of apples, fresh corn, honey, plums and pears. From the middle of August right through the fall the street was redolent with the smells of canning, of homemade jams and chili sauce, and the baking of pies.

Like most women of that day in our neighbourhood, except for a few involved in some war-related factory work, my mother didn't go out to work but spent much of her time preserving fruit and baking. On the hottest days of summer, though, when my sister and I were quite young, she would often make a lunch and, crossing Kingston Road, walk with us down one of the sharply descending streets that led to Queen Street and on to the beach a block or so south. Lake Ontario seemed freezing cold even on days when the sand was so hot it burned your bare feet, and then too it was often questionable, as it still is today, how clean the water was. But we paddled in it and later swam in it without a care in the world.

The maze of lanes behind the houses in our neighbourhood became a sort of badlands for most of our games, from cowboys to Robin Hood, from King Arthur and his knights to daring explorers. As adventurers, we occasionally pinched a potato or two from home and roasted them in small fires behind the rows of sheds or garages. None of the war games had any deleterious effects, and I am grateful to have lived in a time when children were able to experience such freedom from the constant supervision of adults. Our parents rarely knew where we were. When I was fourteen I received a repeating .22 rifle that a friend and I would conceal by stuffing it down a pant leg. Then we'd walk stiff-legged to a small dump at the north end of Lawlor, where we would shoot rats. Today, that site is prime real estate.

There was once a time, not all that long ago, when almost everyone had a religious upbringing of one sort or another. Of course, there were differing levels of intensity or depth, but Canada was a predominantly, actively Christian country until well into the 1960s. Churches and Sunday schools were well attended. Church leaders still frequently made headlines for reasons having nothing whatsoever to do with the sex abuse scandals of the ensuing era. Toronto newspapers regularly reported on Sunday sermons from major pulpits in the downtown core of the city.

Our family was not your average God-fearing household, however—not by any standard. My parents, having dedicated their hearts and lives to God, were very religious indeed. We went to church at least twice on Sunday, and that doesn't include Sunday school, where my father was a keen, energetic superintendent for many years. Although he had left school around what is now grade nine or ten to join the Ulster Constabulary, he had a quick mind with an amazing memory, and he read serious works on theology and church history even while on vacation. He attended night school at Wycliffe Theological College some years later, well after I had been ordained, graduated with an S.Th. diploma and was made a deacon in the Anglican Church of Canada. His job was supposed to be "permanent deacon," a position he could hold while continuing to work at his secular job, but about a year later, Bishop Frederick Wilkinson invited him to his Adelaide Street head office and told him he was needed for a rural parish near Peterborough. He consented, gave up his secular job, was ordained a priest at age fifty-four that spring in St. James' Cathedral, and soon left for the three-point parish of Millbrook, Cavan and Baillieborough, about two hours' drive northeast of Toronto. They soon had one of the finest Sunday schools in the region, and a band in which my mother played the bass drum.

While Sunday was anything but a day of rest as we were growing up, both my parents also attended Bible study groups, prayer meetings and assorted revivalist gatherings on weekdays whenever possible. My sister Elizabeth and I would walk several city blocks with my mother in all kinds of weather to St. Saviour's Anglican Church at Main Street and Swanwick Avenue in Toronto's east end to sit and fidget while a dozen or so women discussed a Bible passage and prayed. There was a fire hall on a nearby corner and I recall being much more interested in that than in what the Scripture Union, as the study text was called, had to impart. I joined the boys' choir at about seven years of age. When there were special children's crusades, aimed at getting as many as possible "to give their hearts to the Lord," I regularly won prizes for bringing in the most recruits.

Looking back, one realizes that the hectic pace of our home life, saturated as it was with religiously based activities of every sort—from visiting English bishops (always of an evangelical bent) coming to dinner, to pressing uniforms and shining buttons for various organizations such as the Boys' Brigade (a passion of my father's) and, during World War II, the air cadets—was, as already hinted, anything but normal. However, to me and to Elizabeth it seemed totally normal at the time. What neither of us realized, of course, was just how ultra-conservative and narrow it all was. It was essentially a fundamentalist theology: the infallibility of the Bible, the literal virgin birth, an atoning death of Jesus Christ for the sins of the world. You were "saved by the blood of the lamb." There was a great deal of guilt in the endless sermons to which we were subjected, and a lot of fear as well. I vividly remember having trouble sleeping after some visiting homespun preacher had waxed eloquent about Armageddon and the coming end of the world.

My parents had a "second family" with the birth of my younger brother in 1939 and sister in 1943, and they were perhaps a little less influenced. By then my father's reading had helped broaden him just a little. But we literally lived and breathed a rigidly faith-filled life. Elizabeth and Jane both played the piano at various Sunday schools my father led in the years before his ordination. He thought nothing of stopping the entire proceedings from time to time to give them a critical appraisal of their lack of preparation should they happen to miscue.

It was made clear to George and me from our earliest days pre-cisely what, as sons, our life's work was to be. I, as the first-born, had been dedicated to God even before I was born—with the Bib-lical story of Hannah's prayer in Samuel, and of Samuel's similar destiny, very much in mind. George, presently an active family physician on the Bruce Peninsula, was firmly pointed towards a career in medicine, preferably as a medical missionary. Girls, it seems, were intended to get jobs, get married, have babies, help out at churches but otherwise keep a low profile.

Was my father chauvinistic? Sexist? Yes, indeed. But my father was a charmer too. The ladies appeared to like him with his twin-kling Irish eyes, his energetic style and his military bearing. He was a disciplinarian with a kindly side and was much liked by his flock when he finally realized his dream and was given a rural parish of his own. He was very much a product of the conflict-riven Ulster of his day, however, and though he left it as a young man in his very early twenties, he remained strongly Protestant to the end. Unfor-tunately, in spite of his many great gifts, he never really overcame the anti–Roman Catholic animus that was born and bred in his homeland and later nourished by his selective reading both of theology and of church history. It was disappointing to my siblings and me that his splendid pastoral ministry during the final years of his life was at the same time narrowed by his steadfast refusal to participate in any local attempts at ecumenicity that meant, for example, sharing the same platform as the area's Catholic priest. However, gradually he had to alter his fundamentalist views on Scripture, particularly the Old Testament, as his theological studies quickly opened his eyes to the impossibility of persevering in a literalist understanding of the great stories he loved so much. And he mellowed in other ways as well. However, he was never a man to cherish the middle position on any matter of controversy—or otherwise, for that matter. In my late teens we had many arguments over when and how I was finally to be ordained, some of them very heated.

Sadly, in 1968 my father died suddenly, but peacefully enough, at age sixty-two in my mother's arms. I still miss him—the haunting sound of the tin flute that was never far from his hands, his incredibly constant optimism and his deep concern for his family's well-being. He expected a great deal from each of us, perhaps even too much at times. But I thank God always for both of my parents' courage in breaking with the past to make a life in Canada. My deep, abiding faith in God, however much it has changed and developed down all the decades since, owes everything to them. It is true, as one of John Wesley's biographers has said, that "mothers are the makers of spirit" in our earliest beginnings. That being said, fathers, for better or worse, have the awesome responsibility of forming some of our earliest inklings about God. As we grow in awareness and self-knowledge, however, shaped by our own individual experiences of the world and of others, both aspects of our lives are inevitably moulded and changed, sometimes quite drastically.

During my high school years, my sister and I attended weekly Youth for Christ rallies at Massey Hall on various Saturday nights. Charles Templeton, full of charisma and eloquence, was at the height of his evangelistic career and, together with his glamorous partner, a Spanish-looking diva with a wonderful voice, regularly held the audience of eager teenagers in the palm of his hand. When, to the haunting but overly repeated strains of "Just as I am, without one plea"—so familiar from Billy Graham's crusades—the invitation was given to come forward and be saved, there was a kind of hypnotic atmosphere in which the pull to go to the front of the hall was close to irresistible.

As a child and then in my teens I had asked Christ to come into my heart and life on more than one occasion, but Templeton made it nearly impossible for many of us not to go forward again. However, both Elizabeth and I usually managed to resist the emotional appeals while enjoying the company of our peers, the entertainment of the music and the movie-star quality of Templeton's leadership. Little did I know that I would one day be a contributor (through my knowledge of New Testament Greek) to his best-selling book on the sayings of Jesus or that we would eventually become friends. He often used to call me on Sundays while I was a regular columnist for the *Toronto Star* to discuss whatever I had written that weekend. We met at his home, on an apartment rooftop overlooking the Don Valley in the heart of Toronto, not many months before he was hospitalized with severe Alzheimer's disease. He showed me many photographs and newspaper clippings of his days as an evangelist and, for a while, partner of Billy Graham. While Charles had eventually become an agnostic, he remained in my view "a God-haunted man" all his life. In *There Is Life after Death*, I outline the story his wife Madeleine told me of a vision Charles had just before he died. Nobody who knew Charles Templeton or who had read his final book, *Farewell to God*, would have anticipated or predicted anything like that.

In retrospect, I see that my childhood, though enviable in so many ways, was a thorough-going indoctrination into the basic tenets of Christian fundamentalism. This cannot be overemphasized. It was an upbringing heavily into guilt and fear. My parents' religion was intensely judgmental of others in different camps, particularly the majority of "unsaved church members" who were regarded as Christians in name only. Sin was humanity's greatest problem and we alone had the answers. To be outside our company of "right" believers was to be eternally lost and headed for hell. It was no easy burden for a teenager, destined by his parents for the ministry, to carry. But, to quote the famous inventor and futurist Buckminster Fuller, "How often I found where I should be going only by setting out for somewhere else."

3

FROM HOMER AND PLATO TO THEOLOGY

I HAVE TO CONFESS to liking high school very much indeed. Compared with the years spent in elementary school education, it struck me forcibly as an entirely new kind of adventure. A powerful lust for knowledge combined with a fresh sense of freedom made what was dull and tedious to many of my fellow students a pure pleasure to me. A course in music appreciation was a part of my chosen curriculum for the entire five years. This opened up a whole new world of classical music that has been a motherlode of spiritual comfort and renewal in my life ever since.

When the Metropolitan Opera Company came to Toronto's Massey Hall, our music teacher was asked by a member of the Toronto Symphony Orchestra to look after the sale of programs and librettos for the week. He then asked me and two other students to assist him. This meant we saw many of the best-known operas, including *Faust*, *Carmen*, *Il Trovatore*, *La Traviata* and *The Magic Flute*, presented by the leading artists of the mid-1940s. The Met came two or three times to Toronto during that never-to-be-forgotten era. Glenn Gould, who grew up in the Beach district and was a student at Malvern during my final two years there, was persuaded to play for the whole student body at auditorium several times. So we were able to hear and watch him before he became the famous artist we know about today.

In high school, it was learning French and Latin that I enjoyed most. Once again there was the recognition of entering new intellectual realms and into a broader experience of the minds and lives of other peoples and cultures—a deepening of one's own *humanitas*. But it was while I was in grade ten that something happened that brought about a truly significant change in my life. We had an English teacher, Ms Enid McGregor, who made studying English grammar, poetry, prose, drama and composition a perfect delight. One day, however, she took one of her frequent side trips (as we called them) and began to show us how many of our most familiar words came from ancient Greek. She began writing lists of them on the blackboard: *geo-logy*, *anthropo-logy*, *demo-cracy*, *pneumatic*, *Christ-ian* and so on. I was absolutely fascinated.

It must have been a case of what Carl Jung dubbed a *synchronicity* (again, a word from two Greek words) or, as they say, "it was meant to be," because I eagerly drank in all she had to say and felt a genuine hunger for more—much more. At close of the class I stayed behind and asked her if she knew how I might be able to learn classical Greek. I told her of my thoughts about entering the ministry and how it seemed a good way to prepare for one day reading the New Testament in its original written form, that is, Hellenistic Greek, which was a popular form of Greek spread over much of the ancient world by the deliberate policies of Alexander the Great. She positively beamed at me and said that a retired friend of hers, a Miss Myrtle Stevens, had taught Greek at one of the only two high schools in the Toronto region where it was on the curriculum. She said I probably already knew her since she had been a supply teacher during the recent illness of Malvern's Latin master. I recalled the lady at once. With the lack of sympathy typical of many teenagers, we had called her Little Caesar and had done our best to make life difficult for her. I now blush to think of how cruel a lack of awareness and compassion can be when a crowd or even a mob mentality moves in before you know it. In any case, an introduction was arranged and I began taking elementary Greek with Ms Stevens as my tutor twice a week after school. In a one-on-one situation with a student keen to learn and eager to work, she was a marvellous inspiration.

Myrtle Stevens lived in an apartment in the Beach directly facing Lake Ontario. I had a rather nondescript but hugely loyal dog at the time, named Pat. He would accompany me down the winding ravine that led almost directly from our home down to Queen Street East and the water. Pat chased squirrels as I intoned Greek declensions and conjugated Greek verbs to myself while hiking through the woods. On the other afternoons I had a part-time job as a delivery boy for Betty's Fish and Chip Shop on Kingston Road. In the winter I was told to keep the newspaper-wrapped food orders inside my parka to prevent them being a cold, congealed mess on arrival. The system worked, but it meant that one's hair, clothes and everything else reeked of deep-fried grease. The good thing about it was that as I pedalled the bicycle through sun, sleet and snow, I repeated the Greek vocabulary and grammar to myself until I had them down thoroughly. This meant I had little or no remaining Greek homework to do at night.

The following year, Ms Stevens introduced me to Homer's *Odyssey*. I had always loved adventure stories, especially those involving travel, the kind of tale told so well by my favourite childhood author, Richard Haliburton. His mysterious and never-solved disappearance in the Sea of China on board a junk in 1939 had captured my boyhood imagination in a major way. Accordingly, to stumble, however slowly—looking up nearly every word at first in a lexicon—in the wake of Odysseus and his companions was a dream come true. The two of us, an elderly spinster and a teenager, sat together over the ancient text and shared a rare sense of harmonious delight. I counted myself fortunate indeed in such a mentor. And Pat was always there afterwards, waiting patiently for me outside. We trudged home happily in the gathering winter darkness up to Kingston Road and home. I little thought then that I would one day be the minister of a growing church situated right on Kingston Road, about ten miles farther east along that same highway.

By grade thirteen, the final year at Malvern, Ms Stevens had me convinced that I had a reasonable shot at winning a scholarship to university if I worked really hard. She said the good news was that the number of students in the whole of Ontario taking their finals in Greek was small—so, more opportunity to win. The bad news, of course, was that these students were amongst the top scholars in their respective schools. The competition would be keen and close.

The results back then were published in the Toronto daily papers. It was early July 1947, and I was up on the roof of a cottage on Lake Simcoe helping my summer boss shingle a roof when a young lad I knew from a nearby farm came up the lane on his bicycle. He had a newspaper in his hand. He blurted out: "You got nine firsts and a second. And you got a scholarship too!" I nearly fell down the ladder in my rush to take a look. There it was in black and white: the James Harris Scholarship in Latin and Greek. I let out a whoop of joy because this meant my complete tuition would be paid for all four years of Classics at the University of Toronto, with a little money for books besides. It wasn't the leading prize; that was won by a student from Riverdale. But for me it was an answered prayer.

There was one piece of wisdom Ms Stevens gave me in addition to tutoring me in Greek. Right at the start she said that if I was serious about my studies, I should find something practical to do as a hobby. Working with your hands, she said, complements working with your brain. "You can do woodworking, manual labour or whatever, but you'll find it keeps you balanced and fit." I took her advice and spent an hour or so after school most days at Malvern in the shop making lamps, birdhouses, bowls (on a lathe) and other household items. In the summers before I started going north as a teacher I did a variety of jobs, from selling fresh fish off a horse-drawn wagon to cottagers at Lake Simcoe to haying, hoeing and cleaning stables on a farm near our cottage. Playing sports of various kinds was another great release from purely intellectual pursuits. I even continued to play rugger while in my first parish as a minister, from 1956 to 1958 at the University of Toronto. By that point I had already played as a forward on the Varsity first-string squad during my two years studying theology at Wycliffe, from 1954 to 1956.

The four years I spent studying Classics at University College in the University of Toronto were a mind-expanding, privileged experience that laid the foundation for everything that followed. The course involved reading in the original Latin and Greek most of the great authors of antiquity, from Cicero, Pliny and Virgil, Horace and Catullus, to Pindar, Aeschylus, Sophocles, Thucydides, Herodotus and Plato, to name only a very few. I could scarcely believe my good fortune, or "blessings" as my mother would have said. There were archaeological studies of art and architecture from the classical and Hellenistic eras in special lecture rooms at the Royal Ontario Museum. In addition there was an English course each year and also one in Oriental or Near Eastern Studies to put our core interests in their wider context in the ancient world.

The terms of my scholarship required that my marks be a "first" each successive year, and I was able through hard work (and prayer!) to maintain that and win additional, smaller awards as well. But the really important thing is that a whole new universe of ideas and of insights into the *humanitas* of our species was gradually opening up for me. It was an incredible inner voyage of discovery.

Two of the encounters that were to be powerful influences on my later thinking about religion in general and my own faith in particular were with Platonism and Stoicism. Plato, to use a colloquialism, blew me away. The myth of the cave, for example, has stayed with me all down the years. There has never been a better depiction of the way we humans often persist in ignorance or half-truths and then resist in anger when someone—a guru, a teacher or even a saviour figure—comes and seeks to lead us to the light of a greater reality.

The soaring heights of Plato's spirituality, especially with regard to the Form of the Good, or God, took me completely by surprise. Here was a writer almost five centuries before the Christian era whose thoughts and even at times his express words echoed in the writings of Saint Paul and in the Gospels. It's not that Paul or the Gospel authors quote the great philosopher, but his ideas and occasionally his actual illustrations foreshadow and influence the New Testament and indeed all subsequent literature in the Mediterranean world and far beyond. All the top theologians of the Church's most formative period were inspired by Plato and by Neoplatonism, most notably of course Saint Augustine. Socrates, Plato's hero and the key voice for all his major works, was widely recognized by these same Christian thinkers as in every way a Christian before Christianity. Meeting him in the pages of Plato in the original Greek text is something one can never forget. What I didn't know then but was to learn later in my research for *The Pagan Christ* was that Plato himself had spent considerable time in Egypt, where he was instructed by the priests in the spiritual lore of that ancient treasure house of wisdom. In the writings of the classical authors, Egypt is described as "the temple of the world."

Meeting Zeno and the Stoics was another life-changing moment of illumination for someone who had been raised in the east end of Toronto by Irish immigrants. Zeno of Citium (335–263 BCE), the founder of Stoicism—the name comes from the *stoa* or porch where he walked as he taught in Athens—set out a philosophy that directly embraced the world or, better still, the entire cosmos. He instructed his followers to think of themselves as citizens of the whole cosmos. He was thus the first truly cosmopolitan man.

It was profoundly liberating to read how he taught that the divine Logos, the rational principle according to which the cosmos was brought into being—and also of course the same term used in the opening of John's Gospel and translated as "the Word"—was actually inherent in the mind and heart of every human being. Zeno called this divine spark of rationality the *logos spermatikos*, the "seed" word sown in everyone. Immediately you are led to think of the passage from John just cited: "In the beginning was the Word, and the Word was with God, and the Word was God . . . That was the true light which lighteth every human being coming into the world." Based upon that kind of foundation, the Pagan, Zeno, taught a universal brotherhood of man and a total commitment to fulfilling one's duty and destiny. Reading the works of later thinkers and writers such as Emperor Marcus Aurelius and Seneca, you quickly realize that they too were "Christians," without the cross.

By this time I was reading some of the New Testament itself in the original Greek, and in doing so I one day came across the famous passage in the Acts of the Apostles describing Paul's visit to Athens and his encounter with the Pagan worshippers on the hill of the Areopagus, overlooking the city. It was thrilling to hear again his purported sermon wherein he takes as his text an inscription he has just noticed on one of the altars there. It said: "To an unknown God." The altar was just a case of the Athenians covering all their bases by ensuring that no deity would be left unappeased. But Paul is shown as turning it effectively to his own ends. He says, "What therefore you worship as unknown, this I proclaim to you." He then goes on to add that the God who

made the world and everything in it . . . does not live in shrines made by human hands, nor is he served by human hands, as though he needed anything, since he himself gives to all mortals life and breath and all things. From one ancestor he made all nations to inhabit the whole earth, and he allotted the times of their existence and the boundaries of the places where they would live, so that they would search for God and perhaps grope for him and find him—though indeed he is not far from each one of us. For "In him we live and move and have our being"; as even some of your own poets have said, "For we too are [God's] offspring."

I wish to emphasize what the Pagan poets being referred to here (Cleanthes and Aratus) actually said because it struck me so forcibly at the time that this is precisely the core message of Christianity also! Every living human—being regardless of creed, colour, sexual orientation or status in society—is a child of God and lives, moves and has his or her being in God, the Ground and Source of all Being. I lay some stress upon this growing awareness of the universality of the Christian message because it played an important part as gradually, through the years of intellectual preparation for the studies and the ministry that lay ahead, I began to challenge little by little the narrower viewpoint of my early years. The discerning reader will already have noticed aspects of my thinking destined later to be fully defined in *The Pagan Christ* and in *Water into Wine* in particular.

The question of whether or not students in training for the ministry at Wycliffe College (where I was in residence while attending University College) would take a summer charge each year even while they were still in their general arts course was never seriously discussed. In 1948, at the end of my first year in Classics, the principal, Dr. Ramsay Armitage, one of the finest human beings I have ever known, simply called me into his office and told me of the assignment he wanted like me to undertake that summer. He told me to go upstairs to my room and "pray about it" and then come down to his office the next day to pick up the train tickets. He told me, "They're expecting you next week." Apparently no need to ask for divine guidance after all!

When I was still a choirboy, all decked out in an angelic white surplice and high starched collar, I used to sit in church during the sermon and fantasize about being a missionary in the High Arctic. The traditional cleric in his dark suit and Roman collar had minimal appeal for me. But I could see myself with the frost ringing my parka hood of wolverine fur, driving my tireless huskies across the vast expanses of snow in search of hapless Natives to whom I could do immeasurable "good" in some very vague, idealistic manner. Later I eagerly devoured books on the North, especially the one about the bishop who ate his boots—Bishop Stringer. In my reveries I elevated myself to the rank of northern prelate, complete with gaiters, flying my own plane into remote Eskimo communities where I would be met with applause and undying loyalty.

When I did finally arrive in the North as a student teacher that first summer, the reality was of course somewhat different from the dream. I was to be a schoolteacher to about seventy Cree children. Big Trout Lake reserve (or Kitchi Numaboos Seepik, as the Cree call it) was a huge expanse of primeval bush, rivers and lakes about 1,600 kilometres northwest of Toronto. It was very close to what today is known as the "Ring of Fire," where vast mineral deposits are currently being prospected by a host of claimants. Chromium, a vital but rare element for the making of steel, is apparently hidden there in very large quantities. Diamonds of a quality equal to those of South Africa have also now been discovered not many miles from the reserve. At that time the Hudson Bay store held a monopoly on all sales there, and the Anglican Church had a monopoly on religion. The only non-Natives on the reserve at that time were the Anglican missionary, the Hudson Bay manager and his clerk, two weather station staff and myself. The Cree children lived with their trapper parents on their remote traplines for most of the year and came in just for the summers. Then they would fish, socialize and go to church almost every day. These children were not a part of the controversial residential school system and got their only formal education during the summer months.

With growing excitement I boarded the train at Union Station in downtown Toronto at midnight, settling into a lower berth and then watching through the window as the farmlands of southern Ontario gradually gave way to the rocks, lakes and pines of the Canadian Shield. I was just nineteen and off on the first real adventure of my life. I arrived in Sioux Lookout at eleven-thirty the following night to find the town in a fever over the recent discovery of gold close to the edge of the tiny community. Even the lawns on the main street had been staked out by prospectors, and, to my dismay, the only bed in town was a cot in the middle of an already full room in a very cheap hotel. I tried my best to sleep, but the snoring of one fellow in the corner and the fact that another's boots kept up an irregular thumping on my head as their owner twisted and turned made it very difficult.

I had to spend nearly a week in Sioux Lookout because bad weather made it impossible for the Norseman float plane I was taking for the final 500-kilometre leg of the journey to attempt to fly. I spent most of my time reading or watching a couple of Chinese men catch pickerel in Pelican Rapids, just west of the town. It turned out they ran the best restaurant in town (there were only two), and I used to order the daily special at both lunch and supper. It was, of course, fresh pickerel, better than filet mignon any day by my reckoning.

With all that time on my hands, however, I was feeling pretty lonely and a little homesick. As in the army or on a film set, a lot of one's time as a missionary is spent waiting. So it was with great relief that I finally received the message to get ready for departure in a couple of hours. Turning up at the dock with my duffle bag, I found the plane loaded with supplies of all kinds, including a couple of drums of gasoline, two or three outboard motors, several cases of liquor "for the boys at Round Lake" and three Indian children who had been waiting for over ten days to get a ride back to their parents' after a fall and winter spent at the Sioux Lookout residential school.

The pilot, a former fighter pilot with the RCAF who reportedly had a problem with drink and eventually, having crashed his plane once too often, ended up driving a taxi in a small northern town, saw at once that we would never get off the water with such a load. So he ordered the three Cree children to get off and wait for some other flight. (Nobody knew when that might be.) He then re-arranged some of the cases, sat me on a motor next to a reeking gas drum and gunned his engine. As we sped across the bay and the trees of the opposite shore rushed towards us, anyone could tell that we weren't going to make it. At the last possible moment the pilot cut the power, cursed loudly and taxied back to his base. Here, at the small dock, he unloaded one or two bulky parcels (but not the booze) and asked me to lean over the cockpit for takeoff so as to get more weight forward. When we headed out again, my heart was in my mouth. As before, there was the furious roar as we picked up speed and shot out across the water. The pilot kept rocking the plane to help free it from the suction on the floats, and at the last second, when it seemed a crash was certain, he yanked the thing up and over the menacing border of pines. "We made it," he said with a big grin. I was too weak even to agree.

It was a very bumpy flight, and as the air grew warmer and the fumes of the gasoline I was sitting beside became stronger, I began to feel very ill indeed. To make matters worse, my ears were blocked with the change in pressure. Just when I thought I couldn't take it any longer, a small cluster of cabins and teepees appeared on the edge of a lake ahead, and in a few moments we had touched down at Cat Lake to discharge half of our cargo. The entire dock was crowded with Cree who had come to shake hands with anyone on board. My leg was seized in a viselike grip by a big husky dog putting the bite on me, and there were howls of laughter at my predicament. One man eventually released me, saying, "He's just trying your leg out for size—he does that to every newcomer."

After what seemed like an eternity, we took off again, and the pilot thrust a large, wrinkled map onto my knees, pointed to a spot between Cat Lake and Hudson Bay and said, "Start looking out for a big lake on the horizon." I looked at the map then out the window. The whole face of the earth seemed to have turned to water since there were hundreds of lakes, muskeg ponds and rivers, all gleaming in the westering sun.

We eventually spotted what he said was Big Trout Lake on the horizon, thanks more to good luck than to my ability as navigator. The pilot chuckled as he prepared to give the Hudson's Bay post manager a good scare. I could just make out the settlement on the end of an island in the most northerly quarter of the 75-kilometre-wide expanse of the lake when suddenly he put the plane into a steep dive. Skimming along barely thirty metres above the water, we did a wide circle out over the muskeg and then roared over the tiny community from behind. We just missed the wires of the Department of Transport (or DOT, as it was called) weather station and the flag of the Hudson's Bay Company store as we buzzed the place for several runs. The Cree streamed out of their teepees and log shacks, waved frantically and ran for the main dock. I was later to learn that everyone who could move always met the plane, even though there was seldom anything on it for any of them. After I had been there a few weeks and grown hungry for mail, I generally led the pack myself, trying not to trample anyone in the rush.

By the time we had taxied over and tied up, the dock was crammed with the welcoming party, and many others sat on the bank. It looked like the audience for an outdoor concert. Babies wailed in their tikinagans (a board with a pouch on it into which the baby is laced and then carried on the mother's back; it is packed with dried moss, which is changed as often as necessary). Several huskies fought each other while I again shook hands with everyone in sight. "Watchy," they all said. So I repeated it. The word, which is spelled differently all over the North, can mean either hello or goodbye, so it's very useful. Apparently it was derived from the earliest days when the fur traders would greet one another with the words "What cheer?" Another sign of the impact of earlier times was the somewhat unusual uniformity of dress. All the men and boys wore old country–style tweed peaked caps, and all the women and girls, even the smallest toddlers, wore brightly coloured kerchiefs or scarves tied tightly under their chins.

Suddenly I was hailed by a very English-sounding male voice. A wiry-looking man in his mid-fifties, wearing a battered old fedora and a collarless shirt bulging out from under a pair of wide suspenders, was paddling his canoe towards the sandy shore beside the dock. It was Rev. Leslie Garrett, the Anglican missionary with whom I was to stay for the next three months. Garrett's weather-beaten face, enormous eyebrows from under which sparkled a pair of the bluest eyes I have ever seen, and baggy, black pants gave him an aura of eccentricity. Some in Sioux Lookout had warned me he was "bushed"—the term used for those who become a little strange from too much solitude—but I was to find him much saner than his critics. He was one of the strongest men I have ever met. He pulled the large freighter canoe onshore with ease, plucked my duffle bag from me and tossed it in, and then nearly crushed my hand in his grip. His enthusiastic smile rearranged the weathered creases in his countenance in a most attractive way as he said: "I'm Garrett—welcome to Big Trout."

He handed me a paddle and pointed to the bow position while he climbed in at the stern. I hadn't been in a canoe often, and I felt every Cree eye on the island watching me as we headed off to the mission dock a short way along the shore. (The next day, just when I thought I was getting the hang of it, I capsized off the end of the Hudson Bay dock and sent several men nearby into paroxysms of laughter.) As we passed by part of the village, it surprised me to discover that while the majority were living in simple one-room log cabins, there were a dozen or more families still living in teepees for their summer home. It gave me a thrill to see the smoke curling up from the hole at the top where the spruce poles intertwined. The silhouette of the teepees against the sky made me feel as if I were living in a movie about the Old West.

The problem with teepees, I was to discover, was that they were never intended for people well over six feet tall. If I stood up in one, my head was up where the racks of fish were curing in the ascending smoke. In a seated position, sometimes on a wooden box but more usually on the floor of spruce branches, one had to lean forward like a yogi to allow for the slanting canvas walls. Since it is impossible to sweep the floor in such accommodation, the family would simply move to another site, spread fresh branches and *voilà!*—the housecleaning was done. It was fascinating to observe that while there was nothing that we would call furniture as such, there was generally a guitar around and one or two radios. The beds were robes of rabbit skins laid on the floor, and the babies rocked gently in little hammocks suspended from the saplings forming the frame of the cone-like dwelling.

The simple log cabins of the rest of the community sometimes had slightly more elaborate fittings, but not always. They were invariably surrounded closely by a solid fence of peeled and sharply pointed poles to keep out wandering huskies and to serve as a drying rack both for any washing and for clumps of moss destined to serve as baby napkins and in general as "the Kleenex of the North." It's worth noting that this sphagnum peat moss—which lies in a deep carpet all through the boreal forests of the Canadian North—was put forward by a Manitoba company as a potential ally in the frantic attempts to clean up the disastrous oil that spewed into the Gulf of Mexico in the summer of 2010. Acknowledged as the worst oil spill in American history, the well churned out thousands of barrels of oil daily for months. The peat moss, according to its promoters, can float on the ocean's surface, suck up oil and then, when saturated, be easily removed for burning or burying in a landfill. It's cheap, exists in almost limitless abundance, and quickly and safely degrades into the environment.

Garrett's mission house was a simple building set beside the white frame church where lengthy services were held on Monday, Wednesday and Friday nights, as well as twice on Sunday, all summer long. Since at that time the residents spent the long months of winter out on their remote traplines and only came together in the spring to sell their furs, renew their trapping equipment and spend the summer fishing and socializing, they felt they had a lot of churchgoing to make up for, and make it up they did.

The mission house itself was much like a plain farmhouse. The largest room was the kitchen, with its polished linoleum floor, huge wood stove for both warmth and cooking, and generous table where, apart from porridge in the morning, I ate what seemed to me better than gourmet meals (fresh-caught lake trout, pickerel and whitefish). Christine Garrett was a rotund, happy Ojibwa woman whom Garrett had married some years after his first wife died of typhoid fever. She baked wheaten bread about three times a week and the aroma, mingled with that of the birch logs burning in the stove, was sheer heaven. My "room" was a section of the upper storey of the house separated from the Garretts' sleeping quarters by a four-foot partition surmounted by a curtain. Through the low window at night I had a splendid view of the wilderness, the boreal forest stretching away forever. On those long, long summer nights the sun seemed barely to set at all. The hermit thrushes sang me to sleep.

The Garretts' three children, Bessie, ten, Herbie, eight, and Esther, five, shared a room on the ground floor. They were very early risers and I was wakened each morning by the strained chords of the only two records they seemed to own and which they played on their hand-wound Victrola as a daily ritual. The songs were "There's a bluebird on my windowsill, there's a rainbow in the sky" and "Come to the church in the wildwood, oh come to the church in the dale . . ." They knew hardly a word of English and so most of the conversation at mealtimes was in Cree, of which I at first understood virtually nothing. They were usually very well-behaved children, except for those occasions when somebody would bring us a large lake trout in exchange for a couple of loaves of home-baked bread. Mrs. Garrett always baked or boiled the head of these monsters (thirty to forty pounds) and always there would be a squabble over who got the cheek pieces and the eyes. I knew we were dealing with delicacies, but I always had to avert my own eyes when the fish's orbs were about to be forked and eaten! There is nothing like a boiled fish-eye rolling on a plate to make one queasy.

The fact that the missionary's own children seemed to know only Cree made me apprehensive about what I would find when for the first time I faced a roomful of my charges for the summer. They say 90 percent of the things you worry about don't come true. Unfortunately, this experience belonged with the 10 percent that do. The morning after my arrival, I rang the church bell, signalling nine o'clock. It wasn't really necessary since the entire class had arrived at least an hour early in their eagerness to see the new teacher. Garrett introduced me to the children, who were between six and sixteen years of age, told them all to behave themselves (all of this in Cree) and then, with a smile, handed me some chalk and left me to my own devices. Now, the Department of Indian Affairs, which had appointed me on the Anglican Church's recommendation, had only sent the briefest outline, which said that my job was to teach school at a fairly elementary level: reading and writing (in English), simple arithmetic, singing, arts and crafts, and sports. But now I realized that no one in the class would understand a word I said. I nearly panicked as I looked in despair at those forty pairs of dark brown, curious, hopeful, trusting eyes. Various maps, some religious art and the large piece of oilskin that was to serve as a blackboard all hung at the front of the church, but I could see no tangible help there. Suddenly I remembered the large boxes of textbooks kindly sent by the government and neatly stacked in the supply cupboard. I hurriedly tore open several cases. To my alarm, they all contained readers in the Dick and Jane series, complete with illustrations and content that was about as relevant to the lives of these children as lessons on how to walk in space!

The Cree of Big Trout were tolerant enough of my bumbling attempts to improve their lot, but the isolation, the mosquitoes and blackflies, and the arduous labour of professional do-goodism on a small stipend quickly dissipated a lot of the romance for me. Frankly, it was a difficult summer as far as teaching was concerned. I did everything but stand on my head to leap the language barrier and teach the children something. I must have looked berserk at times. For example, I would write a simple word such as *jump* or *run* on the makeshift blackboard, get them to print the word in their copybooks and then, seizing one of the smaller boys, would lift him up and down like a rag doll or run with him across the room to act out the word. I taught the alphabet phonetically and made up songs for this and a host of other basics of learning. I brought various objects into the class—cups, knives and forks, a grub box, paddles, traps, items of clothing—and got them to give me the Cree word for each and then had them copy out the English. At other times I used pictures cut from old copies of the Hudson's Bay Company's *Beaver* magazine or old newspapers.

Singing proved the best route to learning of all. They could learn words and concepts in an hour through songs that would have taken much longer otherwise. Besides, the government handbook said singing was good for their lungs, an aid in helping prevent tuberculosis. Several students had one or more relatives in the sanatorium at Fort William (now Thunder Bay) and I soon learned that it was generally accepted at Big Trout Lake that those sent out there very seldom came back.

TB, a legacy of the European conquerors, was endemic, a fact of life. Once a year the Indian agent came to pay out the treaty money— about five dollars a head for having signed over thousands of square miles of their territory to the Crown in the mid-nineteenth century. As well as a Mountie escort, a doctor and a couple of minor civil servants, the agent's party brought along a portable X-ray machine, which was used to check on all the band members. It was at best a very hit-or-miss affair. One time it was scandalous. When the treaty party came that summer, there was the usual annual X-ray marathon. You could hear the little one-stroke motor that powered the generator for the machine running far into the night for four days. About two weeks afterwards, a radio message came to the DOT crew at the weather station asking the schoolteacher (me) to inform a list of eight or nine Cree that they had TB and instruct them to get ready for a plane ride (on a Catalina flying boat) that would transport them out to Fort William. I accepted the unhappy task, and on the appointed day they took teary farewells of their loved ones on the company dock and departed.

A week later, while I was in the midst of teaching, I heard the familiar whisper going around the room: "*Pimosayawin.*" Plane! Since it was impossible to keep them settled while a plane was arriving, not to mention my own curiosity, I dismissed the class and we joined the usual stampede. When the aircraft finally tied up, to my astonishment all of the people I had previously sent out disembarked. There had been a mix-up in the X-ray plates, it seemed, and those with the dreaded disease were still on the island. I was told there was nothing to be done but wait until the next checkup— a full year away. It is a fact that some members of that particular treaty party were drinking almost continuously during the Big Trout Lake X-ray examinations, so the mix-up was not the result of ordinary human error. I was only twenty at the time and politically very naïve. I now realize I should have gone to the media immediately upon returning to Sioux Lookout that fall. I did make a written protest to the Department of Indian Affairs, but nothing ever came of it as far as I know.

After school hours I tried my best to work with the boys in particular, doing what used to be called manual training, and teaching sports. I have to confess that the results were very meagre in both cases. Our first crafts project was a howling failure. I had noticed that there seemed to be a streak of cruelty shown towards animals and birds among my male students. (This has to be seen against a setting where their whole lives depended upon hunting and fishing.) For example, they used to catch field mice, put them in the lake while still alive, and then try to pick them off with catapults while the mice frantically swam for shore.

As a counterweight to this kind of behaviour, I decided we should make some birdhouses. There was considerable enthusiasm for the idea once I had made one to demonstrate. The boys slaved away for hours each afternoon and evening, sawing, hammering and nailing with great gusto. When they were done, I got a primitive ladder and showed them how to erect the birdhouses on slim, tall poles, or in the eaves of their cabin homes.

A couple of evenings later, when I was walking through the centre of the settlement, I encountered a commotion. Several swallows were flying in tight circles around the new birdhouses and making plaintive cries. Something seemed to be agitating them, preventing their entry. When I got closer I found several of my boys hiding behind the wooden fences around their homes and trying to shoot the swallows with their catapults every time they landed on a perch. Of course, I made them stop, but they seemed astounded. Even their elders looked on curiously at my interference. Puzzled, I summoned Mr. Garrett to see if he could find out what was going on. After he had talked with the boys for a while, he grinned broadly and said:

"They don't understand why you're stopping them from shooting the birds. They say they thought that was the whole idea, a new kind of trap!" He went on to say that the parents had shared this view and thought the new *schooniowgamow* (school boss) was really clever for conjuring up such a sneaky device. I realized it was a lost cause, and taught the boys to make stools and grub boxes instead. But they never showed the kind of zeal for these that they had for the birdhouses.

The boys, and indeed all of the able-bodied men of the village, loved playing soccer, using tin cans, a bundle of rags, anything that could be kicked, when there was no ball available. They had no concept whatsoever of boundaries, however. Often two players would disappear into the bushes still kicking and in pursuit of the ball. They would kick it down along the shore, through swampy places full of marsh grass, and finally back out to where the other players were sitting awaiting their return. Some white lime and a marking device were flown in and we set out to make a proper soccer pitch. This activity was watched with enormous interest, and even the men listened politely as I tried to explain with gestures and the aid of one or two older lads who knew some English. When play resumed, however, the game did not change one iota. They completely ignored the outsider's strange views and kicked the ball all over the cleared portion of the island. In fact, they wore out the soccer balls at such an alarming rate that someone in the agent's office at Sioux Lookout sent a wire in via the DOT asking with sarcasm whether we were roasting the soccer balls and eating them for Sunday dinner.

In the summer of 1949, I went north again in early June to teach school a second time. Things went well for the first week, although I was a little troubled one day when I noticed a dead husky floating in the lake just off the small dock where we were in the habit of drawing our drinking water. The missionary and his family had a wooden yoke that went over the shoulders and there were hooks on each side for a pail. The water was carried up to the house and transferred into a large drum. A drinking ladle hung on the wall nearby. Since the dock was on a small bay quite a way from the main dock and other cabins or teepees, and the lake was considered by all to be pristine, nobody thought it necessary to boil the water before drinking it. I was in the midst of teaching the children a simple song one day when I began having the worst stomach cramps I had ever experienced. They continued to grow more severe, and before long I had to let the children out for an early recess while I went to rest at the rectory. I began to feel feverish and then the full impact hit me. I became very ill indeed, racked by a burning fever and serious abdominal distress. I took to my bed at once and, apart from dealing with the seemingly never-ending diarrhea (there was, of course, no indoor plumbing, only a slop pail and the outhouse near the black spruce of the bush), I didn't leave the room until I was carried down the crooked stairs by two of the strongest men in the village one week later. They used a blanket in lieu of a stretcher.

At times I was completely out of it because of the raging fever, and my stomach ached constantly with severe cramping. Mrs. Garrett was next thing to a saint in her unflagging patience in emptying the pail, her attempts to get me to take some soup and her general aura of compassionate care. The missionary himself, who knew some basic first aid but also recognized a serious illness, had sent a message courtesy of the Department of Transport to the small outpost hospital in Sioux Lookout describing my condition. The word came back that a plane would be coming in as soon as some murky weather cleared. It was several days before the decision was made to come in, and it was raining lightly when I was carried down to the company dock and put on board the single-engine Norseman float plane. The cargo area had been emptied to make way for a stretcher. So they bundled me aboard, gave me some morphine tablets and we taxied off across the rough waves.

It was a bumpy ride, and it got worse after takeoff as the plane bucked high winds and I heard the pilot tell his co-pilot that he'd seen lightning up ahead. We flew through a thunderstorm—the roughest ride I'd ever known in the North or anywhere else. I lost track after a while, but I know we put down on a series of lakes all that long afternoon, each time waiting for rain and clouds to pass sufficiently to make possible another "leapfrog" ahead. It was getting dark when I heard one of the two men up front mention "Pickle Crow," and I suddenly felt the loss of altitude. We were about to land at the gold-mining town about a hundred kilometres north of our goal of Sioux Lookout. There, an ambulance was waiting and took me to the fairly primitive runway where a Cessna was ready to go. When we eventually landed safely at Sioux Lookout, another ambulance was waiting. I remember being placed beneath the wing of the plane, out of the drizzle, before being hoisted into the back of the vehicle.

In those few moments a familiar face appeared above me and as if from a great distance I heard a kindly voice asking how I was. It turned out to belong to Rev. Tom Griggs, the rector of the little Anglican church in Sioux Lookout. I had preached for him on the Sunday I had spent waiting for a plane a couple of weeks before. We accidentally met once again in the former Anglican Book Room on Jarvis Street in Toronto some twenty years or more afterwards, and he told me that when he had seen me that evening in Sioux Lookout he had felt greatly alarmed. "I thought you looked in very bad shape indeed," he said. He remembered telling his wife he had doubts whether I'd pull through.

There is now a modern hospital in Sioux Lookout, but in the summer of 1949 it was a small two-storey building with tarpaper brick siding down by the railroad tracks. The town was a major train junction for the CNR, so the noise of steam engines was constant. Natives and whites were kept in separate wards. Nobody on the staff spoke Cree or any other Indian dialect. There were two doctors and a handful of nurses for the entire town as well as the hospital. I was there for five and a half weeks, lost twenty-five pounds, and in the end was a much wiser and, yes, a more compassionate person for the experience. They told me afterwards that for the first two weeks I simply lay there, and I recall feeling so ill that I didn't much care whether I got better or not.

In any case, the dysentery continued and at the same time my abdomen became as hard as a rock—so much so that the senior of the two physicians told the other in my hearing that he thought it would be necessary to perform surgery because of suspected major abscesses. In the end, thankfully, the more junior man, who had been with Allied troops in Italy during the war and had considerable experience with diseases attacking the gut, argued against the knife, opting instead for a new drug he had seen used in Italy near the end of the war, streptomycin.

The drug worked and, though I remained shaky for some weeks, I gradually made a full recovery. The official diagnosis was confirmed as amoebic dysentery. My hair, much of which had fallen out because of the fever, grew back in and had waves it didn't have before.

One night, after I'd been there over three weeks and was beginning slowly to regain interest in getting back to health, they brought in a young miner who had been trapped for several hours by a cave-in at Pickle Crow. He'd been pinned by a large rock that crushed his leg. By the time he was rescued, the injury and resulting complications had necessitated an amputation just above the knee. He was put in the bed next to mine following his surgery and for several days after he had recovered consciousness he was in near-constant pain even though still heavily sedated. At night he would toss and turn and moan that his "foot" was hurting terribly. When he finally felt well enough for us to talk, I learned about what it was like to have a "phantom limb." He described the sense of his foot still being there and of it being trapped beneath part of the tunnel roof.

He was not that much older than me and so we formed a bond in the fellowship wrought by suffering.

As mentioned previously, small as it was, the hospital kept whites and Aboriginals segregated. Most Cree patients were on the second floor, but there was a special room for children on the first, where I was. Since there was no staff person fluent in Cree or any other Native language, and since I had learned a number of key phrases and in particular how to read and pronounce the syllabics (invented by Anglican missionaries in the 1800s), once I was able to get around I was called upon at times to act as a rough interpreter.

In one instance a Cree hunter named Big Beaver, from Bearskin Lake, had been stalking some ducks from his canoe when he grabbed his loaded shotgun by the muzzle and accidentally blew his thumb off. When surgery was required to fix the wound, a nurse came down and asked me to assist them. I went upstairs and found the doctor trying to judge whether or not his patient had had enough anaesthetic injected to leave his hand sufficiently numb for repair. The doctor seemed anxious not to overdo the medication. I could see that whenever he asked Big Beaver (Gitchee Amik) if it hurt or not when he pinched his arm, the man just grinned a stoical smile and said nothing. So the doctor pricked him with a needle and said: "Does that hurt?" He didn't reply, and the doctor made a second attempt. I asked in Cree if it hurt. His eyes widened and he said, "Yes, it does, and it really hurt the last time too!" He was then given a much larger dose of the painkiller and eventually everything was sewn up and his arm was put in a sling.

A couple of days later, a girl of about eight or nine from Fort Albany was flown down to Sioux Lookout suffering from extensive burns to her chest, arms and legs. She had suddenly walked in front of the opening to her family's teepee just as her mother threw a pot of near-boiling water out after some cooking. The girl was suffering from shock and was in extreme pain even after many days of treatment. Since she was in the small private room on our floor, we could hear her screams and almost continuous crying. Finally I was able to make out some words that she kept repeating as she gradually became more articulate. She was saying simply, "I want to go home, I want to go home." I told the nurses and they said perhaps it would comfort her if I could say even a few words she might recognize. I was happy to do so, and read her a hymn in Cree as well.

One would think that after having been so ill I wouldn't return to Big Trout. But I was back again the next summer. The year was 1950. Soon after my arrival I learned that the nurse who had been put in charge of the new, fully equipped nursing station had quit suddenly. The Indian agent's office sent word that they would like me to live in the station and to administer first aid, dispense such simple basics as Aspirin, cough syrup, ointment for scabies and so on, and keep an eye on things until her replacement could be found. I did so, and found myself holding regular dispensary hours three nights a week following dinner. No nurse appeared all summer.

The first night when I looked out there was a lineup of about twenty-five adults and children at the door, and I could see others heading my way. The thought of the gap between their expectations and my woeful ignorance was terrifying. However, with the help of a youth of about seventeen who had been out at the residential school for several years and could interpret a little, I did the best I could. The greatest demand seemed to be for "head medicine," but I soon had to ration the Aspirin when I discovered their approach: if one would help, they believed many would help more. The children came mainly for bottles of cough syrup. It took a few weeks before I realized that they kept coming back to every "clinic," rasping out their request, coughing and clearing their throats, because they loved the sweet taste of Pine Cough Syrup. Watching out the window, I would see them drink the whole bottle at one go. Once a different, evil-tasting remedy was substituted, the ailments suddenly cleared up.

Looking back at those days now, I find it difficult to believe that I, a layman with no medical background other than a few courses in first aid, was in charge of a medical facility, however simple, some five hundred kilometres from the nearest doctor or hospital. Of course, when there was a very serious illness, I could always try to send a radio message out and have a plane come in. But this involved some lapse of time. If there was very bad weather—and sometimes there were periods of two or even three weeks when no float plane could get anywhere near us—we simply had to do our best.

I always found it moving to see the incredible ability of these people to bear pain and suffering with stoical courage and calm. Garrett, the missionary, was often away on canoe trips visiting his far-flung flock, but when he was home he would pull teeth in his living room for those whose toothache had become unbearable. There was no anaesthetic, and yet the "patient" would not utter a sound during the extraction. They even continued to smile in spite of the blood and pain. Once, a Cree hunter came to the dispensary with one barb of a huge triple-pronged fish hook deeply embedded in the palm of his hand. He had been trolling for lake trout far from the post when the accident occurred. Since he was alone and had to paddle back, the hook had worked its way in to the point where it curved around a tendon. There was no recourse but to cut off the other two prongs with wire cutters and then, without any kind of painkiller, work the hook completely through and out at another place. All through this, the man never so much as flinched or changed his overall expression of dignified endurance.

I observed this characteristic repeatedly, but one case stands out above the rest. A man had sliced his knee open with a razor-sharp axe while making the keel for a canoe. When I was called to his cabin, he was lying on some dried moss that was quickly becoming soaked with blood as it spurted up out of the gaping wound. I had to apply a tourniquet to get the bleeding stopped, and then dress and bind the knee as best I could. He too never winced or moaned and, weak though he was, thanked me with a smile as I turned to leave. The good news is that he made a full recovery, though he walked with a slight limp.

The church services at Big Trout Lake held a special interest for me as a future clergyman. The church, which seated about 150, was crammed to capacity at every service. The men and boys sat on one side, the women and girls on the other. The aisles were filled and the children sat on the floor. Often a mother would be nursing one child while its toddler brother or sister would be tethered to the nearest pew by a short "rope" made from rags to prevent straying. The noise level inside the frame building once everyone had assembled was deafening, but inevitably matters got worse once the service began. Any huskies not securely tied up at home would follow their families up the hill to the church. They would then inspect each other, find out how much they disliked one another, and launch into a furious fight. As the din mounted, one of the older parishioners would invariably get up, take a stick and wade into the melee, striking at any animal within reach. The pack would then take off in all directions with blood-curdling howls loud enough to wake the dead.

The services themselves lasted anywhere from two to three hours. The extreme length was partly due to the extraordinarily protracted sermons, whether preached by Garrett or one of the many lay catechists, and partly to the fact that hymns were sung at such a slow pace that they would last for about fifteen minutes each. The Cree loved singing, and since times were quiet and they had nowhere else to go, they got full value at the Trout Lake Mission. Because I had attended church every Sunday throughout the winter in Toronto, I felt no strong obligation to be at every service myself. Instead, while out on the lake fishing, I would hear the resonant Cree voices joined in "What a Friend We Have in Jesus" come drifting over the waters while in the distance loons made the islands echo with their haunting cries.

Looking back, I know I learned a lot from the Natives of Big Trout Lake, much more than I was ever able to teach their young. The following are a couple of my lasting impressions from that time.

The three-summer experience showed me in the most eloquent fashion how non-Natives have, since the first contact, treated the First Nations peoples as little children and not as mature persons, with all that would have entailed. The Church did not consult with them, for example, about who should teach their children in the summer sessions, nor was there any discussion with elders or parents about what subjects were to be taught. At Big Trout every white person was known as the "boss" or *owgamow* of whatever aspect of the community's life he or she was in charge of. So Rev. Leslie Garrett was the church *owgamow*, I was the school *owgamow*, and the Hudson's Bay Company post manager was the boss of all bosses, the *owgamow* over all. His clerk was the *owgamow*'s little boss, or *owgamasis*. Garrett was kind to his flock but clearly defined as their superior in every way. He wasn't called Father as in the Catholic missions, but he played that role to the hilt in most details of the people's lives apart from their dealings with the HBC *owgamow* and their livelihood as trappers. Garrett held the "keys" to their souls, training those chosen to be lay readers and catechists, administering the sacraments, explaining the faith, baptizing the babies, marrying couples and burying the dead. There would be a line of adult men at the rectory door each evening waiting to seek his advice or guidance.

But it wasn't just the Anglican Church that treated the band members as juveniles. The federal government, through its various officials (and in particular the Indian agent, who was ultimately responsible for the welfare of all the bands in the northwest of Ontario and who lived a good three hours by bush plane to the south), treated them in exactly the same manner. There was an abundance of poverty. Most of the residents slept on the ground or floor, had no plumbing or electricity, and thought that the annual five dollars paid to them by the Indian agent was government largesse.

All major decisions were taken off the reserve and directives simply "came down as though from on high," whether it was a matter of whose children should be sent out to the residential school at Pelican Narrows, Sioux Lookout, or how many beaver pelts a specific hunter and his family would be allowed to sell at the post in any given year. In later years, as the plight of both the Indians and the Inuit came much more to the fore of public concerns in the country, Canadians came to see the tragic results of all the many years of such paternalism.

The other issue that shouted aloud to me then was the perverse way in which Aboriginal spirituality was ignored or despised. This problem still resonates with me today whenever I read yet more shocking news stories about the high rate of suicide among young people on the reserves in the Big Trout region and in the various Native communities all around the shores of James Bay and Hudson Bay. Overall, Native spirituality from the earliest days of first contact was deliberately looked down upon, and wherever it dared any open expression it was instantly and crudely stifled. We now know the havoc wrought by the residential schools as tools of this campaign.

Instead of trying to discover and understand the spiritual traditions and rituals of the conquered first inhabitants of Canada, the government, the missionaries and non-Natives in general immediately assumed they were the vestiges of a savage past that needed to be eradicated as swiftly and as thoroughly as possible. One of the most shocking, even appalling, aspects of this situation is the fact that for over a hundred years it was Canada's official policy to "take the Indian out of the Indian." That is an exact quote from Sir Duncan Campbell Scott, head of the Indian Affairs department, as he defined his mandate early in the last century. The results have been a national scandal for years. It does not require a team of experts or a Royal Commission to discover that if you destroy the spiritual beliefs and practices of a people and discourage the use of their languages, you cut off the very wellspring of their being. You rob them of the source of that strength and meaning which made it possible for them to live full, happy and productive lives in one of the harshest environments on the face of the earth. We taught them to earn their living by trapping and then, when fashions or sensibilities "outside" suddenly changed, they were deprived of any viable means of earning a living. Faced with unemployment at a rate that would cause riots and chaos in the rest of the country, the great majority are today left relying wholly on welfare. The young people have nothing to do and nowhere to go. The suicide rate among males from fourteen to thirty is a literal horror story. The same is true for the Inuit as well.

There have been and continue to be attempts to revive Aboriginal religious traditions, but the grim truth is that an awful lot of this past has been forgotten and any meaningful recovery is going to take a huge amount of time and dedication on the part of those sincerely desirous of seeing a renaissance in our day. This is an area where the churches could help, if they could set aside for a while their arrogant assumption that the white man's God and the white man's Saviour is the only way of salvation for the world. My experiences at Big Trout had begun to teach me a lesson that I would take a long time to learn.*

---

* In June 2010, hearings began in a Truth and Reconciliation Event, a five-year project aimed at healing wounds in the Aboriginal communities of Canada caused by the residential schools. It has a budget of $60 million and is a product of the largest class action in Canadian history, brought by former students of the schools against the federal government and four churches who were involved. The church-run, government-funded residential schools began in the 1870s and the last one only closed in 1996. Children were taken, often forcibly, from their parents and traditional way of life. They were forbidden to speak their Native tongues or practise their culture. They were forced to become Christians, and many were physically or sexually abused. See editorials in the *Toronto Star*, July 24 and 25, 2010.

In May 1998, I returned to Big Trout with my wife Susan for a week to mark the fiftieth anniversary of my first visit there. Much had changed. The Hudson's Bay store is gone. In its place is a large Native-run supermarket complex, which includes a clothing store, hardware store, deep-fried-chicken outlet and gasoline pump. The old clapboard church that also served as my school is gone as well. Today's school, with about 270 pupils from grades one through eleven, is much like schools everywhere, down to obscenities scribbled on the exterior. There's a huge gymnasium and a computer room. Modern bungalows stand where teepees once were the norm. Some are in top condition—others are eyesores. But most at least have oil heating, a refrigerator and a TV set.

But there were less positive aspects as well. There is a growing crisis of diabetes, tuberculosis and other diseases. The detritus of consumer technology—machines, twisted snowmobiles, rusting vehicles, a million plastic containers—smother parts of the town in ugliness. Their annual cleanup was scheduled for the month following my visit, but like the rest of us, Big Trout residents have bought into the disposable society. And behind the growth and signs of prosperity is another dark shadow. As some angry teenagers told us, "There's nothing to do here." Hundreds of similar Native communities across Canada still lack safe drinking water. The infant mortality rate continues to be a national scandal. The plight of our Aboriginal peoples remains a disgrace.

When I first came to Big Trout Lake in 1948, these were an economically independent people to a large degree, living off the land. Today, much of the settlement is on welfare.

Susan and I loved the people. I was deeply moved to meet so many of my old students and to make new friends. But I came away feeling very sad. These people, as one former chief said, "need a deep healing of the spirit" in order to find a different future. The current Truth and Reconciliation hearings will hopefully be a small step in that direction.

4

"THE LORD IS MY LIGHT": MOTTO OF OXFORD UNIVERSITY

MY FATHER KNEW all about the Rhodes Scholarships many years before I was eligible to apply. Candidates had to be male (a restriction that thankfully has long since been removed), be in their final year at a Canadian university, and have a thorough track record of academic and athletic achievement together with some signs of leadership potential and of concern for the welfare of others. Cecil Rhodes, born in 1853, an imperialist who had made a fortune in the diamond mines of South Africa, created the scholarship fund in his will in 1902. It was to be the world's first international study program. Ideally, Rhodes wanted the impossible: fully rounded individuals who would take back to their countries of origin the gifts offered by an Oxford education (something he didn't complete all in one session because of poor health). When my father started to campaign and exhort me to apply, I wasn't optimistic.

Several well-meaning but misinformed key people, some of whom I had hoped to put down as my necessary references, told me fairly directly that these scholarships always went to the sons of

the educated "well-to-do" in Canadian life. The not-so-subtle sub-
text was that an east-ender whose parents were working-class immigrants from a family where nobody, at least in recent generations,
had ever gone to university didn't have a hope in Hades of getting
the award. Recent studies of successful Rhodes Scholarship appli-
cants over the years show this perception to have been quite erroneous. Fortunately, my father convinced me to move ahead with
an application. I had the high marks, and while I wasn't extremely
proficient in any one particular sport, I had played intramural bas-
ketball and hockey for Wycliffe College. I was also a member of
the university history club as well as the leader of a growing young
people's Bible class at a downtown church. And I had spent the three
summers at Big Trout Lake teaching Cree children.

All of this was noted in my application, which was sent in early
October 1950. Some weeks went by and then a letter came inviting
me to a reception for the candidates from all over the province. It
was held one evening near the end of November at the large
Rosedale home of Roland Michener, himself a former Rhodes
Scholar, who was eventually chosen by the Queen to be the Governor General of Canada. Although the Micheners were warm and
hospitable, I felt self-conscious because all the guests knew that
only two of us would be chosen to be Ontario's scholars when we
went for our formal interview on the coming Saturday. Quite naturally, we were all busy assessing our competitors while being ultra-
polite. Because I didn't drink at that point in my life, I was one of
the very few people who didn't have a glass of sherry or white wine
to hold on to. I was seized with a kind of stage fright and felt certain
I would be perceived as altogether too shy and awkward. It was a
great relief when the evening ended and we said our goodbyes.

On the Saturday, however, as the hour for my interview drew
closer, I felt increasingly calm and ready for anything. It seemed to
me that I had nothing to lose and everything to gain by going in and

doing my best. Perhaps my lack of optimism somehow lent me a certain poise, I don't know. The interview was held in a lovely, familiar reading room on the second floor of Hart House. When I went in, I was shown to a chair facing a panel of five or six men, all of them former Rhodes Scholars, all of them distinguished in some branch of Canadian life. There were a couple of professors, a noted medical authority and a judge. They took turns asking probing yet friendly questions about my plans should I be selected and go on to Oxford, about my views on the future of religion, and in some detail about what I thought of the federal government's policies regarding our Native peoples. It was in fact a truly relaxed and stimulating experience. As the chairman thanked me and showed me out, he whispered, "Well done."

I went for a long walk around Queen's Park to try to settle down and then went back to my room at Wycliffe to work on a piece of Greek prose composition that was due on the coming Monday morning. It was by then around five-thirty. Because it was a Saturday, the college was nearly empty; almost all of the boarders had gone home or were out for the evening. The theological students had left for the parishes where they assisted on weekends. It had grown dark outside, and the place was almost unnaturally silent.

At about six-thirty, the third-floor buzzer rang out with my particular signal code. I went to the top of the stairs and shouted down to the student who was tending the front hall desk, "Who is it?" He yelled back, "It's somebody for you, Harpur." I tore down the three flights to the phone booth below. A deep male voice asked, "Is that Tom Harpur?" I said it was and he announced, "Congratulations, Tom. You've been awarded a Rhodes Scholarship and will be going to the college of your choice at Oxford next fall." I managed somehow to thank him and hung up. For a moment I braced myself against the back of the booth and said a brief but profoundly heartfelt prayer of thanksgiving to God who had made this miracle possible.

I was momentarily overwhelmed. Then I telephoned my parents to share the news and to tell them I was coming home by streetcar as soon as possible.

My father greeted me at the door simply beaming and nearly bursting with pride. "Where's Mum?" I asked. He said, "She's up in our bedroom on her knees praying that God will show you that you ought not to go unless it really is His will." I had a problem with the logic and the theology of that kind of response, but I knew she loved me and, in spite of her anxious disposition, would at some point admit she too was pleased with this unprecedented event in our family's history. In the end, it was a very happy evening in our humble Lawlor Avenue home.

My parents drove me to Montreal some months later to catch the Cunard liner that would take me to Liverpool and a brief visit in Northern Ireland with our many relatives there before I journeyed on to Oxford. Standing in the crowd at the ship's rail as the engines began to thrum and the small gap of water between oneself and loved ones on the dock began to widen ever more rapidly brought a rush of conflicting emotions. There was all the excitement of a great unknown adventure begun, mixed with premature home-sickness as Canada and home would now be gone from my life for two years, perhaps three.

The last time I had made this same voyage down the St. Lawrence and across the Atlantic was as a boy of nine. I was now twenty-two, this was the first of five crossings by ship I would make as an adult, not to mention many more later by aircraft as a journal-ist for the *Toronto Star* and for pleasure trips. An economy-class berth on a Cunarder was to my mind a luxury beyond compare. It was September and as we sailed downriver the maples along the north shore of the St. Lawrence were already tinged with scarlet. Bright steeples gleamed above every village clustering at the water's edge. There was all the time in the world to read, to walk briskly around the decks, to chat with other travellers and to delight in a succession of simply glorious dining experiences. When we reached the open Atlantic, I found that gazing steadily off at the distant horizon for a fixed period of from twenty minutes to half an hour morning and evening was an effective form of meditation—unless of course one was susceptible to seasickness, as some passengers quickly found they were. However, no mode of travel this observer has ever since employed comes even close to the sheer joy of an ocean crossing in a modern liner. Few things are better for one's spiritual or physical health.

Arriving in Oxford on a late September afternoon was quite an anticlimax. Trains entering the city from the north catch a quick glimpse of spires and towers across a river flanked by a wide expanse of meadow (Port Meadow) before being swallowed up by numerous other engines, dark sheds, stark mechanical devices of various kinds, vistas of cluttered back gardens, and then the looming shadows of what used to be known as the gasworks. Having been primed by all the lofty praise dedicated in poetry and prose to chanting the aesthetic charms, the "towers in the mist," of this ancient city, I felt let down. But by the time the taxicab was out of the station area and whizzing down the High Street, things were looking a great deal better. Even though it is much more invaded by and surrounded with all that makes up a very busy English city than Cambridge is (Oxford has been described as a city that has a university while Cambridge is a university that also happens to be a city), it more than measures up in the end to all the advance notices. It is just more tucked away, more subtly woven into its background, more reluctant to give up all its treasures all at once than "the other place," as Cambridge was known to all Oxonians.

I must have seemed like a very keen "colonial" (as some of the English students liked to dub those of us from overseas) because when the taxi dropped me together with my luggage at the gate to Oriel College, I was promptly told by an elderly gentleman at the porter's lodge that I was more than a week early. "Room's not ready yet, sir," he said. "You're a bit ahead of yourself, you are." He consented to my leaving most of my stuff at the college in spite of this and recommended a small hotel near Magdalen Bridge, farther down the High Street (popularly referred to as "the High"). I took a very modest room at the Eastgate Hotel, where, as I would learn later, the already renowned author and lecturer C.S. Lewis was regularly to be seen enjoying a pint or two with a friend at the cozy bar below. He was an English tutor at Magdalen (pronounced Maw-da-lin) at that time.

Later that night, while having supper at a second-floor restaurant overlooking the High, it was brought forcibly home to me just how much the British were still feeling the effects of World War II. There was no meat to speak of on the menu and not a great deal of choice of other dishes either. I was soon to discover, once properly moved into residence, that several staple foods were still being rationed, eggs, butter, margarine, tea and sugar among them. My scout, as the college servant who looked after the "young gentlemen" on each staircase was called, presented me with a tiny piece of butter, a small block of margarine and a small bag of sugar every Monday morning once I took up residence. You were supposed to use these for tea in your room and bring them along to the refectory at mealtimes.

My scout's name was Cuddiford (I never learned his first name as he seemed more than content to be called by his surname) and he had served as batman to a senior officer in the British army during World War II. He brought each of us hot water for shaving when he came in and flung open the curtains every morning, and then cleaned up the dishes after teatime each afternoon. In hall, as the refectory was known, Cuddiford and the other scouts served the meals—wearing formal wear for dinner. The dons or tutors (officially known as Fellows of Oriel College) took their meals with the provost (principal or president of the college) on a raised dais or platform at the head of the hall. They had much better fare than was served to the students, together with wines from a well-stocked cellar.

In his will, Cecil Rhodes—who was once upset while dining at Oriel to find there were holes in his table napkin—had left a princely sum to uphold the dignity and honour of the college's head table. Dinner each evening began with the provost or one of the dons standing up and bowing to a student whose scholarship or bursary entailed his saying the lengthy Latin Oriel grace or blessing of the food. He would commence with an answering bow and then launch into it. I found that after a couple of weeks I had unconsciously memorized this sonorous-sounding invocation, and even today it resonates in its entirety the moment I recall the scene to mind. The grace was reportedly first recorded by St. John Chrysostom, an early patriarch of Constantinople who played a not insignificant role in this writer's life, as we shall see. It can now be found in full, with a translation, under the Wikipedia entry for Oriel College on the Internet.

While it has changed and grown over the centuries, Oriel College is one of the oldest in the university, having been founded by Edward II in 1326. It will thus celebrate its seven hundredth anniversary in 2026, a short time from now. Because it was a royal foundation, Her Majesty The Queen is the official college Visitor and must pay a formal visit whenever her duties bring her to Oxford. There is a large portrait of the founder at the north end of the hall, over the head table, and one of Queen Elizabeth II at the south end. The hall itself is a stunning, light-filled, oak-panelled edifice with a soaring hammerbeam roof. When the tables are laid with the historic college silver, some of it dating back to the medieval period, and the place is packed with students—today both male and female, since women were finally admitted in 1985—it simply glows with warmth and vibrant energy. It wasn't long before I felt very much at home.

At the same time, I must admit up front that being a student at Oxford and a member of Oriel was a truly humbling experience. People much wiser and cleverer than I have expressed the same feelings about this. You see yourself from a different perspective when you walk amidst the ghosts of all the great names from the past. Just to take Oriel alone: The key founders of the Oxford Movement in the Church of England—John Henry Cardinal Newman, Edward Bouverie Pusey and John Keble—were at one time Fellows of Oriel. Sir Walter Raleigh was a student (*c.*1585), as was Lord Fairfax of Cameron (1710–1713), the patron and friend of George Washington. Winston Churchill's grandfather John Spencer-Churchill, seventh Duke of Marlborough, attended Oriel, as did Cecil Rhodes (1876–78), the poet Matthew Arnold (1845), two Nobel Prize laureates and numerous bishops, including two Archbishops of Canterbury. In short, the full list of notables who walked those cloistered halls is beyond impressive. But, thankfully, as well as being sometimes intimidating, the illustrious history of Oriel, and of Oxford itself, was a source of inspiration. It made you want to do your very best.

Readers who have enjoyed the British television crime series *Inspector Morse* will be interested to learn that the buildings and quadrangles of Oriel College were used as the location for "Ghost in the Machine," under the name of Courtenay College, as well as the following episodes: "The Silent World of Nicholas Quinn," "The Infernal Serpent," "Deadly Slumber," "Twilight of the Gods" and "Death is Now My Neighbour." The college was also used as the location for the actor Hugh Grant's first major film in 1982, *Privileged*, as well as for *Oxford Blues* (1984), *True Blue* (1991) and *The Dinosaur Hunter* (2000). Other television series, a documentary (on Gilbert White) and the book *Tom Brown at Oxford* by Thomas Hughes were also shot or set either in part or wholly at Oriel. When I first walked around Oxford in my early days there, I felt very much as though it were all one big movie set because of the rich and at times nostalgic aura surrounding everything, especially when the mist rose up from the Cherwell and Isis rivers in the evenings. Since then, the city has in fact become the movie set I thought it was in 1951.

At Oxford they talk not of studying a particular subject but of "reading" political science or economics or physics. I read Classics, or "Greats" as it was called, and so was not actually exposed to an English seminary. However, every college had its Anglican chapel and a learned chaplain. Oriel, one of the smallest and oldest of the colleges, was no exception. The circumstances of my meeting our chaplain, Dr. Roy Porter, for the first time were somewhat unusual. I had just arrived to take up residence the day before. My room was on the second floor, off staircase number one, in the main quadrangle. Immediately below me was the large, though similarly bare, suite of the Captain of Boats—head of the Oriel College Rowing Club. On this particular evening there was a club party in his rooms to celebrate the beginning of a new term. The din of the revellers was worsened when, as they drained each glass of beer, they tossed the glass through an open window to crash on the concrete pavement around the quadrangle of grass below. Coming from a conservative background, and being Canadian, I was surprised at both the obvious drunkenness and the wanton waste.

Then I heard a crash of tangled metal. I looked downstairs and saw a student with his dinner jacket askew, bow tie hanging by a thread, climbing the stairs carrying a bicycle over his shoulders. I watched open-mouthed as he staggered past me up to the third floor, paused for a moment before an open window, and then threw the bicycle out and down to the quad below. "What on earth are you doing?" I asked, and he said with an inebriated grin: "My tutor told me that after the party he wanted to see the whole quad filled with bicycles!"

I decided to lodge a formal complaint and went in search of the Captain of Boats. Looking into the crowded room, my eyes focused on a small black-suited figure with a clerical collar: the college chaplain, a man renowned for his knowledge of the ancient Biblical languages and one of the most noted of the translators of the New English Bible. Porter was being held firmly in the grip of two very large oarsmen while a third wound bathroom tissue around him in wreaths from head to foot. A fourth student then mounted a chair holding a pitcher of beer and, reciting some kind of Latin mumbo-jumbo, poured the beer over the chaplain's head in a mockery of baptism. The helpless cleric spotted me and cried out for rescue. Call it discretion or cowardice, but there were twenty "enthusias-tic" young men in the room who were looking for trouble. I decided that anyone clever enough to decipher Hebrew ought to have known better than to be there in the first place, so I retreated and left him to their mercies. The next day I saw him enjoying himself at the head table with the other dons, so it seemed his little encounter had caused him no permanent damage.

With these antics and many more, I suffered a certain loss of innocence during those first few days in the city of mist and "dream-ing spires."

My footsteps reverberated through the deserted quad and the clock tower began to tremble as its inner workings prepared to sound the hour. Peter Brunt, my tutor in Greek and Roman history, had sent a terse note earlier in the day saying he was down with a cold, wouldn't be able to meet with me for the usual full hour, but would I come along at eight p.m. for a brief chat about my studies? I adjusted my ridiculously short commoner's gown as I reached the door of his apartment. As yet we hadn't been introduced, although his rooms were on the front quad not far from my own. As I knocked, the eight strokes of the bell had begun their doleful litany.

The chiming ended before I could make out the distant, excep-tionally nasal voice saying: "Come in, come in—the bloody door is open!" I entered timidly into what proved to be his study-cum-sitting-room. The air was rank with stale cigarette smoke. Books, papers and files were stacked on all sides. Apart from two tired, deep easy chairs in front of the standard electric fireplace, the only piece of furniture visible was a large oak table. There was so much clutter around and upon it, however, that it was very well disguised. The best thing about the room, as I subsequently discovered, was its splendid view of the college's main quadrangle, with the entrance or clock tower on the west and the ancient hall or refectory on the east.

The door in one corner of the study was open and Professor Brunt, my don or tutor, could be seen propped up in bed, surrounded by more stacks of books. He was sneezing loudly, and apparently very moistly, into a dubious-looking handkerchief. His eyes and nose were red and his hair was tousled. When the immediate paroxysms were over, he waved me in with an impatient gesture of his free hand, holding the hanky ready with the other. Since there was no place to sit—the only chair was already carrying its own literary burden—I stood respectfully at the foot of the narrow, astonishingly short bed and tried my best not to stare.

To be honest, I was both scared and intrigued at the same time. I knew this germ-laden, wheezing gentleman was one of the greatest living authorities on the classical period of Greece and Rome. He was later to become the Camden Professor of Ancient History at Oxford, from 1970 to 1982. Brunt, the son of a Methodist minister, was born in 1918 and was eighty-eight when he died. He had scored a rare double first in his own time as an undergraduate and was then, at about thirty-six, still a comparatively young man. I figured he had already forgotten more that I might ever know. What I didn't realize at the time was that I was destined to spend at least an hour a week on my own with Brunt for three eight-week terms every year for the next three, a total of over seventy-two hours one-on-one. It was a schooling in the history of the period before and surrounding the birth of Christianity that few people have been

privileged to receive. Above all, it taught me in depth about this
crucial question: What constitutes genuine historical evidence, or in
other words, what do we truly mean by "historical" and "historicity"? That question was to play an important role in the later controversy over *The Pagan Christ*.

"You're Harpur, are you?" he coughed. I assured him I was.
"You're my eleventh student. The others will come in pairs for tu-
torials, but you'll have to come by yourself."

At the time, this had no significance for me. What I didn't know
was that when there were two students, one would read his weekly
essay aloud; the other would be assumed to have written one if he
made a useful contribution to the discussion. Thus, you could get
away with just making notes on your research every other week.
Being alone for each session, however, meant I had no option but to
write an essay for Brunt every time. He explained that these essays
should be about two thousand words long, which would be roughly
twenty minutes of reading aloud. With a snuffle close to a snort, he
said: "And I don't want you just to regurgitate what you've read in
the books I assign for each topic. I've read them; I know what's in
them already. What we want to know is what you think about what
they think—backed by plenty of evidence."

He was, as I later learned, a very gentle person, but he sniffled
and dabbed his streaming eyes and fixed me with what I thought
was an angry grimace, then shot out: "You do read Greek, don't
you?" When I nodded that I did, he fished around among the books
on the chair and, coming up with a worn copy of Thucydides' *History of the Peloponnesian War*, stabbed a stubby finger down on a page
and ordered: "Start translating from there."

I was barely under way when he asked the same question about
Latin, and hauled out a copy of Tacitus's *Annals*. I exchanged Thucydides for it with a sense of relief. I could handle Tacitus's Latin more
easily than Thucydides' elegant yet knotty Greek any day of the
week.

He seemed to be quickly satisfied, and I began to feel a lot more confident. This sense was shaken, however, when he asked if I read French. "A little," I said. "Do you read German?" "No," I replied weakly. "Mmm, what a pity," he sighed. He arranged the blankets under his chin and added: "Oh, by the way, your first tutorial will be on Wednesday at four p.m. Write an essay on the Athenian law-giver Solon's reforms." He outlined a number of books to read in addition to the Greek sources. A sharp pang of alarm stabbed at my stomach: at least two of the books on the list were in German! My three years of study with Professor Brunt had commenced.

The next time I saw him, he was over his cold and ushered me through his door with a flourish of his lighted cigarette. Standing a scant five foot six or so, he peered up at my height with concern. Once he got me seated in the deeper of the easy chairs, he stood on the raised fender of the fireplace, his elbows crooked against the mantel. Staring down at me now, he seemed to feel more at ease. "You're rather huge, aren't you?" he observed. "The boat club will be glad to see you coming—the rugger club too." In what I was soon to recognize was his habitual way, he sucked vehemently on his cigarette with his mouth open on either side of it. I was later told by other smokers that by hyper-aspirating thus one can maintain a kind of mild high because of an excess of oxygen being inhaled along with the smoke.

There was an awkward period of silence after he expressed his thoughts about the putative benefits that my size might confer on Oriel College's athletic hopes. Then he abruptly said: "Start read-ing." I pulled the product of my late-night labours (the technical term is my "lucubrations") from my jacket pocket and, feeling a lit-tle self-conscious at being one grown man reading aloud to another who was perfectly capable of reading himself, began along the labyrinthine, even tortured paths of my reconstruction of Greek history. Occasionally he would mumble to himself, causing me to lose my place. Once or twice he challenged a statement and watched me try to defend myself. At the end he sat smoking for a few minutes and saying nothing. Finally he said: "That's not too bad. Like a glass of sherry?"

I read him an essay every week during terms. It was an enriching encounter. We were ploughing a narrow furrow, but we ploughed it very deeply indeed.

Since Greats was a two-stream discipline composed of both ancient history (Greek and Roman) and philosophy, I had a philosophy tutor in addition to Peter Brunt. His name was Richard Robinson, a tall, slightly stooped, gaunt-looking man with sad eyes and a trace of an American accent though he had spent most of his life in England. He was in his early forties when I first met him and he died not all that long ago at just short of ninety-five years of age. He seemed a very solemn person and never spoke without giving his words considerable forethought. Robinson's task was to instruct me not just in the philosophy of the ancient masters, Plato and Aristotle—in much greater depth than I had ever gone before and of course in their original Greek—but also in the writings and ideas of philosophers ever since, down to the modern empiricists. Robinson was a long-time atheist (he had written a book on atheist ideals as well as one on Plato's theory of definition) and we often had lengthy discussions that edged at times into disputes over matters of faith and religion in general. We met once a week in term over three years and I knew him very well by the end. He would sit at the far end of a long oak table in his rather bare study and as I began to read my weekly offering he routinely propped his elbows on the table, let his head sink into his hands on either side and closed his eyes. Just when I felt certain that my essay had put him to sleep, he would snap his eyes open and critique or question something I'd said. Often he'd challenge my grammar. "There you go again. You keep splitting the infinitive," he would splutter. I would apologize and soldier on.

It was a painful process at times, but he taught me to think more sharply than I ever had before. I learned a tremendous amount from him and learned also to respect the atheist position while in fundamental disagreement with it—as I remain today. I grew to like the man, but he did seem haunted by an unforgiving melancholy. Whenever I think of him I recall one day when my tutorial was scheduled for eleven a.m. Robinson had just been walking down the High before coming to our meeting. He told me that a few minutes ago he had been looking at the students crowded into a couple of coffee shops nearby. He fixed me with his sorrowful gaze and said: "You know, Harpur, happy people depress me so."

The full richness of studying for three years at Oxford would take a book of its own to attempt to describe. There was the first long summer vacation when four of us bought an ancient London taxi and toured the Continent in it for over a month. There were other vacations where I worked cutting firewood and carrying out many other outdoor chores on a gorgeous Christian-run holiday estate on the edge of Exmoor National Park overlooking the Bristol Channel. There was always a mountain of assigned reading, but it could be done wherever one went. Several times I stayed with my uncle and aunt in Tullyhogue, Ireland, where one could always break the brain work by grabbing a fishing rod and going down to the river. The two terriers used to watch through the window, waiting for the slightest movement towards the cupboard where the guns and fishing rods were kept. They would then almost turn cartwheels in a frenzy to get going.

In spiritual matters, I found myself broadening out steadily. I became good friends with a fellow Orielensis, Andrew Bull, who happened to be Roman Catholic. Andrew rowed next to me in one of the "eights" in many practices and stirring races on the Isis (the upper Thames), and we had many vigorous discussions. (By a curious synchronicity, my annual copy of the *Oriel Record* arrived in the mail the same day I wrote this last passage. It contained updates on the activities of the widely flung, vast family of alumni, and also the obit for Andrew. He was later in life awarded an OBE by the Queen for his work on behalf of education in Portugal.) When I happened to mention this ongoing friendship and our debates in a letter home, I got a swift and tersely worded note from my father telling me to be very careful about my friends, and warning me of the possible risk of being recruited to Rome!

My parents, it should be noted, had picked out the church I should attend while at Oxford (on the advice of their evangelical friends from the "old country"). It was St. Ebbe's, a keenly evangelical, Low Church congregation headed by Rev. Maurice Wood, later named as a bishop by the Queen. The church fairly bulged with students, but after my first year I began foraging elsewhere because there was a certain *everything-down-pat*ness, an overly either-or mentality of a fundamentalist flavour that I was beginning to find intellectually and spiritually cramping and confining. Even so, looking back over the more than one hundred airmail letters I wrote home during those years—my father kept them all and pasted them into a very thick scrapbook, which I still have—I realize now with some shock how extremely pious I was in the earliest days at Oriel. It embarrasses me today to read what I wrote then. Like the folk at St. Ebbe's, I spoke about "real Christians," that is, those who had been "properly (*sic*) saved" and who were quite different from the larger crowd of merely "nominal Christians." Everything had to be seen as "the Lord's will." If evangelicals were the only real Christians and non-Christian religions were wholly out of the loop of salvation, obviously only a very small part of humanity stood a ghost of a chance of reaching "heaven." Even then, however, this sad and mistaken division of the human race into the saved and the unsaved was holding less and less appeal. The seeds were already being sown as I gradually saw the need for nothing less than a spirituality that could embrace not only all of humanity but also the natural world, and the whole of the cosmos as well. Nothing less would be worthy of a God in whom one could believe. It was a long time coming, but the shaking of the foundations of former beliefs was already well under way.

There is a tradition of every Canadian who goes up to Oxford spending part of his time playing ice hockey for the university. I was not particularly good at hockey, although I had played for Wycliffe College at the University of Toronto during my undergraduate days. As a boy I had played in goal once but quit when they started calling me "the human sieve." I loved to skate, however, and my size, which interfered with my ever being really talented at the sport, was considered a plus for a defenceman when truly capable hockey players were few and far between. I might not be able to score goals, but I could bounce the opposition a little and slow them down, or so the coaches hoped.

At Oxford, however, there were problems surrounding this particular sport, mainly the lack of a proper ice rink. We had to travel by chartered bus to London's Harringay, Wembley or Streatham arenas both for practices and for the games themselves. These rinks could only be used after the regular public skating was over, from ten p.m. onwards. This meant long hours of boring rides to and fro and the rigours of "climbing in" over the college walls in the small hours of the morning afterwards, because of course the bus was very late in returning and the college grounds were locked at midnight.

My roommate, Donald Schultz (who was to become Professor of Engineering at Oxford and later an OBE, and who died in 1988 while hiking in New Zealand), rigged up a system for me. He tied a cord to a boot that he placed on his desk and ran the cord out the window to a height of about two and a half metres above the pavement below. I could just reach it with a jump and, by pulling hard, drag the boot off the table to make it clatter into his metal wastebasket and wake him up. He would then get dressed, go down to the quadrangle, through the arch at the other side into the centre quad, and climb up on top of the four-metre wall looking down into

Oriel Street by means of a ladder we had left concealed behind the
shrubbery. Once on top, carefully straddling the rotating spikes set
there to discourage just such exploits as these, he would heave the
ladder up and over to the spot where I was waiting. With all my
hockey gear in a duffle bag, I would climb up and both of us would
balance precariously as we then reversed the procedure. I still have
a small scar on one hand where the spikes took their toll.

After several months of this routine, including a disastrous match
with Cambridge for which I won a Half Blue, I realized the futility
of this exercise and took up rowing instead.

"Come on, Jesus!"

This bizarre shout was followed by three cracks of pistol shots in
quick succession and then a chorus of other loud cheers. I stopped
in my tracks. I thought I had inadvertently stumbled into the making of a film—a weird sacred western of some kind. Otherwise, it
must be cloud-cuckoo-land. A knot of rowdy undergraduates was
surging directly towards me, yelling and firing. But the location
was a towpath alongside the River Thames (or the Isis as it is called
when it curves around Oxford). The occasion was Eights Week, the
annual five-day rowing event to determine which college is "head
of the river."

The cheers were for the eight-man crew and coxswain of the
Jesus College boat. The blank shots were to signal that they were
overlapping the boat ahead of them and could sweep across for a
"bump." Since you row with your back to the direction in which
you're headed, it's impossible for an oarsman to get an accurate
assessment of the right moment to strain to strike. It's even hard for
the coxswain, steering with eight large, toiling bodies in his line of
sight. Hence all the shooting.

Rowing has long been a hugely competitive tradition between
Oxford and Cambridge in the annual boat race that takes place
every spring around Easter. The Captain of Boats at Oriel, as previ-

ously mentioned, lived in rooms on the ground floor of number one staircase. Since mine were on the same staircase, I had to pass his door several times daily. It wasn't long before he invited me to sign up. I soon discovered there was a great deal more to oarsmanship than simple brute strength and determination. To begin with, every initiate had to toil for many autumn afternoons at what was dubbed a "bank tub."

Near the boathouse on the Isis, just off the towpath, was a stubby, squarish-looking "boat" permanently bolted on one side to a dock. It was really a mock version of a section of a racing eight, complete with a sliding seat, foot stirrups and an oarlock. The chief difference from the real thing was that the oar one was given had two wide gaps in it that ran close to the full length of the blade. Once the art of squaring the blade to cut the water at a firm right angle was mastered, the stroke could be carried through with a firm sense of pressure but without the full weight of water caught and carried forward by a normal blade.

It took time, under the critical eye of a member of the crew of the college's first eight, but after a few weeks I was deemed fit to go out on the river in a regular boat. What a mess we made of it! The coach shouted instructions from his bicycle on the towpath, but he was close to losing not just his voice but his temper before the outing was over. It was one thing to pseudo-row in a bank tub, it was quite another to try to coordinate one's oar with those of other beginners just as shaky as oneself. Nobody had warned us that balance was just as important as timing your stroke. The boat rolled easily, so that the surface of the water could be at quite a different place or plane between the time one stroke was ended and another was begun. If once the boat was actually under way your oar "caught a crab" (was too deep in the water), it almost brought the boat to a total halt as the handle was forcibly wrenched from your hands to end up striking your solar plexus while the blade was pulled uncontrollably downwards. The offending oarsman immediately became the focus of a number of intensely cross glares and much shouting from the riverbank.

Once we finally settled in and became the crew our coach was doggedly determined we should be, it was sheer joy to be out on a crisp fall day with a crew on the river. You never forget the crack of eight long oars simultaneously biting into the water as the racing shell beneath you leaps suddenly forward. As you drive your legs, back and arms into the full stroke and then slide ahead, coiling to release the next, the boat becomes a living thing, gliding with barely a susurrating curl of wave at the bow. Eight muscled bodies move as one. Everything melts into a rhythmic single-mindedness. If you close your eyes, as we sometimes were told to do in practice drill, it feels as though you are flying. The wind is on your face and the rest of the world is forgotten. It's a glorious feeling.

In the distance, the towers and Gothic pinnacles of the colleges kept silent watch; in nearby meadows, geese and cattle grazed; close by, the majestic swans sailed on in sublime indifference. It was an almost mystical experience—until a passing barge would occasionally send a swell that would slap over the side of the shell and douse your sweaty back with cold spray. However, after a warm shower later and sitting down to tea in your study—toast and honey or a bit of cheese—before hitting the books, you felt truly alive, glowing and at peace. Our crew managed to win our oars twice and went on to wear with pride the distinctive tortoise ties—a dark blue tie with a white tortoise image sewn into it just below the knot—that marked our membership in the Tortoise Club. It is composed of those who manage to row in the long-distance races held annually on the River Thames at Reading. The college mascot was a big tortoise that could sometimes be seen sunning itself in a corner of one of the college's three quads.

One of our crew members, Ronald Watts, the son of a Canadian Anglican bishop, later went on to become provost of Queen's University in Kingston, Ontario. Ron and I went to the coronation of Elizabeth II in June 1953 by paddling down the Thames from Oxford to London. At night we slept under the canoe, which I had had my father ship over to me during my first term, and we dined off a very large Dutch cheese and a couple of loaves of bread. We spent two full days on the trip, paddling past Eton College, Windsor Castle and Runnymede Island, where Magna Carta was signed, and later brought the craft back to Oxford on the train.

Many years later, in 1983, at the Oxford eightieth reunion of Rhodes Scholars, which we were both attending with our wives, the Queen spoke to us and I was able to tell her of our perhaps eccentric mode of getting to her ceremony all those years ago. Her eyes twinkled as she laughed and said: "How clever of you to have paddled downstream!" A Reuters cameraman caught the happy exchange and it was featured not just in the *Toronto Star* but also in the *New York Times* and several other international newspapers the next day.

This photo op didn't just happen by chance, although luck lent a hand. The *Toronto Star* foreign editor had asked me to cover the reunion since I was planning on being there in any case. So I had arranged for a freelance photographer from Reuters in London to be in the gardens at Rhodes House for the Queen's visit. The former Governor General of Canada, Roland Michener, the oldest Rhodes Scholar on the list of those attending, was supposed to be there to greet Her Majesty. My instructions to the photographer were to capture a shot of the two of them meeting to accompany my story, to be filed later that night by phone to Toronto. Just as the rope line had been set up in the gardens and the crowd of scholars and their partners was buzzing in anticipation, the Australian freelancer whom Reuters had sent came up to me to say that Michener had reportedly been taken ill and would not be available for a picture. I told him: "Do you see that attractive lady with the coral dress and white hat?" I pointed to Susan, who was standing nearby talking to the Wattses. "If you see the Queen come anywhere close to her, get that shot if you possibly can." I went back over to stand with Susan.

Just as the Queen, by a remarkable synchronicity, crossed to where we, together with Ron and Donna Watts, were grouped, I saw the photographer emerge above the heads of the people on the other side of the huge crowd and begin to shoot some film. He was obviously standing on a chair or box of some sort. As the Queen ended her brief stop and chat with us, I looked across at him and saw the palace police pulling him down, but not before he gave me a thumbs-up signal and a huge grin. He had got the shot, and it made the subsequent feature glow.

The following evening there was a special dinner in the gardens of the main quadrangle of Balliol College. It was a formal occasion and large tents had been set up to cover the affair in case of rain. The guest of honour and speaker for the event was the aging but vigorous former prime minister Sir Harold Macmillan. Everyone was given a glass of champagne at the entrance to the quad and with the former scholars and their partners all in tuxedos and black tie or lovely gowns, it was a highly colourful scene. Macmillan was at the top of his form—witty, provocative and wise. The wines were excellent and the fellowship over and after dinner were not soon to be forgotten.

When we finally arrived back at Oriel, where we were staying for three or four days until the reunion program ended, it was about ten-thirty, but we were still too "up" from the evening's events to think of going to bed. Susan said she would love a cup of tea, so I changed into jeans and a sweater and took off up Oriel Lane and the High past historic St. Mary's Church in search of a tea wagon.

The curving chief thoroughfare, graced on each side by some of the loveliest spires and towers of any avenue in the world, with its ancient colleges and famous churches, was strangely devoid of traffic. But in the distance, beyond All Souls, there sat a lone tea van. A couple of customers huddled under the lamplight. As I came up to them, it was clear that they too had been at the Balliol banquet—they were still in formal evening dress—and also that the man had lost something, because he was patting himself down like a pipe smoker in a frantic search for his matches. He and his wife appeared to be in their late thirties. He said to me, "I believe I saw you at the dinner tonight. This is a bit embarrassing, but I forgot to bring my wallet when we came out and we were hoping to get something to drink here." I hastened to pay the small amount involved, and as I did so he said: "By the way, my name is Bill Clinton. I'm the governor of Arkansas, and this is my wife, Hillary." I introduced myself and we had a friendly conversation for a few minutes before parting to our respective colleges.

As in the incident with the Queen, there was a postscript. A few years later, shortly after Clinton became president of the United States, I wrote to him at the White House as religion editor of the *Toronto Star* to register my protest at his firing of twenty-three Tomahawk missiles at intelligence facilities in Baghdad on June 26, 1993. The missiles, fired from American warships in the Red Sea, were a reprisal and "wake-up call" to Saddam Hussein for a thwarted plot to assassinate President George Bush Sr. during his "victory visit" to Kuwait in April of that year. Clinton had called the alleged plot "a particularly loathsome and cowardly" attempt. I began the brief missive on a friendly note, recalling the occasion, which I admitted he had probably long forgotten, when our paths had crossed in the High Street in Oxford in 1983. Then I put the letter totally out of my mind.

One day about four weeks later, a very official-looking parcel came by special delivery to my home. It bore the seal of the White House on the envelope and contained a personal letter, which addressed my comments. While I continued to disagree with his actions at that time, I respected his intentions and courtesy in replying to a critical response from somebody he didn't really know and had met so briefly.

5

THE CURE
OF SOULS

AFTER the three intensive years at Oxford from 1951 to 1954, my parents and younger sister attended my graduation ceremony. In London afterwards, my father and I got into a bitter argument. He had decided that it was time for me to undertake two years at Wycliffe College, the University of Toronto's evangelical seminary, to prepare for the Anglican priesthood through theological studies and practical training. I had wanted to take a couple of years off to go to Greenland and work on a fishing boat while exploring how the Danes had treated their Native peoples. All the reports I had ever read had shown that we had so much to learn from them on that, and this remains true today. However, once again I acquiesced to his wishes, and went back to school.

I was quite familiar with the college, having lived in its residence from 1947 to 1951 while taking the arts degree at University College. While seminary is usually pictured by outsiders as a dull or somewhat staid place, for good reason, the moments one seems to remember are the ones that were anything but pietistic or sedate. They appear ridiculously immature now; however, at that time these stunts served a role as sharp relief from the seriousness of studies. Looking back, it's a wonder that any of us made it to ordination.

There were water fights, usually following a "tubbing party" in
which victims were rousted from bed in the middle of the night and
unceremoniously dumped in a tub of icy water, often creating a
cascade of water down the ancient college stairs. One night a student spied an enemy from Trinity College below his window. He
dumped a pail of water on the unsuspecting foe, only to find that the
innocent man was not a student at all but simply somebody waiting
for a friend.

After the rigours of Oxford, the courses at Wycliffe were rela-
tively easy. I was permitted to condense the three-year course into
two because of the work I had already done in Greek, philosophy
and the history of the ancient Greco-Roman world. Because learning Hellenistic Greek was a major hurdle for most young men
entering the Anglican priesthood, I was made a tutor in Greek to
most of them and so was able to cover the fees together with room
and board. The bishop made me a deacon during my first term and
so I was able to assist or stand in for clergy who were sick or otherwise unavailable on weekends. The Varsity rugger squad persuaded
me to join in, and after a lengthy search for boots large enough—
size 14 or 15, depending on the make—I played with considerable
enjoyment. It's a rough sport and I'm certain that some Sundays the
various congregations must have wondered what I'd been doing
the night before when I mounted the pulpit covered with bruises
and Band-Aids. My preaching, which I would now describe as
"evangelical-lite," seemed popular enough, and overall I found the
experience enjoyable and somehow managed to win the prize in
Homiletics, or preaching, in my first year.

There are some risks associated with preaching, and I learned
early on that communication is a tricky business. Not infrequently
a person leaving the church afterwards would comment on how
much they enjoyed the sermon and then say how they particularly
liked some specific point that was made. The problem was that
what they thought you said and what you knew (or believed) you

had actually said were sometimes not the same at all. That's why later on in the ministry I made a habit of stopping the sermon earlier than before and coming down from the pulpit to take questions from parishioners. The "I talk, you listen" version of communication still prevails in many churches today, although in our highly interactive culture that's about the only place left where this is so. The Internet and the ubiquitous social media now carried in virtually everyone's purse or pocket have changed the way we communicate forever.

The other danger associated with preaching is much more subtle: the way clergy are seduced by the praise into believing they really are as eloquent and wise or spiritual as their flock would have them believe. There is a great spiritual trap there, and nobody at the college warned about it. Often it's only recognized after a fall or in some cases disgrace, as in the episodes we've witnessed in recent years with a few highly popular American evangelistic preachers.

What really interested me most during the two years of seminary was Biblical studies. Though Wycliffe's approach to the Bible was ultra-conservative without being actually hard-core fundamentalist—the college motto was *Verbum Domini Manet* ("The Word of the Lord Remains," or stands solid)—there was a large, up-to-date library and I knew how to use it to full advantage. So, for the first time I was able to research for myself what contemporary scholars were saying about the Scriptures, and what I discovered was quite a shock. It had already become very apparent from what some of our professors were teaching us that there was a considerable gap between what seminaries teach and what people in the pews are told (although that gap was to be greatly narrowed several decades later with the arrival on the scene of the Internet and search engines such as Google). However, what I began to learn as I read more widely for myself was that there was an even larger lacuna between what our professors were teaching us and the latest scholarship of the day. In other words, Wycliffe wasn't exactly in the vanguard of critical thinking at that time. I was a little surprised, for example, to find that there isn't a single teaching in the whole of the Sermon on the Mount that is original. Everything in Matthew chapters 5 to 7, where the Sermon is found, can be matched or found already existing in the Judaism of the time, either in the Old Testament itself or in the Talmud or the Mishnah. Some of the sayings are anticipated in Plato, about four hundred years earlier.

Even more surprising—something that was so cataclysmic in its implications that I deliberately shut it off from full consciousness for many years—was the virtually total dearth of evidence for a historical figure at the centre of Christianity. Because of the fundamentalist "slant" of the overall program, we were never taught to question the Gospels themselves, or the Acts of the Apostles, or the letters attributed to Paul; so it seemed as if there was an abundance of historical material behind Jesus. Certainly the Jesus Story itself had a very long history—but so too had the story of Lucifer! Looking behind the scenes through the eyes of modern critics, I searched in vain for the kind of evidence that my Oxford studies had trained me to watch for: genuinely contemporary eyewitnesses, secular histories, inscriptions, and other archeological artifacts such as busts, coins or artwork of different kinds. This issue would come back to haunt me in future years, but for the time being it had to be repressed. Too much was at stake to venture far into such possibly treacherous waters.

Unfortunately, unless one did as I did and roamed more widely than the courses strictly required, there was little in the seminary experience to kindle either one's imagination or one's intellect with any kind of "divine fire" or passion for Christian renewal. I enjoyed the sports, the company of my fellow students and most of the lecturers, especially the principal of the time, the Reverend Dr. Ramsay Armitage, a truly Christian gentleman and a most Christ-like personality. He glowed with a love of God and a love of people. Most especially he glowed with a love of England. "A stout stick and the Sussex Downs," was his favourite expression, and obviously very close to his idea of heaven. (Once I had been on the South Downs in spring, I knew what he meant.) He is the only person I ever knew who had twice walked the entire length of the Roman wall built by Hadrian to keep the Scots from invading Roman Britain.

When term ended in the spring of 1956, I gave the valedictory address as Senior Student or President of the graduating class. My proud parents were there, together with my two sisters, Elizabeth and Jane, and my brother George. We graduates were ordained to the priesthood in a solemn ceremony at St. James' Cathedral in May.

The Cree Indians of my student missionary days had no word in their vocabulary for the two crucial stages of becoming a deacon and then a priest of the Church. In both ceremonies, as well as in Confirmation, which all Anglicans receive, the presiding bishop puts his hand on your head as he utters a prayer, using a phrase which in Cree quite literally means "having your head squeezed." I felt that I had my head squeezed in ordination to the diaconate in 1954 and then again when I was "priested" in 1956 because I felt that I was being "squeezed" to fit a specific mould. I remember being extremely self-conscious as I donned a clerical collar, black stock and sober suit for the first of these ceremonies. I dressed without once looking in a mirror and it was only upon walking along Bloor Street to the ceremony that I first caught sight of my image in a restaurant window. With a sinking feeling, I felt as though I were now part of a sort of "third sex"—cut off from others as a "professional holy man." It was what I had been planning for and studying for over many years, but the reality gave me a genuine shock. I fervently hoped I was making the right choices. I wanted to serve God and my fellow men, but I honestly didn't feel very religious per se. I knew what the martyr to Nazism, Dietrich Bonhoeffer, meant when he wrote about "the end of religion" in its narrowest sense.

Of course, at that time the ministry was still considered a noble calling and a great deal of respect was paid to clergy. In time I got used to looking different from other people, and even found the collar a help in pastoral care. Contrary to popular mythology, however, it in no way brought me special favours from authority figures. I got more than my fair share of tickets for speeding, illegal parking and other minor traffic sins. The officers were polite: "And where are you going at such a clip, Father?" they would query as they drew out their ticket pad. Then, trying to be funny, "We wouldn't want you going to your own funeral, now, would we?" Garage mechanics saw the collar as a sign of worldly naïveté and adjusted the bill upwards accordingly. Panhandlers seemed to spot the collar a block away. Drunks were particularly moved by the sight of it and would often embark on a recital of their entire life's story at the sight of a clerical collar.

The worst part, though, was the way the round collar dampened down the repartee and social ease of ordinary people. The Scottish evangelist Tom Allen once put it like this when describing the effect of a minister's garb: "When an ordinary chap realizes you're a clergyman, he ceases to be the man he really is and instantly becomes the man he thinks that you think he ought to be." They'd apologize for swearing, and tell old jokes about religion, all of which most clergy had heard by six weeks after ordination. At six foot four, I would get a lot of "How's the weather up there?" and "I didn't know you were such a High Churchman."

Once, just before ordination to the Anglican priesthood, the bishop summoned us to a rural centre north of Toronto for a spiritual retreat prior to the ritual on the following Sunday. He was a stickler for upholding the dignity of the cloth, and we were told to bring our full ministerial equipment—surplice and cassock and so on—as well as casual clothes for recreation. I arrived late at the retreat centre, well after the first session had begun. I dumped my suitcase and, dressed in casual slacks with one of my favourite red-and-black-checked open-necked shirts—looking a little like an after-hours lumberjack—raced to the main seminar room. As I entered the room, the bishop was laying down the law about always being sure to wear white shirts with French cuffs and cufflinks underneath our black bibs and Roman collars when on church duties. I squeezed into a chair at the back of the room, trying to avoid his eyes. He abruptly interrupted his colloquy and beckoned me to a seat near him at the very front. As I slunk forward, I saw to my embarrassment that every one of my fellow ordinands was dressed in an official, flowing black cassock and round white collar. I squirmed uncomfortably until the lecture's end, and then bolted to my room to change. Less than ten minutes later I arrived at the next session dressed in full clerical splendour only to find to my total chagrin that the rest had decided to follow my relaxed example and had changed to casual clothes.

Eventually it was time for the profoundly moving ceremony when we were to be ordained in historic St. James' Cathedral, in the heart of the city. I had purchased a new and very expensive top-coat for the occasion. Unfortunately, I made the mistake of leaving it over a pew at the rear of the cathedral at the rehearsal the night before, and it was stolen, probably to buy a bottle of cheap wine. The police were cheerful when they said, "It's an ill wind . . ."

Following ordination in May 1956, I was married the next month to my first wife, Mary, who had been a student at Trinity College across the street from Wycliffe, and three daughters, Elizabeth, Margaret and Mary Catharine, were born over the next seven years. Desperately needing money, I obtained a menial job as a sweeper at the Ontario Exhibition Park for a few weeks as my first posting in the ministry didn't commence right away. (The only thing I learned there was that general labourers prefer a boss who wears big boots, because then you can hear him coming long before you see him, and thus get busy sweeping.)

My first position was curate of St. John's York Mills, one of the most affluent and influential parishes in the diocese. As a curate (or junior assistant), my mentor and boss, the Venerable Archdeacon Arthur McCollum, presented me with a leather-bound parish list and said he expected me to make a minimum of five visits every afternoon. To be honest, I found this part of the ministry less than fulfilling. It worked well in rural charges where one could go out to the fields or barn and talk with the menfolk. But in the city, in such a wealthy suburb and at a time when many if not most women didn't go to work, the lady of the house was usually the one there to greet you. We would make polite conversation about the weather, the children and Sunday school, but it seemed a pale image of the kind of muscular Christianity I thought I had been called to.

This part of the work often left me feeling trapped, and it was sometimes a relief to find nobody was at home. One could then leave a card and tally one more visit in the book. One hot afternoon I knocked on a door and was greeted by a little boy of about four years old. I asked if his mother or father were in, and he said in a bright and chirpy manner, "Come on in," and ushered me into the living room. I was just about to sit down when a startled pair of eyes peering out through a tangle of wet and still-soapy hair appeared like an apparition from behind a half-open door. Spying my clerical form, the woman gave a sudden cry and shouted at little Ricky to "Show the gentleman out, I'm having a bath!" and slammed the bathroom door. I retreated in a hurry.

The following year, I accepted the position of rector of St. Margaret's-in-the-Pines, West Hill. In 1957 there was just a small chapel and a very sad-looking concrete-block parish hall, but the fourteen-acre setting with its tall, ancient pines and well-kept cemetery was magnificent. The road through the property was part of the old stagecoach route from Toronto to Kingston—the Kingston Road, as its modern successor is still called today. The first church was built in 1832, thirty-five years before Confederation, and the victims of early cholera and other epidemics were said to have been buried along the way, not far from the rectory.

Unlike doctors, until recently most ministers, priests and rabbis still made house calls. In the course at seminary called Pastoralia, we were taught that the typical day should go as follows: sermon preparation and/or hospital visiting in the morning; systematic house-by-house visiting of everyone on the parish rolls in the afternoon; meetings or individual counselling in the evenings. I took over the parish at a time when traditional farmlands and the spread of suburbia were still intermeshed around Toronto. Once, I was visiting a family who lived in an old farmhouse not far from the edge of the Scarborough Bluffs, the cliffs which mark that part of the shore of Lake Ontario. It was a chilly October day and there was a warm fire in the old wood stove. Things looked very cozy and I accepted a cup of tea and biscuits. Just then, a large, elderly dog came in from outside, padded over to me, collapsed at my feet and fell asleep. Unfortunately, the poor animal had recently been in close contact with a skunk, and the heat from the fire on his wet coat made the odour rise like steam from a kettle. Nobody else appeared to notice, but my stomach started to do cartwheels and I knew if I didn't make a run for it I would soon be sick. I put down the food and drink and beat a hasty retreat. I remember the stunned look on my parishioners' faces. I didn't have the courage to tell them the truth. The suit had to be sent to the cleaners twice before it was fit to wear again.

There were always some members of the church who had to be approached with special care. Everyone had warned me that an elderly widow in my first parish, Mrs. Barnfather, could be fierce and that she disliked me sight unseen, on principle, because I was replacing her friend, the previous rector. I very much wanted to make a good impression and win her over to my side. When she opened the door, I realized she was almost as tall as I was, with grey hair pulled into a prim, tight bun on the top of her head. She invited me into her formal parlour and served up tea and fruitcake. She had provided me with a table napkin that I tried to keep on my knee while balancing the cup and saucer and eating a piece of cake. Unfortunately, the napkin kept falling to the floor. To make conversation, I ventured a weak joke. I said, "I wish I had a wooden leg—then I could use a thumbtack to keep this napkin in place." She glared at me ferociously and replied, "My late husband had a wooden leg, and that's anything but humorous!" It was to be a long time before we eventually became friends.

Churchgoing was then very much in fashion, and new homes were springing up on all sides in my parish. Soon the church and hall were filled for morning services and the numbers were continuing to grow rapidly. Our congregation decided to build a large new church, as many other growing suburban congregations were doing. Architects were hired, endless planning and fundraising dinners were held, and in the spring of 1960 the cornerstone was laid. The dedication of the completed sanctuary was set for late that fall. In good time, a splendid, lofty building went up, with lots of clear and tinted glass through which the worshippers could still appreciate the natural beauty of their surroundings. The soaring arches inside were of British Columbia fir and the roof was made of cedar shingles. The whole impression was one of woodsiness and airy heights.

The contract for the pulpit, lectern and altar had been let to a craftsman in downtown Toronto—a friend of a key parishioner. He did excellent work, but unfortunately he found it hard to keep to a schedule. As the much-awaited day of dedication of the new church approached with no pulpit in sight, I went to his downtown workshop and was greatly alarmed to find everything in the most elementary form, half buried in piles of shavings. He assured me, however, that everything was proceeding as it should. I tried to smother my fears, but when the day before the event came and went and still there was no altar, lectern or pulpit, I began to panic.

We were expecting several hundred people at the dedication, including local politicians and, in particular, the Lord Bishop of

Toronto himself. In the Anglican ceremony of dedication of a church, there are special prayers of consecration to be said over all three items that were still missing. How to explain their absence? I cajoled, pleaded and begged, and the craftsman continued to assure me he would be on time. But when the Bishop arrived for dinner at the rectory on the evening of the affair, there were still no essential furnishings. The Bishop, the Right Reverend Fred Wilkinson, who terrified me at the best of times, had to be told. I took him aside and broke the news. He was quite annoyed. "I suppose you expect me to ask God to bless the altar, pulpit and lectern which one day will be seen here," he grumbled. I gulped and told him that was about all we could do.

Finally, the service was ready to begin. The church was filled to overflowing and the choir was assembled at the doors to commence the processional hymn. As the sexton tolled the hour and I was in the middle of announcing the opening hymn, there was a roar at the gates of the churchyard and a cloud of dust as an antique truck lurched its way up the drive. It screeched to a stop and the driver, my tardy cabinetmaker, leaped out crying: "Don't start yet!"

The red-faced Bishop, holding on to his ceremonial shepherd's crook, curtly gave his permission to delay the proceedings until the contents of the battered truck were brought in. The altar came first, in four pieces, and had to be assembled up at the front while the packed congregation looked on in astonishment. Next came the pulpit. It seemed enormous and looked more like a chariot from *Ben-Hur* than an ecclesiastical podium. The maker and four men and I had all we could do to carry it up the aisle. Since it wouldn't fit in the aisle, it had to be carried waist-high above the pews on either side. While we struggled with it, my accountant, who was also the insurer of the property, rushed up to say that he would not accept liability if the pulpit were to tip and fall on anyone. So an announcement was made and people scurried for cover or scrunched up together, and we struggled on. The craftsman, who was carrying some of the weight on his shoulders and dropping wood shavings all over the new carpet, was nearly crushed when we finally set it down too quickly.

When my former "boss," the Archdeacon of York Mills, the Venerable A.C. McCollum, eventually climbed into the pulpit and launched into his sermon, he began, "I can't tell you what a privilege it is to be the first person ever to preach from this pulpit. What's more, I'm certain I'm the first because I saw it come down the aisle with my own eyes!" Afterwards, some people told me that it was the most dramatic church service they had ever attended, and others said they thought I had staged the whole thing for effect! This is one of the moments in my life that would be done differently if I had another chance.

Christmas in the 1950s and 1960s, while the source of a certain delight, was also a season of utter exhaustion for the ministry. There was private communion to be taken to the sick, children's concerts to be endured, gift and food boxes to be delivered to the poor, and extra sermons to be given. After several years had passed, it became almost impossible to say anything new on the subject, I found.

On the afternoon of December 24, 1959, I was almost dropping in my tracks from weariness. Earlier that day I had delivered a box containing a large turkey and trimmings, with toys for the children, to a "needy" family who lived in a high-rise apartment building. The elevator wasn't working and I had to carry the package up several flights of stairs. I rang the doorbell, and after an eternity a child of about five opened the door. The living room was dominated by a huge colour TV set going full blast, which made my little black-and-white one at home seem like a relic. "I've come with gifts from St. Margaret's-in-the-Pines Church," I said. The father of the house, who was reclining on a sofa with his head propped on pillows watching *I Love Lucy*, looked irritated and said, motioning with a casual wave, "Put it over there," indicating a table in the cor-

ner. This little encounter didn't do much to put me in the right
frame of mind to deliver my midnight sermon that evening, entitled "Sharing as the Essence of Christmastide."

I spent the rest of that afternoon pacing the church grounds
with my pipe (my crutch at that time) and trying to think, but by
suppertime nothing had really gelled, and I also learned that my
organist had suddenly come down with the flu. By nine-thirty I had
an outline in my head and headed over to the office to type out my
notes. I threw my coat over one of the benches (we were using the
parish hall until the new church was ready), and at about ten o'clock
I added the final touches to my sermon. Then I smelled smoke. I
dashed down the stairs three at a time and into the hall and stood
there, transfixed with shock, as flames leapt five feet high from
my overcoat and the bench, which was also on fire. I realized I must
have forgotten to empty my pipe of its ashes before putting it into
my pocket. Fortunately, a rush of adrenalin freed me from my
immobility, and after several pails of water I had the fire out, but it
left the hall completely filled with clouds of acrid, choking black
smoke. The service was due to begin in less than an hour. I tore
around, opening as many windows as I could, and to my relief blasts
of freezing air soon cleared most of the haze. But the place simply
stank of burned cloth and paint, and by now it seemed to be border-
ing on too cold to serve as a church. I felt on the verge of a nervous
breakdown! I ran for my car, drove to the nearest convenience store
and purchased several cans of air freshener, drove back, closed the
windows and furiously sprayed in all directions.

By the time the congregation began to arrive, there was the
oddest scent in the air, but nobody remarked on it.

Preaching is either a clergyman's greatest delight or the one thing
that can keep him tossing at night like a harpooned fish. At that
time, sermons were prepared with great diligence in an effort to
impart something original and inspiring. Usually I enjoyed it, but

there were times when I would have given anything for a copy of a
medieval collection of prepared sermons aptly titled *Dormi Securi*
("sleep without a worry in your head"), reportedly much used by
clerics of that feisty period in Church history. Interestingly, the
Internet has enabled some clerics today to use generic sermons.
They're easy to spot because they invariably conclude with a
question: "How would you [pointing a finger at a sweep of pews]
respond to such a commandment today?"

Soon after I was ordained a deacon and during my first year of
theological training, I was sent on weekends to a country charge
with three churches. All the services were in the morning, beginning with the farthest point at nine o'clock, where I did a "preach
and run" and then moved on to the next and the next in order to get
everyone home for their Sunday dinner at one p.m. My very first
morning was a beautiful, sunny fall day that was so warm all the
windows in the little rural church were wide open. I mounted the
pulpit feeling confident, apart from a certain tension I always had
while gazing down into such trusting eyes. It was a harvest home
service and the oaken pews were crammed with families, including
the front rows, a rare phenomenon in Anglican churches even then.

Unfortunately, I got off to a rather shaky start. There was a banner attached to the reading stand on the pulpit by a piece of elasti-
cized ribbon. As I gave the opening prayer, I inadvertently toyed
with the ribbon. I said, "Amen," looked up to announce my text,
accidentally freed the elastic, and with a *whoosh* the banner shot into
the lap of a matronly woman wearing a straw hat. She stared at me
as if I had done it on purpose. I apologized and waded into the
homily, but found it hard to keep up the enthusiastic momentum
my notes called for. As I laboured on, the congregation took on that
fixed, glazed look of those whose minds have wandered far away.
Then an extraordinary thing happened. A sudden, quirky gust of
wind came in the window, lifted the paper with my sermon notes on

it and gently wafted it outside, where it tumbled like a falling leaf to the lawn below.

Now the congregation came to life and started to look interested for the first time. I did my best to smile and, putting a look on my face that I hoped would show I was better off without the notes anyway, tried to improvise. It was a losing battle until I suddenly remembered my concluding points. I seized on them like a drowning man and worked and reworked them until I had successfully filled the remaining ten minutes.

Afterwards, several parishioners told me they had enjoyed such an "interesting" sermon, but I knew that "roast parson" would be the main course at Sunday dinner in more than one home that day.

"The cure of souls" is an old-fashioned way of speaking about ministering to people's spiritual needs. A good deal of time in the parish was spent presiding over the rites of passage of funerals and weddings, and administering the sacraments of baptism and Holy Communion. During the course of my ministry I had, like all clergy, to face human tragedy and sorrow times without number. I found it a tremendous privilege and responsibility to be admitted into the tender arena of grief and attempt to bring comfort, renewed courage and hope. There can be no point at which a minister comes closer to people, who are very often today total strangers to him or her, than when a death occurs.

The one thing I tried to avoid at all costs was the habit of some overzealous clerics of seizing the occasion of a funeral, where one has a captive audience, as an opportunity to preach to the "unsaved." It still goes on today and has always seemed to me an unfair tactic. Words of comfort—yes, of course, but anything more is not truly compassionate. My very first funeral was that of a three-year-old. She was a little girl, the joy of her parents and grandparents, who lived on a farm together at the edge of town. The only grandchild, she was tragically run over by the grandfather's tractor one morning as she ran to him unaware that he was going to back out of a nearby shed. Everyone was devastated and my heart was particularly touched to the depths by the plight of the old man. He was utterly inconsolable. I visited him and his wife, as well as the young parents, several times before the funeral—mostly just to be with them, saying very little, except to try to assure them of the presence and love of the Eternal always with and within them and their darling little one. At the service I studiously stayed away from syrupy truisms or the, to my mind, wholly misleading pronouncements often heard at such events as people try to make sense of the incomprehensible, to the effect that "God took her because he needed her in heaven" or "She was too good for this world." But it was very difficult, even at times exhausting work, if you really loved your people.

So close a walk with death and dying takes its toll on many ministers and priests. If not for the ability to receive the gift of humour, most clergy would find it impossible to continue. You could even, with no disrespect, call it "putting the fun back in funerals." Often I found that when hearing about amusing things the deceased person said or did, the bereaved may begin to sense that healing is taking place. This was especially true when the deceased was on in years and had lived a full life. In the midst of the saddest funerals, I sometimes found my own spirits start to lift, for example, at the incongruity of the professional grief of the undertaker and his staff in their mourning clothes or the syrupy and sentimental funeral chapel hymns.

Once, I was conducting a funeral in mid-winter. I felt I looked rather resplendent in my new floor-length black funeral cloak, which was designed to ward off the chill that only cemeteries in winter provide. However, as I strode by a group of mourners, a young lad of about eight pointed at me and, tugging at his mother's arm, said: "Look, Mum, it's Zorro!" It helped my humility, but it did more—it introduced a note of laughter and saved an otherwise very bleak day. I was reminded of Robert Frost's poem "Dust of Snow," about being in the woods on a depressing winter's day. He wrote that the way a crow in a hemlock tree shook down a dusting of snow on him lifted his mood and "saved some part of a day I had rued."

Weddings are usually a pleasant part of any minister's duties. It's a privilege to be close to a couple at such a key existential moment. The pitfalls are many, however. Often I would find that the reception hall, flowers, rented tuxedos and even the wedding cake had all been booked and partially paid for long before I was asked if the church and I would be free and willing on a particular Saturday in June. Being the busiest month of all for weddings, compromise was often necessary.

The media got involved at the first wedding I performed after receiving my licence as a newly ordained deacon. It was my sister Elizabeth's wedding, and it was a tasteful ceremony carried out at St. Peter's Anglican Church in Churchill, Ontario, where I was serving a summer charge. I was mortified, however, to pick up a copy of a Toronto daily (the now-defunct *Toronto Telegram*) the following Monday and read a report under the heading BROTHER MARRIES SISTER.

During my last summer at Big Trout Lake in 1950, on one occasion the groom failed to show up at his wedding. The missionary, Rev. Leslie Garrett, had told me to be sure to come because it was to be a double wedding and there would be a colourful send-off at the end when all the men of the band would line up on either side of the path as the couples left the church and fire their shotguns off into the sky in a grand salute. Frankly, I was a little nervous about this part of the celebrations because, for people who lived most of their lives by hunting, these particular Cree seemed very unlucky in the number of injuries they did both to themselves and to others through accidental discharges of their weapons. But I resolved to go anyway.

Two brides showed up, but only one groom. We waited for at least a half-hour, and in the end I felt so sorry for the woman without a man that I would have liked to volunteer one of the other young men present. At last someone was sent to find out what had happened to the missing man. It turned out he had fallen asleep and forgotten that the event was set for that afternoon. He was too chagrined and ashamed to show his face that day, and his girlfriend was asked to sit down while the other bride was married. Most girls would have been insulted to the point of rejecting such a sleepy suitor entirely, but the pair were married the following Saturday. I'm happy to report that no one was injured when the shotguns finally were fired for them.

The Anglican service of baptism, intended mainly for infants of very tender age—the Book of Common Prayer actually says "as soon as possible after birth"—always has as its Gospel reading the passage where Jesus bids the disciples to "suffer the little children to come unto me." Although church attendance today has suffered dramatic declines, for very good reasons, many young parents still want the traditional baptism for their babies. The principle seems to be that once the baby has had all its shots against temporal diseases, it should then be inoculated against any possible spiritual harm. Ironically, the process for many years now seems to have served as an immunization against ever catching Christianity. Of course, the other motivation is the family party afterwards, or it may simply be done to please the doting grandparents.

One morning around 1960, as a consequence of the flood of newcomers taking up residence in the West Hill region, the parents of sixteen children came for the sacrament of baptism. Their many relatives and friends added significantly to the already large regular congregation. Several of the more influential parishioners glared at me when I first came in because they had been forced out of their usual pews by the invasion of these strangers. As I strode into the centre aisle to begin the various prayers for the "remission of sin by spiritual regeneration" of the assorted babies and toddlers before me, one three-year-old decided to make a break for it, running down the centre aisle with his father in hot pursuit.

The escapee was returned, but not without howls of outrage. This unfortunately made the rest of the baptizands apprehensive that something might be lurking ahead to cause them pain. The first set of parents approached the font and handed me their baby while holding their other toddler by the hand. Normally I never had any trouble with small babies, holding them very firmly in one arm the way we were taught to do, and pouring a small amount of tepid water on the forehead with the other hand. This baby, however, yelled bloody murder the moment I took him. I tried the usual technique: smile sweetly at the baby, speak as loudly as possible and give it back as swiftly as you can while not looking too relieved. Now it was his older brother's turn, and I made the mistake of picking the child up, trying to handle him as one would an oversized infant. He screamed and struggled, delivering some very energetic kicks to my midsection. The entire group of little ones had now joined in and begun wailing loudly.

By the time I had fought my way through the entire batch, I was soaked, my preaching scarf was hanging askew, and my patience had almost given way to something else. I then needed to deliver the sermon, repeating the passages about childhood innocence I had so unsuspectingly prepared the night before.

Later that afternoon I was having a brief nap when I was awakened by a phone call from a woman I had never heard of or met asking whether she and her husband could have their baby "done" soon. In weariness I couldn't help myself and said, "And how would you like it done, madam? Well, medium or rare?" She hung up at once.

Those who have read *Water into Wine* will know something of my own understanding of what baptism actually means and how it can be seen as so much more than a churchy ritual of convenience.

Were I to be back in a parish today, I would present it quite differently than in that bygone era. One thing is certain: there would be a great deal less said about sin and much more about the acknowledgement of the presence of the divine spark in every newborn child of God.

Certainly the most sacred service for most Christians is the Eucharist, also known as the Lord's Supper, Holy Communion or Mass. The risks for clergy are many: losing one's place in the prayer book, dropping the chalice, or running out of bread and wine. One morning at St. Anne's Church in the heart of Toronto, I nearly electrocuted a parishioner. I had walked across the carpet of the chancel area several times and had unknowingly picked up an impressive charge of static electricity. I learned later that I should have discharged it by touching the metal radiator before handing the cup to anyone. Not knowing this, however, I blithely offered the cup to the first gentleman on his knees, and watched as a spark leapt between the cup and his lip. It was audible to the entire group kneeling at the altar rail, and badly frightened the poor man as well as myself.

One thing you are taught as an Anglican minister is that any bread or wine which has been consecrated for Holy Communion and has not been used must be consumed by the clergy at the close of the service. In order not to run out, I would frequently overestimate the size of the crowd and have quite a lot to deal with at the end. My father, when he had his own parish in his late-in-life career as an Anglican parish priest, had his own ideas about leftover bread: he would simply throw it out on the lawn for the birds well after the service, believing it did more good that way. Eating leftover bread or wafers is one thing, and can be at times an embarrassment, but drinking any remaining wine after the chalice has been passed around to two hundred or more people and contains small wet crumbs from the bread the communicants missed is enough to make a person gag. This practice is seldom thoroughly discussed or even mentioned anywhere. Fortunately for the clergy, the practice of drinking from the common cup has changed somewhat in this day and age of fears of pandemics, but it is still a contentious issue in some parishes.

Outwardly, it appeared at that time as if my parish career was proceeding just as it should. All the external marks of success were in place. St. Margaret's-in-the-Pines was one of the few parishes in the diocese that had more men than women in the pews on any given Sunday morning. Inwardly, however, trouble was fermenting. Issues were arising, both theological and personal, that one day would have to be squarely faced.

Sometimes I am asked whether I would like to be back in a parish ministry today and, if so, what I would do differently. A full answer would again require a book-length treatise, but a few points can sketch at least a general direction. If possible, I would simultaneously have a teaching or writing post so that my preaching and teaching could be quite financially independent. Put bluntly, it's very hard, if not impossible, to speak out freely from a pulpit when those who pay the bulk of your salary and the church maintenance fees are sitting in the front row each Sunday. I would also initiate a parallel church for agnostics, atheists and seekers of every kind. There would be no formal prayers, sermons or lectures at such a gathering. Rather, it would be a place and time for honest questioning and debate.

My understanding and experience of prayer have evolved gradually in the process of living in the real world and not that of the cloister or the seminary. Whereas, like most people, I once prayed as though God were indeed some super-parent in the sky with a switchboard dedicated to my plaintive demands, I slowly matured through various stages to a point where prayer is most often not verbalized at all. I still believe in clearly stating my fears, uncertainties and doubts as well as my joys and gratitude, either silently or aloud (when alone), because God is everywhere throughout the cosmos and we live constantly with that Presence about us and within. This wish to put things into words is not based on some assumption that my wants or joys are unknown to the Deity, but on my need to express them and on what this does for others and for me. I speak of what I know. Prayer has power, but according to universal spiritual laws, not because God needs to hear either our whimpering or our praise. The best prayer for me—and for millions around the world of all religions or of none—is that of pure silence. Sometimes one wants to meditate by using a simple mantra while calmly observing the breath moving in and out. At times I simply repeat a verse of Scripture or of sublime poetry. For example, the word *Amen* can itself become a mantra. Or the verse "We have not received the spirit of fear but of power, of love and of a sound mind." In the end, I have found that I pray because I must express my thanks for being alive and all that means. We are wired to pray, but the puerile "bless me, bless me" days of one's childhood need to disappear.

In the "parallel church" there might be readings, not just from Holy Scriptures (of various faiths) but from so-called secular writers, poets and journalists. The music would be as varied as the "congregation" decided. There would be a wide use of modern media in a spectrum of presentations—and always with time for feedback or discussion. When I was at St. Margaret's, I wrote an entire Sunday school curriculum based upon a series of major films dramatizing the life of St. Paul. The teachers and children loved it. In parish ministry, as everywhere else in religion, it is time for some truly radical change.

Harvest home and Thanksgiving would not be the only occasions where our total dependency on and "interbeing" (to use a Buddhist term) with the whole of the natural world would be acknowledged and made the focus of prayer, readings and meditation. One thing I have learned from my own experience as well as from my research into pre-Christian or Pagan beliefs is the centrality of the Creation to a full and balanced spirituality. When the early Christians gained temporal power through the conversion of Emperor Constantine and then gradually proceeded to denigrate and destroy all that Paganism held dear, they turned away from the deep connection religion had always had with Mother Earth and the cycles of the cosmos at the same time. Literalism too played its part, as the whole myth about God cursing the earth and Adam's destiny in it was read as a fact of history. Part of the vast environmental crisis we face right now is due to the Western world's inheritance of an attitude towards nature of negativity and indifference. You can find it even in the hymns we sing in church. "Joy to the World," one of the best-known of all Christmas carols, for example, in stanza three celebrates belief in the "Curse of Adam" upon what we call "the environment." The verse says in part, "far as the curse is found," and repeats it three times for emphasis. At best the natural world is regarded as there to be exploited and used as we see fit. All religions need to rediscover the reverence and awe that link us once again to the womb out of which we come and that nourishes our inner spirit as nothing else can.

On my eightieth birthday we had the great privilege of visiting Zion Canyon National Park in southwestern Utah. Our hiking path through the valley followed the Virgin River, alongside the canyon heights, which were named by the early Mormon settlers as the Altar of Sacrifice and the Thrones of the Three Patriarchs. As we stood and gazed mutely at the soaring rock walls, I had a deeper, more awesome awareness of the reality and the power of the presence of God than I had ever known before or have experienced since in any cathedral or in the presence of even some of the holiest personalities I have met. Lorne Greene, the famous Canadian TV personality, put it very simply but perhaps best in his recording of the song "Oh, the place where I worship, is the wide open spaces, built by the hand of the Lord." Many millions today can say amen to that.

6

LIVING MY
FATHER'S DREAM

MOST OF US, particularly when we have had some measure of success in life, are reluctant to reveal or discuss our weaknesses, failures or defeats. Certainly this is so for me. Yet as Jung and others have made clear, facing one's shadow with all its latent strength as well as its more negative powers is essential to one's individuation and growth towards greater maturity. As the great "doctor of the soul" points out in *Modern Man in Search of a Soul*, anything of substance must of necessity have or throw a shadow. Evil walks *pari passu* with the good.

There were a couple of major events that, if not necessarily failures, at any rate highlighted a need for a radical change of direction in my personal narrative. Some aspects of these are necessarily painful, but the ultimate meaning and outcome were enormously fruitful and liberating. There was no voice from above, no heavenly vision, no sudden inner light, but throughout even the most difficult, yes, even the darkest hours, the realization of a divine Presence close by me and within made it possible to carry on. And I discovered that coming to terms with one's shadow, including the darkness of disappointment, depression or loneliness, can be the prelude to a release of fresh creativity and of deeper joy.

Each of the events about to be described is connected to the others by a common thread: a hitherto largely unconscious bondage and subservience to the parental matrix, with all its many-sided demands. In particular, in the early 1960s, when I was a married man with children of my own, the rector of a large and thriving parish, and a budding lecturer at Wycliffe College in the University of Toronto, I was still thoroughly in thrall to the authority of my father. Just as my parents had chosen a career as a minister for me from the moment of my conception, so too it was they who had first suggested that I apply for the post of rector at my first parish, St. Margaret's-in-the-Pines. As mentioned earlier, they had even picked out the evangelical Anglican church I would attend when I went to Oxford!

It was of course no accident that West Hill, where the church of St. Margaret's was located, was only about a twenty-minute drive from my parents' Scarborough home. They began to attend the services, even Bible study groups and other mid-week activities. Sometimes they would show up at the rectory early on Saturday morning and begin tidying up the garage or our other casual belongings in the vicinity in order to preserve the proper dignified image for any chance visitors or passersby. Worse, they interfered frequently with Mary's routines and disciplines for our two children at that time, arriving without warning just when they were being put to bed or handing out candy even after hearing they were not to have any. As they say in England about such unwanted or misdirected activities, "they meant well." That's a warning, not a compliment. The truth is that I was not as outspoken or as direct as I ought to have been in warding off or stopping the interference.

In fact, in retrospect I see that I was not yet prepared to face what my unconscious was screaming in my dreams and in a general sense of inner tension and unease. Things in the parish were going very well, but I always felt under the strain of not doing enough. My father would ask from time to time, "How many conversions have there been?" And there were signs of trouble in the marriage as well.

Mary had reasons enough, but my failure fully to understand what lay behind the many outbursts only made them worse. When there were the inevitable arguments and quarrels, I would piously blame myself for lack of grace and so resorted to prayer instead of looking deeper for the root causes.

Against this backdrop, as the struggle to build the congregation continued at the same time as the planning for the erection of a new church building was proceeding apace, my father had begun a fresh campaign to persuade me to return to academic life and obtain a Ph.D., or rather the Oxford D.Phil. I had already spent nine years at university preparing for my ministry, so the thought of at least two, possibly three more years of slogging completely left me cold. I had fear, not of being unable to do it, but of ending up in total poverty. My years of study even on scholarships had not been conducive to a bank balance worthy of the name, and while the Anglican Church may be generous with titles and other honours, it was not at that time very supportive where clergy salaries were concerned.

At the same time, I knew that my father's vision for his firstborn was that one day I would teach as a professor at the bastion of Anglican evangelicalism in Canada, Wycliffe College. Though by that time I would have shied away from being labelled a fundamentalist, I still saw myself as very much a part of the conservative evangelical point of view, with its emphasis upon Scripture and upon the need for a personal commitment to Jesus Christ. My friends in the clergy of all denominations and my other personal contacts consisted chiefly of those with a similar outlook. Even though I did not share my father's far-fetched dream that I would one day be the leader of a movement that would transform Canada into a national evangelical base for a worldwide mission, I was enjoying the part-time teaching I was already doing. I loved reading and research, and the prospect of being relieved of some of the more tedious aspects of parish ministry held some appeal. Also, I was concerned about the future of Christianity and convinced that the training of young people for ministry was absolutely critical for any hope of renewal.

So, about a year after fulfilling the eleventh commandment for young clergy in the late 1950s and early 1960s, "Thou shalt get thy church deeply in debt," by building the new St. Margaret's, I applied for acceptance as a doctoral candidate at Oxford. The choice of Oxford over an American or Canadian university seemed wisest because, as a graduate student there, I had already fulfilled the basic residence requirement. By returning to my old college, Oriel, for one year, I could then be approved and come home to write the thesis on my own turf. The bishop, Rt. Rev. George Snell, was not very happy about my decision when I announced it to him in a hastily called appointment in his Adelaide Street office. He grumbled about my leaving the parish so soon after the dedication of a new and costly building. But he was somewhat mollified when I said I would come back for at least a year after Oxford to "round things off" properly.

Unfortunately, the entire Oxford project was not planned or thought out as fully as it ought to have been. Wycliffe was pressuring me to rush ahead because the New Testament professor, Rev. Dr. Ronald Ward, had served notice he would be leaving his post in the spring of 1964. It was already about mid-March 1962. There was no scholarship money available and, since I had decided to take the family, there would be considerable expense involved: the boat passage there and back for two adults and two children, house rental, food and transportation for a year, plus the university fees and other sundry expenses.

In retrospect, one can see only too readily that it was one of those times and places where youthful exuberance combined with failure to consult one's own inner wisdom rather than that of others. The result was undue haste and poor planning. In any case, I arranged for my father to sell our car, and having contracted for a retired American Episcopal (Anglican) priest to live with his wife in the rectory and administer the parish in our absence, we set sail for England in August 1962.

It proved to be one of the most conflicted years of my life in spite of some moments of great illumination as well. The house we rented on Aston Street, off the Iffley Road in east Oxford, was dark and dingy beyond belief, its walls and furnishings every possible shade of brown. The only heat, until purchase of a coal oil–fuelled space heater, was a small fireplace in the kitchen. Coal for it had to be purchased at an ironmonger's shop, brought home in a bag on the handlebars of the "sit-up-and-beg" antique bicycle I used for transportation, and then hammered into usable pieces in a dark dungeon of a cellar. There was no refrigerator, just a "cold cupboard" near the rear wall of the kitchen that actually had mushroom-like fungi growing out of one or two shelves because of the dampness. We managed to make the kitchen and upstairs bathroom reasonably bright and cozy, but the whole experience had a lot of the features of a year-long camping trip.

The really important thing was getting on course for my research. Because of my own ongoing interest in and commitment to a practised faith, one that made sense not just intellectually but experientially too, I had decided to do my research on one of the greatest preachers of early Christianity, St. John Chrysostom. His very name in Greek means "golden-mouthed" or, in other words, superlatively eloquent. Chrysostom (*c.*347–407) was made the Patriarch of Constantinople in 398. The city had been inaugurated in 330 by Emperor Constantine as the capital city for the Eastern Roman Empire. I knew that all of Chrysostom's hundreds of sermons and commentaries had been faithfully recorded in Greek (with a Latin translation added later), and it seemed logical to me that a faithful investigation of this huge store of wisdom could be worthwhile. What, I wanted to ask, did such a great expositor of the Bible and of earliest Christianity teach as the essence of a living faith in day-to-day experience? Eventually, I sharpened the focus: the work and experience of God's Holy Spirit in the life of a believer, according to Chrysostom.

Two problems immediately presented themselves. In the first place, Oxford was at that time totally out of sync with graduate studies programs at American universities. There was a system in place in the sciences, but in the humanities it was a very mixed bag indeed. Very few of the college dons had doctoral degrees themselves, and not all professors had one either. The MA (Oxon.) in Greats that I had earned previously was considered equivalent to a doctorate and sufficient academic preparation provided the person concerned had gone on to make good use of the tools already given to him or her. More particularly, however, amazing as it seemed to me, there was nobody in the theology or other faculties of the numerous colleges who was judged, on inquiry, sufficiently well read in the work of the great "doctor of the Church" to become my supervisor. I spent several anxious weeks in September and October interviewing nearly a dozen of some of the best-known Biblical and patristic scholars at the university, including Henry Chadwick, George Caird, Samuel Greenslade and the Dean of Christ Church, Dr. F.L. Cross, who edited the first edition of the well-known *Oxford Dictionary of the Christian Church*. These were all noted scholars and acknowledged authorities on early Christianity; their collected published books would make a small library. But none of them saw Chrysostom as his "cup of tea," as one of them put it. One or more of them nevertheless urged me to bring my knowledge of German up to speed, and so I added a German tutor to my schedule.

Finally it was decided that my best recourse would be to seek out the guidance of a non-university Anglican priest of immense learning who occasionally helped out with unusual situations such as mine. His was a small but very ancient parish deep in the countryside south of Oxford. It was arranged that I should go down by train to meet him, have lunch at the rectory, discuss my aims and return to Oxford the same afternoon. The Reverend Father Chitty was an energetic, wispy-haired man of advanced years whose agile quickness belied his age. His black outfit and white collar at once marked him out for me on the platform as the train pulled into the station, and I soon was having the ride of my life as we careened around narrow, winding lanes at breakneck speed in his beaten-up old Austin. As we lurched around one particularly sharp bend, the passenger door flew open, struck the stone wall and banged shut again. This happened twice more as he shouted out something about meaning to get "the blessed thing" fixed.

I counted us both lucky when we at last pulled up in a lane with a picturesque Norman-style church on one side and a three-storey eighteenth-century rectory on the other. It was a labyrinthine, drafty old place within, but we were soon in his study with its stacks of books not just on sagging shelves to the ceiling on all sides but piled high on every available inch of space on chairs and on the floor itself. In spite of a glowing coal fire, the air seemed damp and smelled of mildew.

We talked for a while about Chrysostom and he pulled out a couple of tomes and hunted for a particular passage he wanted to share. When he found it and urged me to take a look, I found the Greek text almost impossible to read because of something I had never come upon before: some of the characters were illegible because there were actual wormholes through the pages. One hears of bookworms, but apparently they're very real. Their presence in his library didn't affect his obvious enthusiasm, however, and the time passed very quickly.

My spirits had been sagging badly, but the possibility of being mentored by such a learned and lively character gave a glimmer of hope. Chitty had kindly invited me to stay for the noonday meal, and since the impression it left with me has lasted all down the years, a brief description should be forgiven. At the ringing of a bell, a most varied collection of people—relatives both distant and immediate, plus a couple of elderly parishioners—descended the stairs and gathered around a large oval table in the capacious dining room. Some wore several sweaters and scarves. A couple were wearing rather soiled neckcloths or bandages denoting, I supposed, some kind of throat ailment. One had a racking cough. As we assembled, I was rather wickedly thinking of the colourful verse in the Book of Revelation: "And the sea gave up its dead." It certainly could have been a scene out of a Charles Dickens novel. The crockery was of noble vintage but cracked and worn. The soup and the other dishes were excellent, however, in spite of everything, and the conversation was highly entertaining. I had a lot to ponder on the train journey back to Oxford. I wondered more than once, though, just what I was doing and where the path would lead.

Study of Chrysostom's voluminous sermons now consumed many hours each day. Sometimes I worked in the Oriel College library above the senior common room. At others, for a change of atmosphere, I toiled in the world-famous Bodleian Library or went over to Pusey House, several blocks west of Oriel and built on a much smaller, more intimate scale. The connecting thread of my growing notes was anything that threw light on the central theme of the life of faith as viewed through a towering early Christian understanding and perception. When I tired of the Greek, I read the Latin translation, and my facility in both languages steadily deepened and grew apace.

Every month I sent a newsletter back to West Hill to be read aloud at a Sunday service in order to keep my congregation up to date with our activities and our impressions of life in a thriving though ancient university city overseas. On one occasion I even gave a sermon by telephone link-up that was broadcast from the pulpit in St. Margaret's-in-the-Pines at a regular eleven a.m. service. The late Aubrey Wice, religion reporter for the *Toronto Telegram*, did a special feature article on it in a Saturday edition.

Few places I have known can be more depressing, in spite of all its beauty, than Oxford in the autumn when the fog rises up from the Isis and from the Cherwell River, blotting out the landscape and colleges alike. One rather dismal, foggy afternoon near the end of October, I was walking past Christ Church College garden when I had a most significant encounter. Walking towards me in the semi-gloom was my old Greek and Roman history professor, Peter Brunt. He carried a cane, as was his habit when he took his obligatory exercise break each day, and his hair was as tousled as I remembered it being when last I saw him nearly a decade earlier, in 1954. He always ran his hands through it as he listened to one's essay or strove to make a point in his critique of the same.

Brunt, who was to go on to hold the prestigious chair in Ancient History not long afterwards, told me that he had heard I had come back. Pointing his cane at me, he then demanded, "What are you doing here?" I explained that I had returned to do a Doctor of Philosophy degree (D.Phil.) in order to teach at my old theological college. He almost snorted with surprise and not a little indignation. He said, "What kind of American nonsense is that? You have an excellent MA in Greats from here that is certainly the equivalent of any doctoral degree elsewhere. You have the brains and have gained the tools for research to add to the overall sum of knowledge. I should have thought you would have been better to stay at home to get on with it!" I was left practically speechless by this, and after promising I would bring Mrs. Harpur and the two girls to tea at the college the following week, I mumbled a hasty farewell and walked on into the gathering night.

Brunt's words came as a numbing shock. I thought about them over and over as I walked around Christ Church Meadow and listened as the melancholy bells of the college clocks and the churches, more per acre than in any other city on earth, counted out the passing time.

During the weeks that followed, the research went on as before, punctuated by breaks when I attended specific lectures to broaden my knowledge of the state of Biblical studies and of the latest thinking about the origins and nature of early Christianity. But the words of my former tutor kept sounding in my mind. As I thought about returning to the rush and pressure of a busy, growing parish, teaching one day a week at Wycliffe, and at the same time trying to pull my research together and begin to write the thesis, it began to sink in that I had really taken on a vastly tougher assignment than I had originally bargained for.

A letter soon afterwards from Rev. Dr. Leslie Hunt, Wycliffe's principal, informed me that I had been appointed *in absentia* as Associate Professor of New Testament and Greek. I was to assume part-time duties in the fall of 1964, one year after my return from fulfilling the residence requirement in Oxford. My duties—and, not insignificantly, my salary—would be part-time to permit me to complete the D.Phil. It was expected I would augment my wage with an honorary appointment as assistant on weekends in one of the more well-to-do suburban parishes. Lodging for me and the family would be a large, drafty apartment in the college itself overlooking Hart House. The previous New Testament professor, Dr. Ward, had also lived there for some years during his tenure.

The prospect of the next few years—seemingly endless studies, insufficient funds with more debts already beginning to accrue, a family to provide for and, at the height of my vigour and ability, having to be in effect a sort of second-grade professor alongside the rest of a faculty who were all full professors—began to depress me. I seemed engaged in one of the world's most solitary tasks, sitting for hours by myself in a chilly library surrounded by voices from the past. Oxford in the deep mid-winter is not, as already hinted, the most jocund spot on earth. The depression grew darker and I began to find it hard to concentrate. Sleep was difficult and troubled. Praying seemed to be in vain. In one way, it was a dark night of the soul. I became aware of a growing, pent-up anger. It was rage, but with an unknown cause or object. I began to blame myself for a lack of faith. But more prayers and attempts at piety—Bible reading and churchgoing—only seemed to make things worse.

Then one Sunday evening I went to a lecture called "A Christian Psychologist Speaks Out" at an Anglican church in the city centre. The speaker was Frank Lake, MD, a former counsellor to Christian missionaries in India (whoever would have thought that missionaries needed clinical counselling?). He impressed me so much and I was feeling caught in such a quandary that I went up to him afterwards and asked if it might be possible to see him sometime about my problem. We agreed on a time and place for a week later, and it proved to be one of the wisest steps I had taken in a very long time.

We met for two very lengthy conversations overall. Gently, but at the same time firmly, he helped me to bring to consciousness my undue anxiety to please my parents, especially my father. He helped me to see the sources of my anger, so long and so carefully concealed under a "nice guy" persona. He helped me to unpack all of my reasons for being back at Oxford and showed how some were noble, some were much less so, and how one stood out above all: "because my father said I should go." Most helpfully, he said there is a place for right-directed rage. "You will be depressed because you are holding down so much anger," he said. "That takes great energy. Get out in the country alone somewhere and shout it out. Allow yourself to be angry with God, too. He can take it!" He added that whatever I decided to do about my future, it was very clear that I had some big decisions to make.

I have necessarily condensed this episode, but it was a turning point in my life in so many ways. I felt gradually a great sense of release and of returning energies. It was as though I had been standing with a foot on the hose while at the same time hoping for water. I wrote home to my parents to say that I was going to accept the post at Wycliffe, after fulfilling my promise to the bishop of a full year back in the parish, but that I was reconsidering whether or not to pursue a D.Phil. My father's dream had been of my being a staff member, a professor, at a leading evangelical place of higher learning. Well, he would have his dream, but no longer on his terms.

Experience has shown me that once you make the right decision, events have a way of coming together so as to confirm it, sometimes again and again. I was about to receive a couple of very clear signs of my need to change tack.

I had been attracted to Chrysostom in the first place because of my deep interest in a theology not of the academy but of the heart. He had the reputation of being the most eloquent preacher ever to grace a pulpit and of garnering packed crowds whenever he spoke. I wanted to discover and lay out for myself and others his power to connect. My thinking had been particularly influenced by a passage from Carl Jung that I had read while in the parish some months earlier. In his marvellous little book of essays already cited, *Modern Man in Search of a Soul*, Jung speaks of the many hundreds of people from every race whom he had treated over the years. He writes: "Among all my patients in the second half of life—that is to say, over age thirty-five, there has not been one whose problem in the last resort was not that of finding a religious outlook on life . . . Every one of them fell ill because he had lost that which the living religions of every age have given to their followers, and none of them has been really healed who did not regain his religious outlook." My interest was in finding ways of expressing such a "religious outlook" in terms people today could readily understand, in the same way that Chrysostom had touched the people of his own time. The year back at Oxford had helped to deepen my awareness that merely repeating the old evangelical dogmas was not the path to such an end.

Keeping all of this in mind, the reader can imagine my shock and sense of dismay at gradually discovering two things that somehow had been either wholly forgotten or not sufficiently well grasped by the various scholars whom I had consulted both before and after my return to Oxford. The first unpleasant surprise came one day while I was reading more of Chrysostom. I happened across his Discourses Against the Jews. They were given in 386 and 387 during his preaching days in Antioch, capital of Syria and one of the leading centres of Christian learning and teaching in the fourth century and beyond. There are eight sermons, and while much of the anti-Semitism in them is directed against Christians who were observing certain Jewish rituals and festivals, the racism against Jews and their religion is absolutely virulent and shameful. (Note that the term "anti-Semitism" only appeared in 1879, and so is a modern idea; but anti-Judaism and antipathy to Jews as a race predates Christianity itself.) To my shock and dismay, Jews are called pigs by Chrysostom and accused of drunkenness. All Jews are "Cains," that is, murderers. He denounces Jews as lecherous, rapacious, "perfidious murderers of Christ." God, he rants, "always hated the Jews. It is essential that all Christians hate them." In another passage Chrysostom, the leading light of the emerging faith that was to conquer what was left of the Roman Empire and spread around the globe, declares: "The other disease which my tongue is called to cure is the most difficult . . . and what is the disease? The festivals of the pitiful and miserable Jews which are soon approaching."

There is more, much more, some of it much worse than this. One is reminded of the disgraceful vituperation against Jews by the renowned Protestant reformer Martin Luther, in his *Table Talk*. Anyone interested in learning more about all of this can research it on the Internet, looking especially at "The Surprise of Finding Anti-Semitism in the Heart of the Early Church Fathers."

My mind was reeling from the impact of my discovery. The next day I forsook the libraries and my customary work of translating Chrysostom in search of nuggets of wisdom and instead spent a day walking for miles out along the towpath by the Isis, north of the city. I paid scant heed to the horses and cattle grazing in the vast expanse of Port Meadow or to the occasional college "eight" that rowed past with a repetitive crunch of oars hitting the water as a single stroke. I was too deep in thought to be distracted by any of that. I realized there was no way I could devote any further time, let alone the next couple of years, to, as they say, "learning more and more about less and less," in trying to distill a thesis from the life and work of such a remarkable bigot. I am aware of the numerous attempts since then to whitewash this aspect of Chrysostom's preaching—to "see it in context" or allow for this or that allegedly ameliorating factor. But the unvarnished truth is that he preached hatred against Jews on theologically based grounds, and it remains what it always was—a scandal.

The second, and by then unnecessary, confirmation of my decision to surrender the whole plan of doctoral studies on Chrysostom also came from my ever-deeper immersion in his thinking. In the kind of ironic twist that life at times confronts us with, it was gradually dawning upon me that Chrysostom's approach to the Bible was in essence diametrically opposed not just to some of the Fathers whom I most admired in earliest Christianity (most notably Clement of Alexandria, followed by the great Origen, *c.*185–*c.*254 CE) but to my own deepest instincts. I was learning day by day that the greatest preacher of the early centuries was himself a rigid literalist as he expounded Holy Scripture. In fact, he was the key advocate for the entire Antiochene school of Bible exegesis based upon wholly literalist principles. In short, he was a fundamentalist roughly 1,500 years before the term was even coined! The more I was learning about theology in general, the less appeal this entire approach had for either my heart or my brain.

That Easter I attended a two-week special seminar in Switzerland held by the World Council of Churches. It was designed to immerse budding theologians of different denominations in the world of Eastern Orthodoxy, both the theology and the worship. The first week was spent hearing lectures and participating in discussion groups at Château de Bossy, the WCC's unique conference centre by the lake, about fifteen miles from Geneva. From there we travelled by bus through glorious scenery to a Russian Orthodox monastery in the nineteenth arrondissement of Paris for Holy Week and Easter Day. Since I knew very little about the Orthodox churches, it was a mind-expanding experience of the first order. The choir of the monastery was made up of a group of Serbian men, and listening to them brought back memories of hearing the Don Cossacks singers at Massey Hall years before. The unaccompanied singing was powerful, haunting and beautiful at the same time.

The balance of my year of graduate studies at Oxford was spent in attending the odd lecture in the general field of New Testament and in pounding the books in the libraries to get up to speed on the latest scholarship with a view to eventually taking on the job of teaching at Wycliffe College.

On our return to Toronto, I still had to fulfill my commitment to pick up my ministry at St. Margaret's-in-the-Pines for an additional year, as promised to Bishop Snell. At the college, the New Testament chair or professorship was now vacant and the principal, Rev. Dr. Leslie Hunt, was anxious to have me give at least one two-hour class a week while the rest of the faculty filled in the gaps as best they could. Since there were plenty of loose ends to be picked up in the parish due to my absence, and inasmuch as the teaching, with preparation and travel time included, meant a whole day at least downtown, I had a busy schedule indeed. As well, there seemed to be more demand for baptisms, weddings and funerals than ever before. And in the spring, our third child, Mary Catharine, was born and our family was complete.

In the late summer of 1964, the men of the parish helped us to move into our new quarters at the college with the aid of a large rented truck. Our lodging was to be an ancient, rambling two-storey apartment above some lecture rooms in the college itself. The living and dining rooms looked out upon the athletic wing of Hart House to the south and Queen's Park, behind the Ontario Parliament buildings, to the east. The children loved the storybook nature of the place, with its high ceilings, numerous staircases and even a quaint former coal fireplace. Being in the heart of downtown Toronto and yet in the midst of such a park-like setting, with the university campus all around, was a major change from the rapidly expanding suburb of West Hill we had just left. They enjoyed it all to the hilt.

In many ways academic life suited my particular personality and training. I had always had a love of learning and an interest in communicating ideas to others. So I threw myself into the ongoing task of thoroughly updating my awareness of where Biblical studies were going and where they had been in the past. There were fresh lectures to prepare and graduate seminars as well. What interests me most looking back is the way in which my entire approach to the Bible in general and the New Testament in particular was changing as my knowledge increased. Serious questions, some of which have not yet been answered to my satisfaction, others of which came to fruition in the research leading up to *The Pagan Christ*, began to occupy more and more of my study time. To understand what was going on, one has to realize that the average person in the pew, never mind the average person in the street, hasn't much more than a faint clue, if that, of just how incredibly complex the task of interpreting the Bible has become in the light of all that is now known. Take for example the Gospels. At first sight they seem to be simple, straightforward narratives. In its outline, the Jesus Story that they all tell is quite transparently set forth. But whole libraries could be composed of commentaries and a host of other books and dictionaries struggling to explicate their true nature and meaning.

The Gospels may appear to be biographies of a historical person who was also the "Son of God." But looked at with discernment and in the clear light of day, it soon becomes very apparent that they are not like any other biographies ever written. In fact, they are not biographies at all; they are best described as a benign form of Christian propaganda. In other words, their aim is to convert others to the Christian faith. They have little or no concern for the five Ws of any normal historical narrative: who, why, what, where, when. None of the authors (or editors) of the Gospels is known for certain. Nor are their precise dates or places of origin. The earliest of the four, generally agreed to be Mark, has no birth story or reference to anything in Jesus's life until John the Baptist comes out of the desert preaching and he is baptized by him. We know nothing about Jesus's appearance, whether he was bearded or clean-shaven, short or tall, slim or chubby, with long or short hair, blue-eyed or brown. Absolutely nothing. To add to the confusion, the Gospels frequently contradict one another. For example, Matthew and Luke disagree over Jesus's place of birth, and the Resurrection accounts differ markedly, as I have shown in *Water into Wine*.

I found it difficult at times, since the students were almost uniformly conservative in outlook—that's why they came to Wycliffe in the first place—to raise these kinds of issues with them. For certain, the question of whether or not Jesus was a truly historical person was a cloud "no larger than a man's hand" on my horizon at the time, so it was never mentioned at all. Some of the largest and growing questions in my mind were accordingly kept *in pectore*, as is said when the Pope wishes to keep secret the names of certain cardinals whom he has elevated until it is politically safe to reveal them. Nevertheless, the Form Critics (scholars who study the literary form of Scripture material) had to be dealt with. They had given evidence that many if not most of the Gospel stories had had a lengthy history outside the New Testament before being included, and that they conformed to certain recognized literary formulae, whether they were stories of miracles or brief anecdotes ending in a pithy saying. And there was much, much more. While expounding familiar texts in the classroom, I was privately busy with some more acute academic puzzles and difficulties of my own. They would be many years in the background of my thinking and research.

In the sixties, when I did most of my seminary teaching—apart from the lectures given on the theology and practice of mass media in the first half of the eighties at the Toronto School of Theology— one of the foremost themes in New Testament scholarship was the increasing interest in the alleged Jewishness of Jesus. I duly relayed this to the students in class, but at the same time there was a dimension of this development that it seemed nobody was addressing. I had no immediate answer myself, but the question niggled away on the fringes of my consciousness all the same. The problem was this: The scholars were (and today still are) convinced that if there was a historical Jesus in first-century Judea, he undoubtedly spoke Aramaic, a Semitic dialect, as his native tongue. It makes perfect sense that his words and deeds would later be translated and put forth into the wider Mediterranean world in Hellenistic Greek, the lingua franca of that world ever since Alexander the Great's conquests in the fourth century BCE. But where are the supposed Aramaic originals of the Gospels to be found? Since obviously the redactors or editors of the four Gospels, whoever they actually were, purported to believe that the acts and sayings of Jesus were those of the divine Son of God, why were these not held worthy of being preserved in their pristine, original form? True, there are one or two Aramaic words preserved in the Gospel records, but their amazing paucity merely serves to highlight this lacuna in the "birthing" materials all the more. Let it be stressed that this is no minor matter for scholarly quibbling; it is an omission of huge proportions to be faced by traditionalist thinking. Yet for the most part it is—like many such issues—simply glossed over or ignored completely.

While it was clear to me that the New Testament documents, at least in the form they have come down to us, were chiefly the work of Jewish hands and minds, certain other aspects of this situation troubled me as well. There were two specifics in particular that raised for the first time in my mind the possibility that perhaps the Jesus Story might be the telling of an older, more universal tale in a carefully Judaized dress or terminology. Accepting for a moment the Jewish matrix for the story, that of a Saviour figure for the world, how can one explain the wholly remarkable fact that the central sacred, ritual meal—the chief sacrament—laid down for all times in these texts, sets forth and celebrates the eating and drinking of the body and blood of the God himself? Anyone who has ever read Leviticus or who knows anything whatsoever about Judaism then or today, anyone who understands even one iota of the beliefs about the kosher killing of animals and kosher food in general, knows how utterly abominable all of this sounds in Jewish ears. Abominable and blasphemous too. Indeed, it was commonplace in the various Mystery Religions and other circles in the ancient world, but we are talking about one of the most un-Jewish of all conceivable ideas. Even if, as surely most reasonable people do, one understands the terminology to be symbolic or metaphorical in nature, the problem for Jews remains simply enormous.

The second problematic "specific" in relation to the growing emphasis upon the Jewishness of Jesus—and let it be said that in general I believed this to be an overdue and hence welcome correction of a previous tendency to overlook the Jewish content of the New Testament almost entirely—has to do with the very nature of the Jesus Story itself. As said above, it is the narrative of a Saviour man-God come for the deliverance of all mankind. But as the earliest critics of Christianity in its infancy were quick to point out, this dying/rising God soteriology (to use the technical term for a theory of salvation) was already well known in the other religions of Mediterranean and other Middle Eastern antiquity. Even the very first Christian apologists, Justin Martyr and Irenaeus for example, were profoundly embarrassed by the obvious parallels with the

Mystery Religions and came up with far-fetched and even contradictory explanations. I was to become more aware much later in my
career of the extent to which this was a thorny obstacle to the traditional telling of the Christian story, but it troubled me then also
from time to time.

Unfortunately, I had more than enough on my plate in meeting
the demands of a fairly heavy lecture load, plus doing Sunday duty
to supplement Wycliffe's less than bountiful salary schedule, to
be able to devote the kind of time it required to further research
just at that moment. But the question was there to be pondered
at odd breaks in the college rhythms, even at times in chapel when
thoughts should have been elsewhere. It returned again repeatedly
throughout all the following years. Here is the question starkly
put: "How do those who deny that there is direct input to Christianity from Pagan religions account for the glaring fact that there
is no basis or pattern in ancient Judaism for a dying/rising-again
Saviour motif?" Yes, there is the Suffering Servant of Deutero-
Isaiah—who seems to represent or personify the Nation of Israel
as a whole—but no suffering-dying-rising God. From today's vantage point I realize that I was far from ready for the answer. The
stakes at a very deep level were much too high.

Early on in the course of preparing a series of lectures on the
Sermon on the Mount one summer, I realized that the latest commentaries and Bible dictionaries were now emphasizing the to me
radically disturbing truth that, as hinted at already, virtually none
of the material was original. The "Sermon" pronouncements—
Matthew chapters 5 to 7—are now recognized as a collection of
logia, or sayings, rather than as one continuous discourse. Interestingly, the mountain on which the Sermon is supposed to have taken
place remains unnamed and its situation vague. (In Luke a shorter
version of the same "Sermon" is said to have taken place, not on a
mountain, but on an equally vague plain.) I discovered, I must say

with a certain sense of shock, that most of the key sayings could also be found in the Talmud and Mishnah, and even at times in earlier Pagan authors. For example, the saying of Matthew "Many are called but few are chosen" and the *logion* or saying that it is hard for a rich man to enter the kingdom of heaven are both found virtually verbatim in the writings of Plato, roughly four hundred years earlier.

The motto of Wycliffe College, *Verbum Domini Manet*, "the Word of the Lord Abides" (or stands firm), now had to be viewed from a different perspective. That, together with my growing recognition that the Greek text of the New Testament had at least 150,000 variant readings in the different manuscripts (many of them minor, but some very serious and important for the overall meaning), combined to force me to review and correct my view of Holy Scripture. In this latter connection it is worthwhile to look at the work of Christian Lindtner, Ph.D., author of *The Secret of Jesus*. Lindtner, a Sanskrit scholar, believes he has proven that much of the Gospel material is anticipated in earlier Buddhist scriptures. There are other noted scholars who agree. It was becoming very clear that, rather than being the product of pure visionary revelation or sudden inspiration from Above, all sacred scriptures were the product of composite human effort, from varying sources, in some cases over a long span of years. In other words, God does not write books—human beings do. I was of course aware that this was a stage in my own inner development that could well be pregnant with significance for the future.

As I look back at over a decade of training clergy and Christian educators—including the years of lecturing both before and after my seven years as a full professor of New Testament and Greek— I see that I remained fairly conservative in outlook. For example, Wycliffe College in particular, and Christianity at large, held as a central doctrine the teaching that God sent his only begotten Son into the world to "save sinners"—that is, all of humanity—by dying

on a cross at a specific time and place under a specific Roman official in the Roman province of Judea. In other words, certain events
rooted firmly in history were at the core of this theological schema
or plan. Quite apart from the huge question of what happened to
the millions of humans who lived before this salvific action came
into effect, not to mention those since then who never even heard
the Gospel story, there was another increasingly nagging dilemma
with which I had also begun to struggle. The whole story of salvation climaxes, it seems, in the "historical" events just noted. But the
cause of the entire problem being dealt with at the Cross, the pri-
mal "Fall," or the sin of Adam and Eve, is, and always has been, presented in purely mythical terms. Nobody today except the most
fundamental of fundamentalists believes in a literal Adam and Eve,
in talking serpents or the like. So we are asked to accept that a historical solution is in some utterly inexplicable way required for
what is clearly a problem presented by means of mythology. The
great "sin" of Adam's disobedience never happened in time or
space, anywhere on earth; it is purely mythological. Thus, when
Paul says, "As in Adam all die, even so in Christ will all be made to
live," he balances the equation. Just as Adam is mythic, so too is the
risen Christ. The full truth one day struck me like a bolt of lightning: just as the story of the Fall is mythical, so too is the story of its
undoing, or Redemption! None of this, however, changes the *inner*
truth of what is being said in any way whatsoever. It simply means
that one more of the five "fundamental truths" of fundamentalism
cannot stand.

Over the years at the college, these and other issues began
increasingly to trouble me. But it would be some years yet before I
was able to see my way clearly out of this maze.

Canada celebrated its one hundredth anniversary in 1967, and I
spent the summer driving with my family to the Yukon Territory.

The Bishop of the Yukon, Henry Marsh, had invited me to take over two churches for a couple of months and to hold some seminars for the handful of clergy in his vast diocese. That was a camping trip to remember, especially travelling up the as-yet-unpaved Alaska Highway. The rough terrain tore the little tires on the tent trailer to ribbons every few hundred kilometres. Taking one of these tires to a garage—they were very few and far between—I realized it looked as though a grizzly bear had slashed it. I asked the lone mechanic-cum-gas attendant, "Do you sell many of these?" and he replied, "We sell them like doughnuts." But memorable as the Yukon was, the truly important step for me in 1967 was making my first foray into a world that was to change my life and my approach to spirituality forever.

Much as I enjoyed teaching at the college, the questions and friendship of students and staff, I was becoming more and more dissatisfied. The theological college atmosphere, far from being a fellowship of eager, kindred minds engaged in the quest for truth and a better understanding of how to engage and change for the better the world outside our doors, was in reality stifling and incredibly inward-looking. New thinking of any kind was discouraged. The daily morning and evening services in chapel struck me as increasingly boring, cold, and out of touch with the aspirations and needs of ordinary people. I have elsewhere described seminary life as "the Church busy talking to itself." In all too many well-known schools of theology today, the same description still applies. Outside in the larger world at the time, major events were shaking the very foundations of our society. Inside, it was the old refrain: "As it was in the beginning, is now, and ever shall be, Amen."

In theology, the "God is dead" ferment of the early 1960s had been followed by the Anglican Bishop of Woolich's 1963 paperback shocker *Honest to God*. Everywhere in the Church and beyond, it was causing a furor. The bishop, John Robinson, whom I was later to come to know well, spending time with him not only in my home near the University of Toronto but also in Canterbury, where he was born and raised, focused on serious issues revolving around the New Morality and the need to change the traditional thinking about God. In Canada not long afterwards, broadcaster-author Pierre Berton wrote his soon-to-be-famous indictment of a sleeping Anglicanism, *The Comfortable Pew*. Readers' opinion pages in traditional Church publications frothed with outrage for months. Internationally, the United States, torn by years of the civil rights uproar, the Kennedy assassinations and a host of other problems, was slowly but inevitably being drawn into the war in Vietnam.

In 1966 the college sent me to some scholarly meetings in New York, held at the stunningly opulent Riverside Church. Sitting for hours listening to deeply learned lectures on Biblical themes and then travelling back to my hotel on the graffiti-covered subway trains late each afternoon, the question I had been asking myself in Toronto grew to a roar in my ears: "What on earth has any of this to do with any of that [the secular world beyond]?" I realized that for me it was time for a truly seismic shift. The longing filled me to find a way or means to move beyond the world of purely academic pursuits to communicate spiritual truths in terms any modern layperson could readily understand. I felt drawn to mass media. The problem was where or how to begin.

One day after my return from New York, between classes, I was in my study praying about this dilemma (this was before my thinking about prayer had been transformed) when there came a knock at the door. It was an Armenian friend, a keen but unconventional, evangelical layman who fashioned fine jewellery for a living. He said that God seemed to be telling him to come and talk to me about a need for me to be somehow involved in media. He cited a series of brief meditations I had done at one time on CBC Radio. It was a nod by the corporation to the churches called *Plain Talk* and was something I had enjoyed.

I could scarcely believe his words because of their apparent syn-chronicity. I told him of my deep sense of being "called" to find a voice in the public forum and shared my growing bafflement over how to break in. He bluntly asked: "What are you doing about it?" I told him of my prayers and was priggishly surprised when he retorted: "Well, it's time to stop praying right now. How many radio or television station managers or newspaper editors have you talked to or taken to lunch? You teach New Testament. You know how the story of the raising of Lazarus begins with a command to move the stone. That's what you need to do. Move the stone, i.e., do for yourself what you're busy pestering God to do!" It was clear that he had a valid point.

I knew of only one person who might be a possible contact, an Anglican layman and lawyer named John Graham whom I had once met when he was a delegate to synod meetings at the Adelaide Street head office. He was, I had been told, co-owner of a small radio sta-tion called CFGM in Richmond Hill, just north of Toronto. I called him that afternoon and asked if I could see him about doing some sort of program on his station. To my complete surprise he said at once, "Let's meet in your study tomorrow." So we did. On arrival, he came right to the point: "Would you be interested in doing an open-line show one night a week, and if so, when would you like to begin?" I replied that I'd be keen to do so and that since it was then around the end of April, the fall sounded good to me. He said: "I was thinking about next week. How about next Thursday?" That was shock enough, but he followed up that with his idea for a title for the hour: "How about *Harpur's Heaven and Hell*?" A vision of the bishop, Right Reverend Frederick Wilkinson, flashed through my mind as I blurted out: "The Bishop will be mortified. We can't go with that." But Graham was not a man to be easily put off once he knew what he wanted. And a prophecy he made at that moment eventually came true. He told me: "Some people, especially your colleagues and other prissy Anglicans, may not like the name, but

I guarantee you that once heard, it will never be forgotten." I little expected then that my first book in 1984 would go on to be a bestseller under that name, and that an hour-long interview series I hosted and that ran nationally for three years on VisionTV would bear the same title.

Daily radio had never really been on my radar screen—apart from CBC News occasionally and the programs featuring classical music. Life had simply been too full. But I immediately began tuning in CFGM to discover what it was like. To my initial dismay, I found it was a country and western music station with such theologically insightful songs as "Drop Kick Me Jesus through the Goalposts of Life" and "When It's Round-up Time in Heaven." A genuine feeling of alarm befell me when I heard the first promo for my maiden show. The promo itself was fine, but the disc jockey followed it immediately by announcing the next record: "I Won't Go Huntin' with You Jake (But I'll Go Chasin' Women)."

The principal of my college and I had not been on the very best of terms before this, but there was a further coolness suddenly emerging that was to mark our relationship from then until I left my post to become the religion editor of the *Toronto Star* in 1971. The news that I would be hosting a radio show was definitely not appreciated.

The program itself had a slow beginning. A country and western audience didn't have a lot of use for professors of Greek and New Testament, especially one who knew next to nothing about them, their interests or their heroes, musical or otherwise. For some weeks I had to get family members and friends—even the Old Testament professor, my esteemed colleague, the late Reverend Dr. R.K. Harrison, a close friend who sounded a little like my mother on the phone—to call in and voice opinions or simply argue with me. Afraid to face an entire hour void of commercials on my own, I routinely had a guest to talk to when there was nothing but terrifyingly empty air.

Graham kept encouraging me to "lose the guests" and launch out unaccompanied into the deep. Gradually, I began to do this and surprisingly it worked—much better than I had hoped. I still had guests from time to time, including John Diefenbaker, our former prime minister, a stripper who had "found God," and eventually the famous Beatle John Lennon and his wife Yoko Ono, by a direct line (for an hour) into their room in the Montreal hotel where they were holding their 1968 Bed-In for Peace. John spoke eloquently about his front-page comments on how the Beatles were "better known and communicated with modern young people better than Jesus Christ." Unfortunately, though the station supplied me with a recording of that encounter, the tape of it was lost in a move long ago.

A number of things began to happen as a result of the radio involvement. I discovered that I was communicating better with my students. I was using fewer technical, learned-sounding ecclesiastical terms (such as *eschatology, epistemology, pneumatology, ecclesiology*) and more contemporary illustrations. A recent study of seminary students in Britain had shown, according to a news story I kept pinned up at my desk in my office, that the men and women who were to be future clergy were far better able to communicate effectively with their fellow human beings *before* entering theological college than upon graduation! I was afraid of that happening at Wycliffe. The radio experience helped me to determine that this would no longer occur, at least on my watch, if I could help it.

At the same time, the other media began to notice. Allan Spraggett, then the *Toronto Star*'s religion editor, came to the college to do a major feature for his popular Saturday page. He said his readers would be intrigued to learn more about an Anglican cleric and professor who spent time on that kind of station instead of in a pulpit. More importantly, he issued an invitation for me to write occasional opinion pieces for the weekend paper's religion page, and I was soon turning out articles with headlines such as THE

GOSPEL ACCORDING TO JAMES BOND and BISHOPS — WHO NEEDS THEM?
Would You Believe, a regular CBC TV Sunday morning religion show
of that day, began using me as a member of their panel discussions,
and *Man Alive* producers started calling upon me to write scripts for
the prestigious TV religion program hosted every Monday night by
broadcaster Roy Bonisteel.

One morning I woke up with the realization that what had begun
as a very timid, tiny adventure had become my passion. When, in
the early weeks of 1971, I learned that Spraggett would soon be
quitting his post as religion editor of the *Toronto Star* to focus on
writing a book, I immediately called him and we met for a long talk
about the full nature of the job and what he thought I might bring
to it if I applied.

After prayer and much thought, I knew it was time to make a
move. I was going to be forty-two that April. There would be sacri-
fices to make. I had full tenure then as a professor at the college,
with a residence in the college itself, over four months for reading, writing and vacation each summer, and, in spite of a typically
Anglican low salary, many other perks besides. Working with the students had provided innumerable highs (along with some inevitable
lows). Some things would be missed very much.

Among these was an important development that was ripe with
promise for the future. Discussions had been going on for some
time among the key institutions devoted to theological training
in the Greater Toronto Area about the possibility of creating an
ecumenical federation. In 1970, in a historic move, the Anglican
colleges (Wycliffe and Trinity) joined with the Roman Catholics
(St. Augustine's, St. Basil's and Regis), the Presbyterians (Knox
College) and the United Church (Emmanuel) to form the Toronto
School of Theology (TST). It was the first such school in Canada
and remains the largest, although other centres have followed suit.
Lutherans, Baptists, Mennonites and Christian Reformed now also
have affiliated status in TST. What matters most about this change

is that, for the first time, future clergy and other Christian educators are now sharing classes. What's more, it means that Anglicans can learn about Catholics from Catholic professors. Catholics can grapple with Reformation theology under the leadership of Presbyterian or United Church professors and lecturers. Speaking personally, as one of the founding faculty members responsible for the setting up of TST, I found great pleasure in teaching students of other denominations. This was particularly the case with the Regis College participants. As Jesuits in training, they were characteristically very bright and, above all, eager to come to grips with my subject, the New Testament. The reforms of Vatican II (1962–65) had opened a fresh window on Biblical studies for the Church of Rome.

Nevertheless, overall, nothing essential had really changed at Wycliffe. I had a deep awareness that for me theological education itself had become a dead end. I used to think it was the place to begin to make a difference—to renew the Church. I had come to realize it was really a big part of the problem and not about to change much any time soon. From my sources I am aware that today's theological students are, if anything, more conservative than when I was teaching almost forty years ago.

During my years as a journalist I had the privilege upon several occasions of interviewing in some depth Robertson Davies, the noted novelist and for many years Master of Massey College at the University of Toronto. One of these encounters was an hour-long conversation for the VisionTV series already mentioned above, *Harpur's Heaven and Hell*, in the late 1980s. I remember at one point we were discussing the crucial turning points in his career, and particularly his decision to leave the newspaper business that he had inherited from his father to take up writing full-time. It was a huge decision, one with great significance not just for his own career but also for the future of Canadian literature as a whole. He said he had observed that very often in life the death of one's father signalled the release of hitherto untapped creative powers. Since this intriguing insight gave rise to a strong sense of affirmation within me as he spoke, I pressed him to elaborate. He made it clear that he wasn't speaking of instances where there had been a lack of filial love, respect or admiration for the departed parent. Simply put, the death of one's father, he thought, very often left a son, however grieving, feeling a sense of much greater freedom to be true to his own inner allurement or genuine bent. In his own case, he said, it had led to whatever success he was enjoying in the world of fiction and beyond.

I was keenly interested in this observation. Without comparing callings or achievements, it was becoming increasingly clear to me that certain of my decisions, such as leaving academia to write first as a journalist and then as a columnist and author of books on ethical and spiritual themes, would not likely have been possible for me while my father was still living. His vision for me was as a bishop of the Church. It turned out it wasn't mine. Whatever the reasons, my creative juices began to flow much more freely some time after my father made the transition in late 1968 to what I believe is a new and fuller state of being. Living my own life thus began for me, in a very real way, with the approach of what used to be called pejoratively middle age. A much larger world beckoned, and so I made the best decision of my life to that date.

7

"ST. PAUL, HAD HE LIVED TODAY, WOULD HAVE BEEN A JOURNALIST"

– Pope Paul VI, Vatican City, 1975

I N THE SPRING of 1971, I applied for the post of religion editor at the country's largest-circulation newspaper, the *Toronto Star*. Within the shortest possible time, the publisher, Beland Honderich, had his secretary telephone to set up an interview in the old Star building at 80 King Street West (now the Bank of Montreal building) in the heart of the downtown financial district.

Going through the splendid brass doors and on up to the inner sanctum—the offices of the "Beast," as some staffers referred to him—reminded me of how intimidated I used to feel as a student in the presence of the Provost of Oriel on the final day of term, when my tutors sat on either side of me and gave an account of my progress and overall conduct. Honderich could be a formidable force to encounter. He had little or no gift for small talk, a razor-sharp mind, and a reputation for a flaring wrath when crossed or displeased by shoddy performance. But he seemed genial enough to me when we first met, and over the years I was to find him a generous, wise mentor whose word was always utterly reliable, come what might. He asked why I would consider making such a major change in my career, listened carefully to my answer, and asked me what I thought I should be paid. He then wanted to know when I could start, and showed me out of his office with the words that were to determine the shape of the next twelve years of my life and beyond. Honderich said, "Tom, I want you to travel the world and bring us stories from wherever you find them. The managing editor is up on the fifth floor. Go up and have a talk with him before you go."

I had no idea just how much my life was about to change. A door had opened into a huge new arena and an experience about as far removed from my past—the halls of academic, conservative ecclesiasticism—as anyone could ever imagine. There was a surge of fresh energy and excitement within, but also a tinge of anxiety. There was risk involved. Bridges had been burned. The road to priesthood, with ten years spent in my college education and then a very minimum wage for eight years in a parish, had been intellectually rich but financially close to a disaster. With no house (a residence had always been provided and counted in as part of my remuneration or stipend) and very little in the way of savings, and unused to deadlines, I had to follow the course of everybody else at the *Star*: three months on probation and a very steep learning curve to boot.

Writing articles for a newspaper is definitely not the same thing as composing sermons, lectures or pious talks for the Women's Auxiliary. Mr. Honderich believed a story should be such as your average cab driver could understand. He had little use for technical or deeply theological terms. He read every line of every issue, and was particularly critical with regard to any "artwork"—photo illustrations—especially on the Saturday religion page. It is said he had a habit of coming into the newsroom and throwing a quarter onto the head in a person's photograph. If the head wasn't at least the size of the coin, there was hell to pay for the editor who had approved the photo.

I had never been to a school of journalism. Having been shown around the newsroom on my first day, May 1, 1971, I sat down at the old Underwood typewriter and realized I didn't even know where to find a pencil sharpener. I knew nothing about how to file stories from overseas—say, from London, Rome or Jerusalem. The first time I went down to the newsroom to ask for a photographer to take a shot for a feature story, the man who turned out to be the one in charge took one look at me as I approached and roared so all could hear, "Just what the hell do you want, Harpur?" I was so shocked that I almost forgot what I had come for. I didn't know a photo editor from a copy boy.

I would go on to write about ethics, spirituality and religion for the paper over the next thirty-five years.

There was a time in the sixties when, as a professor at a seminary, I had felt a lot of pressure to publish a book—something, anything, that would have my name on it. It was the old "publish or perish" syndrome. I even canvassed a few publishing houses with a couple of what I now realize were pretty vague, pious ideas. Not surprisingly, they turned me down. I didn't write my first book—though I was part of the three-man advisory team of Biblical experts for Charles Templeton's book *Jesus* in 1977—until, in that same year, the popular American publisher of rather conservative Sunday school and related books, Thomas Cook, approached me. They wanted to see if I'd be interested in expanding a series of front-page articles I had written for the *Star* leading up to Christmas 1976. The series had been called *The Road to Bethlehem* and was accompanied by some remarkable photos by *Star* photographer Dick Loek. The original articles came from an idea I had had while walking to work from my home, which at that time was near the Robarts Library on the University of Toronto campus. I proposed to *Star* managing editor Martin Goodman that I would go to Israel, hire a donkey and walk the 160 kilometres from Nazareth to Bethlehem, staying at border kibbutzim each night. Accompanied by a photographer, I would file stories giving an account of what such an experience was like today as opposed to two thousand years ago. When I laid the proposal before him, Goodman asked one question: "Have you ever been to Israel before?" When I said no, he said: "You're the religion editor. Isn't your not having been there a little like the sports editor having to say, 'I've never been to Maple Leaf Gardens'? I think it's a great idea, and you've got to go." I was to go to Israel several times over the ensuing years—and to Egypt as well.

The series was a huge success for the paper, especially the day they were able to run a headline saying STAR MAN FIRES DONKEY accompanied by a large picture of the stubborn animal being led along the road near Jericho. He (we were told his name was She-mon, or Simon) was supposed to carry our packs, but he was just too slow and so we had to call his owner in Nazareth to come and pick him up on the second day of our trip. With the coloured photos and a coffee table–type format, the book itself looked attractive and sold well. In retrospect, however, I think of it (as indeed I do of Templeton's book, *Jesus: A Bible in Modern English*) as a well-meaning mistake.

While one can never forget the intimate sense of that severe yet awe-inspiring landscape brought on by walking all that distance down the Jordan Valley, I realize now that I was really helping to further literalize a story that was never meant to be taken that way in the first place. The account in Luke, the only place in the New Testament where a journey to Bethlehem from a putative home-town of Nazareth is mentioned, is flatly contradicted by Matthew's Nativity story. According to Matthew, the star that allegedly was followed by the Magi "stopped over the place where the child was" and "on entering the house, they saw the child with Mary his mother . . ." In other words, in this version, the house of Mary and Joseph was not in Nazareth at all but in Bethlehem. Luke's story of a birth in a manger resulting from a lack of room in the inn is totally ignored by Matthew. There are other technical details that add to one's unease over my *Road to Bethlehem* venture. Suffice it to say that when one is dealing with myth, it is always folly to lapse into the literal and/or historical. I still had far to go and much to learn on my own inner intellectual and spiritual journey.

For some time, as already mentioned, I had been deeply concerned about the failure of religious institutions to communicate their message to ordinary men and women, especially those on the edges and those completely outside. I was almost painfully aware of how much we in the religious establishment relished talking about spiritual matters in a language few others could understand. It seemed time that somebody "religious" made the effort to learn how the media work and how to use contemporary means to spiritual ends. Apart from Malcolm Muggeridge and C.S. Lewis before him, I knew of very few Christians who had made such an attempt.

The past three and a half decades have been a fantastic experience for me. Perhaps in some small ways I have been able to help in pioneering or attempting to set certain standards in the mass communication of religio-spiritual truths. But that's not the big news for me as I look back. It's what I learned through the privilege of being a religion journalist at a top paper during one of the most exciting periods of theological and spiritual change in our history. Yes, and how this experience has shaped me as well. It has been a far more thorough and radical course of instruction than all the years at university and theological college ever were. In particular, the twelve years as religion editor were a whirlwind, but they gave me a global experience and held a richness that enlarged my heart and mind beyond measure. All of it formed a new and fertile matrix out of which the many columns and books of my later life as a free-lance author and broadcaster were to be born.

I had only to come up with a compelling idea for a story in order to receive permission to go—to Israel, to Japan, to Africa, to Central America, to Scandinavia, to Rome, and to more other places than I have space to list. *Star* photographers and I travelled deep into the territory east of James Bay with Aboriginal hunters tracking caribou in the depths of winter while we did a story on the James Bay hydro project. We flew into the Sinai Peninsula and slept on the mountain where Moses is traditionally said to have received the Ten Commandments. We travelled to Central America to report on Canadians working with children orphaned by war. We spent time in San Francisco with the world's first all-gay police squad, and we went fishing for Arctic char out on the ice beyond Baffin Island with an Inuit Anglican priest. We spent time with film director Franco Zeffirelli while he made his epic *Jesus of Nazareth* in the Moroccan foothills of the Atlas Mountains. Anne Bancroft and the other stars were eager to discuss Jesus with a former teacher of New Testament in the long breaks between scenes. One day, during a shoot in Meknes, a small Biblical-looking town, there was a sudden downpour and I found myself sheltering in a doorway with Bancroft and Zeffirelli. We had a lively discussion. Zeffirelli told of his difficulty in maintaining a sense of majesty or divinity in the Jesus character while at the same time portraying him as human. "He cannot yawn or burp," he said. Bancroft, who was surprisingly well informed about the Gospels, had some challenging questions, such as why no actual description of Jesus's appearance or mannerisms seems to exist. It was a very stimulating half-hour before the rain ceased.

Money was no object in those heady days of the 1970s. For my first trip to London, the secretary for the Insight section, which at the time included the religion pages, decided I should stay at least one night at the Dorchester Hotel. She seemed very pleased with herself when she told me. I had no idea at the time that it was considered at the top of London elegance or that such notables as T.S. Eliot, General Dwight Eisenhower, Sir Winston Churchill and a host of others had at various times regarded it as home. The Queen, when she was still Princess Elizabeth, and Prince Philip had announced their engagement there, and today it remains the first choice of Hollywood film stars and leading politicians from all over. Situated on Mayfair's stylish Park Lane and overlooking Hyde Park itself, it is in the very heart of London. I was naturally more than pleased to be able to tell the cabbie at Heathrow the name of my destination.

However, pride indeed goeth before a fall. When the cab pulled up in front of the hotel, a doorman wearing more gold braid on his hat than a rear admiral, stepped smartly down the front steps and opened the cab door for me. I was suddenly somewhat self-conscious. My one suitcase had seen much better days and in fact was of lowly origin to start with. In short, it was cheap and old. The doorman whipped it out of my grasp and turned to lead me up to the entrance. Suddenly, to my dismay, the handle came off in his hand and a sort of yellow, fluffy stuffing burst out of it. The unfortunate suitcase landed on the edge of one of the steps and popped open, spilling the entire contents—socks, underwear, shirts, everything—all over the entrance. Red-faced, I hurriedly grabbed the bits and pieces and packed them away while wilting completely under the scornful eye of my former helper. I could tell he wanted nothing more to do with me and I avoided him thereafter by using another door. I changed hotels the next day.

Writing for the *Star*, one had the rare privilege of meeting and speaking with all the great spiritual leaders of our time, from the Dalai Lama to Billy Graham, Malcolm Muggeridge, three Archbishops of Canterbury and so many others. In many ways it was like a dream fulfilled. The most striking thing about the Dalai Lama was the great aura of calmness that radiated from him, as well as his constant smile and his deep humility. Muggeridge was noted not for humility but for his rapier wit, his ability to communicate through shock (he once told a Toronto audience that the two symbols of today's culture are "the raised fist and the raised phallus") and his fervent approach to religion.

Although he is now well over ninety, when most people think of Billy Graham they conjure up a tall, craggily handsome man standing at a podium with a large bible in his hands. His face is earnest, the eyes commanding, as he urges the crowds at his feet to make their decision for Christ. With the choir singing softly over and over again, "Just as I am, without one plea," he presses his broad brow into his hand and stands seemingly lost in prayer. And the people stream forward by the hundreds.

Having been at many of his crusades both in Canada and abroad, I too can picture him that way. But it's not the first image that springs to mind. Instead, I see him during his last crusade in Toronto. Wanting to get an edge on the competition, the *Star* had sent me to Minneapolis to travel with Billy to Toronto for the week-long series of sessions at Maple Leaf Gardens. We had already become good friends over the years, and as usual he and his staff proved very gracious indeed. I had a long interview with him in an airport hotel in Chicago, where we stopped over to enable him to be present at a crusade his brother-in-law, Leighton Ford, was conducting in Cicero. Then we sat together during the flight from O'Hare to Pearson airport. It was interesting how patient he was with all who wanted his autograph or to shake hands with the world's best-known preacher. Several people on the plane, including a nun in very traditional black garb, interrupted him. He even autographed a cigarette package for a young woman who said she had nothing else for him to write on.

In an earlier book I told the story of once interviewing him at the boardwalk of the Beach area in Toronto, and of how the photographer attempted a very creative photo while I was busy speaking to the press officer. He asked Billy to remove his socks, roll up his pant cuffs and walk on a slimy concrete breakwater. He wanted to show Billy appearing to walk on water. Once the press officer and I realized what was happening, we quickly put a stop to it. The photos had already been taken, but Graham simply asked for assurances that we wouldn't do anything "unwise" with them. They never ran in the paper, although they probably still remain somewhere in the *Star*'s photo files.

Since then I've always remembered Billy Graham with a chuckle. He was one of the best-dressed and most admired men in America, and the most famous of all contemporary evangelists, but to me he'll be remembered with his pants rolled up, a stub of a hot dog still in his hand, graciously accommodating an overzealous photographer by doing his best to walk on water. Even at that time I differed greatly from him on matters theological, but he will always rank highly in my esteem for his integrity and humility of spirit in the face of fame.

As is the case for any would-be objective journalist, I wasn't always welcomed in certain places. As the *Star*'s first ombudsman, the late Borden Spears, once told me, "Your beat causes more reaction than the crime reporter's!"

I once was sent to interview the Archbishop of Canterbury, who was at that time the Most Reverend Michael Ramsey. He was in Toronto giving an address to the Canadian and Empire Clubs at the Royal York Hotel. Next to His Holiness the Pope, the Archbishop of Canterbury, head of the 63-million-member Anglican Church, is undoubtedly the most prominent of all Christian leaders. Those who occupy this ancient position are nearly always distinguished scholars and have the bearing proper to such an exalted ecclesiastical rank. Like the Pope, they live in a palace—in this case Lambeth Palace—and are treated with extraordinary tact and respect even by those who have no religious faith.

Ramsey was to me the quintessential Archbishop of Canterbury. His bald dome of a head was covered with fly-away wisps of white hair (it was said that even as a student he had looked ancient); his great hook nose was set between two darting bright eyes that seemed to pop out from under a thick thatch of eyebrows; he had a broad figure and a booming voice. He seemed a character ready for the stage in a real-life drama about a sturdier, bygone time. Added to his physical appearance were certain eccentricities of manner and character that he seemed to exploit. For example, he had cultivated a way of stuttering slightly when he spoke. Many English aristocrats and leading academics have affected this speech defect as a method of lending importance to their words. When someone of note stutters, it has the effect of keeping people on the edge of expectation—their attention is much keener. Ramsey was interviewed once on CFTO television in the early 1970s, on the usual topics one discusses with a world religious leader. When he was asked what he thought of the current "sexual revolution," especially the growing trend towards sex before marriage, his eyes sparkled and the massive eyebrows jumped up and down as he began: "The Church has always been opposed to f-f-f-f-f-fornication!" The producer was holding his breath and on the edge of his seat, but Ramsey continued on, beaming like a cherub.

The Archbishop had consented to give me an interview over sherry after his TV appearance. At the end of the questions I told him I was an Anglican priest. He looked at my casual dress, a turtleneck sweater and tweed jacket, and quipped: "My, what an excellent disguise!"

In fact, I had first met him ten years previously, in 1962, while doing the year of postgraduate study at Oxford. I was walking up the High Street one October afternoon when just ahead of me I made out the figure of a stockily built man all in black who looked like the sheriff in a TV western. He was wearing gaiters and a frock coat together with a wide-brimmed hat. With his back to me, it was impossible to see the white clerical collar, but as I drew closer I could tell from his shape and the locks of bushy white hair fringing his neck that it was none other than Canterbury himself. I fell into step beside him and, plunging in, told him my name and that I was a visiting student priest from Canada. I can only describe the look in his eyes as one of startled alarm. He managed to mutter something about how nice it was to see me, but it was obvious from his body language that he wanted nothing to do with this philistine from the colonies who had dared to interrupt his reverie without a formal introduction. Suddenly he spied an opening in the walls on our right and, with a stuttered reference to "somebody I must see immediately" and a wave of his black arm, he darted down Magpie Lane beside Oriel College with the alacrity of someone trying to avoid a rattlesnake. Later, when I told some English clergy friends about my chance meeting, their merriment knew no bounds. Apparently it just wasn't done for anyone to walk up to the Archbishop of Canterbury without having been at least spoken to first or introduced.

Ramsey was a great gift but also a challenge to the media, not only because of his style but because he knew well how to deal with reporters when he wasn't keen on talking. In 1975 I was in England attending a conference of doctors and theologians on non-medical healing. After it ended I went to London to meet the Dalai Lama at a press conference and, perusing one of the papers, I learned that Ramsey was to attend a reception at Brompton Oratory the following day. Since there was a considerable debate at the time over the ordination of women in the Anglican Church, I decided to go in the hope of either talking with the Archbishop or setting up an interview for later in the week, and perhaps doing a news story for the *Star*.

I arrived late at the reception and was told by an antique verger that everybody was downstairs. I walked down to the large church basement wearing a trench coat and carrying my tape recorder, in search of His Grace. People were trying to navigate from conversation to conversation while holding cups of tea and plates of sandwiches and cakes. Looking about, I spied Ramsey sitting all alone at the head table, with an empty teacup and a plate with crumbs on it. I walked over boldly and was about to introduce myself when he looked up suddenly, got me in focus, held up his cup and saucer, and said: "How very kind of you . . . a little milk and sugar, please." There was nothing I could do but go and fetch his tea.

When I took it over to him, he immediately dropped his eyes and seemed to withdraw inside himself into a world of his own. Coughing slightly, I quickly asked whether we could talk on the record for a few minutes. He gazed up very benignly and said he was much too busy with the reception just then to give his attention to so important an issue as women's ordination, and he returned to his tea with Buddha-like concentration. Daring to interrupt once more, I asked whether I could call his secretary in the morning and arrange an interview for later that week. The enormous brows did push-ups and he said twice, "Don't count on it." And with that he rose, collared a nearby Greek Orthodox prelate and became instantly engaged in a ferocious dialogue. I knew I was beaten. I had a cup of tea, climbed the stairs and reluctantly went out into the London fog.

During the summer of 1978, the bishops of the Anglican Church met at Canterbury, England, for the Lambeth Conference. The sessions were held at Canterbury University, up on a hill overlooking the ancient cathedral, but most of the religion journalists and some of the bishops stayed at hotels in the old city itself. I was covering the event for the *Toronto Star* and was lodged at the centuries-old Queen's Head Tavern. The ground floor of the topsy-turvy two-storey building was the site of a very busy pub. My room, reached by way of a crooked set of stairs and a winding wood-panelled hall with a roof so low I was always in danger of increasing the size of my bald spot, was comfortable enough, but the floor, walls and closets all slanted in the most alarming fashion. One evening I had a couple of bishops up for a drink. As I put a glass for Archbishop Lewis Garnsworthy on the small table, only his quick reflexes saved it from sliding onto the floor. To my embarrassment, none of the closet doors would stay closed. No matter how firmly shut, after a moment's pause and with the creaking of antique hinges, out they swung at you again.

Of course, this was before the era of computers and cellphones. Getting messages and stories back to the *Star* was a nightmare. There was one phone in the building other than the manager's, and that was in the entrance to the pub below. One night, having written what I thought was a front-page story on women priests, and after waiting in line for the phone, I tried to dial the long-distance operator. You could hardly hear for the din of singing, shouting and banging glasses coming from within. When I did get through, the operator told me that the British post office workers and thus long-distance operators were working to rule over a labour grievance and it would be some time before we could get a line. Meanwhile, others behind me were starting to make noises about it being time they had a "go" at the phone. Then, inspiration struck. I told the operator to call me back when we had a line free, and then I put an "out of order" note on the phone. Eventually the manageress spotted the note and asked me what I was doing. I explained my dilemma and she said, "Come to my office. You can use my phone." To my delight, I got an international line at once. I finally was answered by a familiar voice in the *Star*'s newsroom. But before I could get the words out, he said: "Hey Tom, that's a terrible connection. Call back on another line." Click! And he was gone. I almost cried with frustration. It was nearly two hours before I got through again and was finally able to dictate the piece. I don't know if it made page one or page sixty.

During my two-week stay at the Queen's Head two of my teenage daughters came to England for a holiday and we were able to spend a few days together in Canterbury. The hotel moved us to newer rooms at the rear of the second floor. I learned very soon that the rooms were directly above what was called the Golden Bar section of the pub. It was a rather sad episode with a bidet that caused my embarrassment. The girls had never seen a bidet before, and were amused by turning the tap on and off to see how it worked. What neither of them noticed was that the tap continued to trickle after it was shut off and, worse, that the plug was rusted in place. We went off to dinner and returned two hours later to find a stream of water flowing under the door of the room. I could hear sudden shouts and raucous laughter from the bar downstairs. We went inside to a mess with water everywhere. Just then there was a furious thumping at the door and the manageress thundered: "Whatever in the world is going on in there?" When she saw the extent of the flooding, she ran for her husband to fetch a plumber and for the hired help to bring mops and pails. "You should see what you've done downstairs," she shrilled. "You've ruined the Golden Bar!"

Sheepishly, I descended to the bar area. Water was dripping down a series of light bulbs above the bar, having blown them all out. Some had popped in a mini-explosion and lay in puddles. One of the bishops' wives, also staying there and who had imbibed somewhat freely, was catching the murky liquid in a cocktail glass and challenging all comers to drink "a Queen's Head cocktail." I retreated from the semi-dark pub as quickly as I could and discovered my bags being moved to yet another room.

I was not the only one who disgraced himself at Lambeth in 1978. There was an awkward moment at the special garden party at Buckingham Palace for the bishops and their wives. Normally, the attitude of British churchmen towards journalists is that of those who bask in their secure superiority to "lesser breeds without the law," but at the last minute the reporters covering Lambeth had been invited to join the gala affair. We went through the palace gates, past a series of guards and footmen of various ranks, each of whom inspected our invitations, and then through the palace itself and on out to the magnificent lawns and gardens beyond. In the foreground were several large, open-fronted canvas marquees where maids in white and black uniforms poured tea and iced coffee to accompany the myriad plates of thinly sliced sandwiches and mountains of iced cakes. The bishops in their crimson ceremonial robes, together with their wives who were decked out in straw hats and white gloves with long gowns of every hue, made a splendid contrast to the emerald green of the immaculately cut turf. Behind it all lay copses of trees and, in the middle distance, a mirror-like miniature lake where pink flamingos preened themselves in the sunlight. A regimental band in smart uniforms provided a musical background.

The Queen was away on a tour at the time, but Princess Margaret was there together with the Queen Mother and the Duchess of Kent. They made their rounds to meet their guests accompanied by six Yeomen of the Guard from the Tower of London, each carrying an enormous halberd. It was a most impressive sight. The royal party was just passing the group where we were standing when one of the Canadian bishops' wives, who was on the plump side, sat down firmly on one of the canvas lawn chairs. There was a loud tearing sound as the seat gave way and she sank through the frame to lodge there. The members of the royal family had been schooled not to look back, mercifully, but since the military band was silent at that moment, everyone else within earshot heard the ripping noise and stared at her as one man. Several bishops rushed instantly to her aid, their red cassocks matching the colour of her face. They tried to raise her to a standing position, but unfortunately the frame was wedged around her hips and the entire chair came up with her. It took some delicate manoeuvring to get it off, and as she finally struggled free she caught sight of me. With a hiss she threatened that if I ever wrote a word about this she'd come after me herself.

Two highly controversial stories came out of that garden party, one of which I filed for publication in the *Star*; the other I deliberately kept to myself. Idi Amin, the ruthless dictator of Uganda, figured in both of them. During the sixties and until 1971 there were a number of young Ugandan clergy who came to study at Wycliffe under a special "Ugandan program" that was conceived and directed by the principal, Rev. Dr. Leslie Hunt. Several of these men later became bishops soon after their return to Africa. One of them came over to me during the affair at Buckingham Palace and we had an enjoyable few minutes together catching up on what we had been doing over the intervening years. As we talked, I noticed a couple of black men with press credentials hanging about and obviously attempting to listen in. The bishop glanced over at them and, gently tugging at my shirt sleeve, motioned his intention of moving away. He whispered, "We must get away from them." He led me quite a distance towards a small bandshell where a band of the Grenadier Guards was now playing. Out of earshot of the two (as it turned out) ersatz reporters, he grinned broadly and said, "You know why we're here?" I said that obviously he was there to attend the conference. He shook his head while, still maintaining his smile, he swore me to secrecy and said, "Well, that's not all. We are here to get guns to fight Amin!" I was somewhat startled, but agreed to keep it off the record.

As it turned out, the bishop, who still referred to me as Professor Harpur, had another revelation to make. He told me that the two men whom I had observed eavesdropping on our earlier conversation were not journalists at all. "They are spies for Idi Amin," he said. When I pointed out that they seemed to be wearing proper press identification tags, and in the case of one, to be carrying a large Nikon camera, he explained that the men were intelligence agents of the Amin regime whose presence was being countenanced by Canterbury as part of a negotiated "deal" with Amin. The dictator had flatly refused permission for the Ugandan prelates—there were three or four attending—to leave their country unless his two fake reporters were accredited to come as well. I felt this was a scandal of some proportion and told the bishop I intended to report on it in my daily file that night. I assured him I would not reveal my source.

As luck would have it (bad luck), back at the University of Canterbury later that evening, I was dictating my story over a phone that was well away from the main concourse when the wrong person happened to intrude. Quite unexpectedly, the Archbishop of Canterbury's press secretary, who was responsible for organizing all media coverage, came down a nearby staircase and heard some of my report. He made some angry gestures at me and grew very red in the face as he indicated he wanted me to hang up at once. I waved him off, finished the last couple of sentences and turned to face his wrath. He was very upset with me indeed, charging that I had gone totally against some "contract" he had made with the press not to make any mention of a "Ugandan deal." He alleged that all the journalists covering the event had solemnly agreed to keep this matter out of their reporting for the sake of the safety of the Ugandan contingent and the required conditions of their being there at all. I replied that I had never been part of any such "contract" of silence and that I felt the safety of the bishops would be better protected by full disclosure of the intrigue. He refused to accept that and left in high dudgeon with a threat to report me to the Canadian Anglican primate, the Most Reverend "Ted" Scott.

I met Archbishop Scott during a coffee break the following morning. He confided he was "on a bit of a high" since he had just been offered, and had accepted, the prestigious post of Moderator of the World Council of Churches. He then told me he had been complained to by the press secretary but that, off the record, he thought I had done the right thing. Ted Scott remained a personal friend for many years, until his tragic death in a car accident on June 21, 2004. The Right Reverend Desmond Tutu, the former

Archbishop of South Africa, preached the sermon at his funeral in St. James' Cathedral.

The year 1978 was to become known as the Year of Three Popes because of a series of major events that began to unfold rapidly in Rome in the late summer and autumn of that year. I had been home barely a week after the Lambeth Conference in Canterbury and London when the *Star* switchboard managed to trace me to a poolside dinner party. It was a hot, lazy afternoon and to be honest the last thing on my mind was going anywhere on a story for the newspaper. However, the operator said that wire services were reporting that Pope Paul VI, who had been in poor health for several weeks, had died at his summer retreat of Castel Gandolfo, not far from Rome. According to the managing editor, the *Star*'s London bureau chief would head to Rome and cover the story until my arrival, but a hotel room near the Piazza di San Pietro in the heart of Rome had been booked for me, and airline tickets and money were waiting at the airport for a flight that night.

Rome was enduring one of the hottest summers in recent memory when I arrived there the following morning. The news of the day was that a crowd was expected to line the streets as the cortège carrying the dead Pope delivered him to the Vatican for some final rites and preparation of the body for his lying in state before the altar of St. Peter's Basilica. Paul, who was baptized Giovanni Battista Enrico Antonio Maria Montini, had been in office for fifteen years. He never smiled much and was perceived as a rather Hamlet-like figure by the media and also by many of his followers. He is no doubt best known for his 1968 encyclical *Humanae Vitae* ("Of Human Life"), which, in contravention of the proposals of the commission he himself had established to study the issue of the birth control pill, firmly banned its use by the faithful. It was to become a principal source of discontent and of the erosion of the moral authority of the papacy in our time. Rome's stand on abortion made some sense to the majority; the simultaneous stand against birth control and contraception did not. Paul VI was eighty when he died in the late afternoon of August 6.

One of the wonderful things about covering a story like this one was that once a daily report had been written up and then wired home from the Reuters office in the Via Propaganda Dei Fidei, close to the Spanish Steps, I then had the rest of the day to spend as I wished. It was one of the greatest pleasures of my life to be in such a romantic and historic city—my favourite over any other city on the planet—and to be able to wander at will through the narrow, twisting streets in search of the distant past. I was able to make several visits to the catacombs beneath the ancient sites, especially that of St. Sebastian along the old Appian Way, outside the crumbling walls of the earlier medieval town. Also there was the opportunity to do some research on the Mystery Religion that was so much older than Christianity and that was such a rival in the first two centuries of the Christian era, Mithraism.

The cult of the Persian-originated man-god Mithras had arrived in Rome in approximately 100 BCE and had so many similarities to Christianity that the early Fathers and apologists of the faith were forced into some very strange contortions in the attempt to discredit them or explain them away. Unlike some modern ultra-conservatives who try to deny the parallels altogether, the earliest defenders of the faith knew only too well that such an approach would be in vain since the Mithraists lived as neighbours and their places of worship and their rituals were only too well known.

Mithraism is in fact a primordial form of sun worship whose Roman version ultimately worshipped Sol Invictus, "the Unconquerable Sun." Mithras was believed to have "slain the bull of heaven"—perhaps a reference to the timing of his appearance with the close of the zodiacal age of Taurus. There are several hundred monuments or ruins connected with Mithraism in and under Rome, including more than one Mithraeum, or cultic shrine. These were built over a cave or hole in the rocks. In other words, the saving light was thought of as having been "born" in the womb of a cave. Mithras was believed to have had a virgin birth and twelve followers or disciples. He was viewed as a saviour figure who died and rose again from the dead; his birthday was December 25; he performed miracles of healing, laid down a high standard of personal morality and was called, among other things, the Light of the World. Mithraism had its sacred meal of bread, water and wine, and these elements were consecrated by priests who were called Fathers.

In the light of all of this, it is not surprising that the great African Church Father Tertullian (*c.*160–*c.*220 CE) was so disturbed by the similarities that he tried to explain them away by the highly unconvincing dodge of saying that the devil had inspired them to parody the Christian counterparts or "originals." In any case, I knew that Mithraism had had considerable appeal for soldiers in Rome's armies and that its monuments could still be found today in abundance all along Rome's ancient and far-flung frontiers. The time I spent in first-hand examination of some of these remains while awaiting the funeral of Paul VI played an important part in my research over a decade later for what became *The Pagan Christ*. The influence of Mithraism and the other Mystery Religions upon earliest Christianity cannot be denied.

Rome, which is always thronged with eager tourists in the summer months, was filling up even more with every passing day. Meanwhile, the blazing heat of August baked the streets and squares relentlessly. In St. Peter's, where the body of the pontiff was beginning to emit an increasingly distinct odour, making it plain that the limited embalming and the hidden ice beneath the flowers were no longer adequate to the task, large fans were installed and the crowds filing past were kept at a greater distance than earlier.

There were still three days to go before the funeral itself. The 116 cardinals who were eligible to vote in the upcoming conclave (after the death of a Pope a conclave to elect his successor must be held not fewer than fifteen days or more than twenty days following) were already flying in from around the world, and speculation about the likeliest candidate was the sole topic of lively journalistic debate over the wine and pasta in the trattorias flourishing in the streets surrounding the Vatican. Rumours of all kinds were flying, but the consensus was that the next Pope would be Italian as well, given the more than four hundred years of tradition—the last non-Italian to be elected Pope was Adrian, a Dutchman—and the fact that with a total of thirty-three candidates the Italians were by far the largest single bloc.

In his will Paul VI had made it plain that he wanted his funeral to be "pious and simple," with no elaborate catafalque—a raised platform to facilitate public viewing to the end—or other special frills. So the man in charge, Cardinal Villot, the Secretary of State, did his best. Nevertheless, the decision was made to have the funeral Mass outdoors in the Piazza di San Pietro itself. On the day, the TV cameras rolled and the Vatican choirs, the scarlet-robed cardinals and the hundreds of white-surpliced priests, against the magnificent backdrop of Bernini's great colonnades and the Basilica of St. Peter, accompanied by some of the most sublime music on earth, combined to make the day indelibly memorable. The following day I left for Toronto and a brief return to the *Star* before preparing to come back again for the papal election two weeks later.

By the time I arrived back in Rome, August was all but over and the city was recovering slowly from the "tourist shock" of midsummer. I was able to book into my favourite hotel, the De La Ville, on the Via Sistina close to the top of the Spanish Steps and not far from the Villa Borghese, with its classical artifacts including sculptures by Bernini and Michelangelo. The roughly half-hour walk from there down the steps to the Piazza d'Espagna, along the Corso to the Piazza del Popolo, across the Tiber and along its bank past Castel St. Angelo to the Vatican press office just off St. Peter's Square was one of the joys of being in the Eternal City.

The assembled cardinals met briefly on the evening of August 24 to prepare for the conclave, and the first session in the Sistine Chapel was held on the following morning. A Vatican press officer pointed out the quaint, somewhat frail-looking metal chimney now sticking out from the roof of the chapel and told the large crowd of reporters crushing around him in the piazza that after each ballot it would emit black smoke if there was no clear winner and white in the event of an election. The tension around St. Peter's was palpable as banks of TV cameras were mounted and uptight journalists stood around in buzzing knots on every side swapping rumours and floating theories about a liberal–conservative split among the cardinals. The first ballot was cast before noon the next day. The first wisps of smoke that emerged were a pale grey, causing some confusion. However, it soon changed to black and everybody relaxed. In the afternoon there was a similar flurry of excitement but with the same result.

On the Saturday morning, a very hot and sunny day, I met Ken Briggs, religion editor of the *New York Times* and a former Methodist minister, and we had coffee at a sidewalk table on the Via Conciliazione, just outside the Piazza di San Pietro. Our location afforded an unobstructed view of the roof of the Sistine Chapel. Our work had thrown us together a number of times in unusual places around the world, and there was a lot to discuss and learn from one another. Eventually there were some puffs of black smoke again; the third ballot was over. We agreed to meet at the same spot later that day.

It was a sleepy, simmering kind of afternoon, and we were again at the sidewalk café enjoying a cold drink while speculating that nothing would now likely happen until Monday when suddenly a plume of white smoke billowed up and everybody began running around and shouting at one another. A Pope had been elected on the fourth ballot! Almost miraculously the word spread and thousands of excited people began streaming through the colonnades and streets into the square. By the time the official announcement "*Habemus Papam*"—"We have a new Pope"—was made from the loggia above the entrance to St. Peter's, the piazza was filled to overflowing. The sense of anticipation as we awaited the name of the new pontiff was a unique experience for nearly everyone there. Then it came: Albino Luciani, the Patriarch and Cardinal of Venice—a man not on anyone's list of likely contenders—was the surprising choice. The crowd, chiefly Italians though heavily laced with representatives of virtually every country, roared its approval as the man who would shortly be known far and wide as Il Papa di Sorrismo, "the Smiling Pope," was introduced and waved his greeting to a sea of upturned faces.

I have seldom worked harder in my life than I did for the rest of that Saturday and well into the early hours of Sunday, reading up on Luciani, writing and rewriting the story of who he was and how surprised everyone was at his being chosen. He was the total opposite of Paul VI and in every way a breath of fresh air for Christians of all backgrounds everywhere. What made it doubly difficult was that my right arm had become sore and inflamed during the day, and it was soon clear as I typed away that an infection of some kind was making the elbow red and badly swollen. When he saw me the next day, Briggs thought it was clear I was running a fever and he persuaded me to go to a small clinic near the Colosseum run by some Irish Catholic nuns. I stayed there for two days receiving wonderful care, minor surgery and an eventual clean bill of health. The important thing was that the account of the election was filed in time and ran on the front page at home that Sunday.

With regard to Luciani, I was startled from the outset at how much this man resembled my own father, especially when the latter was showing his kindliest, most winsome side. Their backgrounds could not possibly have been more different, but I truly liked Papa Luciani from the start. Perhaps what was most appealing about the man was his complete lack of any pretence or side. He was open, unassuming and apparently bent upon a fully reformist approach to the papacy. Luciani had already scandalized some Church authorities by the way in which, while Patriarch of Venice, he had sold off certain Church assets in a determination to live more simply on the one hand and to do charitable works with the proceeds on the other. There were rumours he would do the same in Rome. He made it clear from the beginning that he intended to humanize the Church's leadership and to dispense with unnecessary frills. For example, shortly after his election it was announced that instead of the customary coronation ceremony and the wearing of the papal tiara, symbolic of worldly power and status, he had chosen a plain investiture without the crown. Luciani was only days in office when he gave a sermon in which he said it was right to speak of God as "Mother" as well as "Father." He also made it clear he intended to clean up the Vatican Bank scandal that was ongoing at the time.

People were genuinely moved by the gentle simplicity of the new Pope when it was learned that in his book *Illustrissimi* he had written a series of letters to famous people, including Charles Dickens, Mark Twain and even Pinocchio. In short, while he was soon said to have many critics and even enemies within the Vatican itself— one senior official was reported to have said contemptuously, "We've elected Peter Sellers to the Chair of Peter"—people were quickly growing to love him. Mother Teresa called him "the greatest gift of God, a sunray of God's love shining in the darkness of the world."

Because of the incident with my arm, the foreign editor sent a message to my hotel telling me to take myself out of the coverage in Rome and return to Toronto as soon as possible; the wire services were always available, and the major news was now over in any case. Things returned to normal as I resumed the religion page responsibilities and made several appearances on CBC and CTV television with commentary on the new leadership in the Roman Catholic Church. And then the wholly unexpected happened. At 1:30 on September 28, I was awakened out of a deep sleep by the telephone. I answered and heard a familiar voice saying, "It's the night editor at the *Star* . . . The Pope is dead!" Annoyed, I said, "That's not very funny," and was just about to hang up when he insisted I should hear him out. As everyone was soon to discover, Luciani had passed away—apparently while sitting up in bed reading—and the Catholic Church had once again been "orphaned," as one Italian paper described it. He had been in office only thirty-three days, one of the shortest pontificates in the Church's history.

My immediate task was to contact Cardinal Roy, the Archbishop of Quebec, who was the senior Canadian Roman Catholic prelate at that time, to get his reaction to the tragic news. My call to his residence got him out of bed, and I leave it to the reader to imagine how completely stunned and upset he was as he struggled to come to grips with what had happened. I made several other calls to some key contacts, both Catholic and non-Catholic, and then took a cab downtown to the *Star* newsroom. We watched TV and wire services from Rome for a while and then I sat down to write the story for the earliest edition. Meanwhile, arrangements were already under way for a flight to Rome that evening. The cycle was to begin again: funeral, a two-week break, another conclave, another papal election, and an enthronement or investiture. I was back and forth so many times that, taken with all that had gone on in the previous months, including the Lambeth Conference in England, the job of religion editor seemed more like that of chief foreign correspondent.

One of the problems with covering stories in Rome, I found, was that one arrived for work after a long, tiring overnight flight during which it was seldom possible to get comfortable enough to catch even an hour or two of sleep. When the story was hot, as tired as one might be, you then had to hit the ground running. First there was the long cab ride to the hotel, getting settled, then racing to the Vatican press office to find out the latest. Confusion seemed the order of the day on September 29. At the first briefing, reporters were told that Papa Luciani had possibly suffered a heart attack but it was too soon for a full verdict. At the same time, it was made clear that there would be no autopsy. There never was, although at one point a couple of days later the Spanish Conference of Bishops sent a message to the Vatican expressly urging that an autopsy be held. Apparently the late Pope had had a history of low blood pressure, but as skeptical journalists told the reporting press officer, that didn't usually result in a myocardial infarct. There was confusion also over who had first discovered that the pontiff had died, and when. In the first account we were told that a nun, Sister Vincenza, had found Luciani sitting up against a pillow with a book propped against his knees. Then, realizing that the notion of a nun having access to the papal sleeping quarters was open to considerable mis- understanding, the story changed. At a hastily called subsequent briefing, it was announced that a male papal secretary had made the find. Unfortunately, when the press asked to have either the sister or the secretary appear and be questioned, we were told that nei- ther person was available. It seems they both (separately) had had urgent reasons for leaving the city. In any case, no more was heard about either, with reference to the Pope's demise.

For these and a host of other reasons, all of which are fully dis- cussed in journalist David Yallop's book *In God's Name*, where he puts forward the view that Luciani was murdered, Rome was under- standably full of rumours. (Several books on this theme besides Yal- lop's have since been written.) On my first day there, coming down the Spanish Steps, a headline on a satirical journal pinned up at the news kiosk caught my eye. The cover had a full cartoon-style pic- ture of the small figure of Luciani propped up in bed reading while a cassocked man looks back over his shoulder at him. He is in the act of pouring a vial of what is obviously poison into a mug with the symbol of the papal keys on it. In case anyone should miss the point, the caption below asked bluntly: "Who killed the Pope?"

The newspapers in Rome were filled with speculative stories and commentaries. The Vatican kept making the situation worse by repeating answers that were either evasive or wholly contradictory. A further example of this was the simple matter of what it was that the Pope was reading when he met his demise. The first response seemed to say (piously) that it was *The Imitation of Christ* by Thomas à Kempis. That soon changed to a report on some scandalous state of affairs in a large, prestigious American diocese (unnamed). One account I heard being set forth as gospel truth by a well-known religion journalist said that Luciani had been reading an insider's analysis of the conduct of Archbishop Marcinkus, head of the Vatican's banking institution. (Marcinkus was soon to be under investigation by the Italian police and would have to remain under virtual house arrest inside the Vatican's walls to avoid going to jail.)

There was so much more, but with so very little light shining on any part of it, it still remains muddy and unclear and to many, myself included, all very sad. Oddly enough, it rained without let-up day after day all through the lying in state, the funeral and its aftermath. Rome gets rain in the autumn, but even the native Romans were saying that it seemed as though nature itself had been saddened by the passing of Il Sorrismo. I wrote a letter to him in the style of his own letters to the famous cited earlier, and the *Star* ran it front-page on the day of the funeral itself. I have to admit that, standing as I was on the steps of St. Peter's when Luciani was carried out on a bier for the service and seeing up close the bright red papal slippers, still so new and shiny, I felt quite moved. Because of the resemblance between them, I was reminded very powerfully of my father and of his sudden passing exactly ten years earlier.

The second conclave of 1978 opened on the morning of October 14 with a High Mass for the participating cardinals in St. Peter's Basilica. The buzz among the international press corps as it gathered once more was that there was again a liberal–conservative split in the college, with two strong leaders emerging. Both were Italian. There was Giuseppe Cardinal Sin, the Archbishop of Genoa, on the conservative side, and Giovanni Cardinal Benelli, the Archbishop of Florence, on the other. Later speculation in the Italian press had it that the conclave was very quickly deadlocked between the two opposing forces and that the Cardinal Archbishop of Krakow— who had received a few votes in the preceding election of John Paul I—was put forward as a compromise candidate on the second day. In any case, late on the afternoon of October 16, just as dusk was descending on the city, the white smoke could be seen twisting up in the glare of the searchlights now flooding the facade of St. Peter's and the Sistine Chapel roof. A thunderous roar went up from the crowd already swiftly gathering below when the announcement came ringing out once more into the piazza, "*Habemus Papam.*"

Knowing from experience that it would be some time, perhaps thirty minutes or more, before the official proclamation of the identity of the new pontiff was made, I made my way quickly through the growing crush of people to the press office just off the square. Inside, there was a bank of about a dozen phone booths. I immediately put through a call to the foreign desk at the *Star* and told them the election had just taken place on the eighth ballot. I asked them to have the *Star*'s highly skilled operators keep the line open until the new Pope was named and said I'd be back at once when that happened. I quickly drew up a note, as official-sounding as possible, indicating that the line had been reserved, said a brief internal prayer and tore back to the edge of the still-growing throng. It seemed I waited an eternity and I was sure that in the meantime somebody else would take the line. But in less time than in the case of John Paul I, Cardinal Villot appeared on the balcony and announced that Karol Josef Wojtyla, the Cardinal Archbishop of Krakow, had been chosen to fill the "shoes of the fisherman."

The crowd's first reaction was one of utter astonishment. There was a vast hubbub of murmuring as people asked one another, "Cardinal who?" Though I didn't see this reported in any of the accounts I read the next day, the largely Italian gathering was frankly stunned at first with sheer disbelief: the conclave was the first to elect a non-Italian in almost five hundred years! (The last non-Italian elected was Pope Adrian VI of the Netherlands in the 1520s.) I had with me a book of dossiers on all the eligible cardinals—part of an earlier Vatican press office handout—and quickly checked to read the brief description of Wojtyla. Then, rushing back, I found to my immense relief that the line in the press office was still free and that there was an editor waiting on the other end in Toronto. So, in a matter of moments, there was the thrill of being told that I had got the news to them before any of the other available services had reported it. Because of the time difference—six hours between Rome and Toronto—the brief story I dictated was just in time to make the front page of the final edition of the day. Considering just how significant a role the new Pope was to play on the international stage for the next twenty-six years (he died in April 2005, after one of the longest documented pontificates in Church history), it was a great privilege to be able to be there and to have had a tiny part in making his arrival on the scene known to the wider world beyond. All of this, of course, was before the current wizardry of the Internet and all the other instant news-gathering technology of the present day. Newspapers and radio were still the primary sources of breaking news for the world back then.

Cardinal Wojtyla chose the title John Paul II to signify his intention to walk a middle path between the adventurous liberal spirit of Pope John XXIII and the quieter, more conservative stance of Paul VI. Papa Luciani had had the same kind of dream a month or so earlier, hence his choosing of the title John Paul I, but fate had cut him short. John Paul II also followed Luciani's example in refusing

a coronation, and so was inaugurated, or invested, in a stately ceremony on October 22. Then things promised to grow quieter for a
while, but what nobody knew at the time was that this Pope was to
become not just the most travelled pontiff in history but one of
the most travelled world leaders of all time, eventually visiting 129
countries in all.

While the moment of his election is still fresh at hand, I want
to set out briefly my own take on Pope John Paul II, formed after
years of observing him up close on his earliest travels and then
many years as a religion columnist watching from afar. He clearly
was one of the most influential men ever to lead the Roman Catholic
Church. He was all the things the media said about him—or nearly
all. He was obviously charismatic, eloquent, courageous, and persistent in carrying out his vision for the Church. But to me it was
clear from the first long peroration he delivered at his first angelus
to the crowded Piazza di San Pietro that he loved too much the
limelight and the feel of his own personal power. Throughout his
papacy he gave speech after speech and sermon after sermon, but
he never ever listened to the cries for help coming from his clergy
or indeed from his own enormous flock. The media adored him
and gave him a wholly free ride as far as critical analysis went. Few
figures in the modern era have so completely escaped a truly objective, balanced reportage as he did. He was portrayed as a fully
modern man when he was in fact anything but. Underneath the
charismatic exterior was a wilfully stubborn, undemocratic tem-
perament ill suited for the huge task of giving guidance to a Church
heading into the third millennium of the Common Era. His successor, Benedict XVI, is just beginning to reap the fruits of his
planting, and there will be much more to come. (As a matter of fact,
Benedict is in many ways very much like Pope John Paul II in mind-
set—but without the charisma.)

People forget that the New Testament emphasis upon loving
your enemies is there not because it sounds pious but because there

is a terrible spiritual truth behind it. Those who have enemies and are unable to love them (not "like" them, but as far as possible wish them nothing but good) are fated to become like them. Wojtyla knew life under the hated Nazis and then under the Communists in his native Poland. Unfortunately, in dealing bravely with them, he also became very much like them. At heart he was to prove every bit as autocratic as they—only in a much kinder environment. That is why, for example, though on the surface he gave every appearance of being willing to make overtures of peace to the Orthodox churches, the Anglican Church, the Jews and other non Catholic religious groups, nothing really solid resulted from any of it. The words were there, but the action was not. As a matter of fact, at times even the important words were wanting. The Buddhist leader and leading spiritual figure Thich Nhat Hanh, in his bestselling book *Living Buddha, Living Christ,* rightly points out the latent intolerance in the late Pope's thinking. Commenting upon Wojtyla's manifesto, *Crossing the Threshold of Hope,* he chides him for maintaining that Jesus Christ is "the one mediator between God and humanity," that he is "unique." The Buddhist monk writes: "The idea behind the statement . . . is the notion that Christianity provides the only way of salvation and all other religious traditions are of no use. This attitude excludes dialogue and fosters religious intolerance and discrimination. It does not help."

Wojtyla did, of course, assist in the dismantling and fall of Communism in Poland and then the rest of Europe. But he was very far from accomplishing this by himself, as most uncritical and overly enthusiastic commentators would have us believe. It was instead rather like the case of a large decaying tree that eventually takes little more than a firm, strong push to make it come crashing down. The signs of Communism's decay and imminent collapse were in evidence on all sides before the Solidarity movement began. Of course, the question of whether or not I personally liked Pope John Paul II is not of great consequence. But for the record, I did not.

There was much about him to admire, but the total package, spiritually speaking, was a matter for regret.

Early in December 1978, with Toronto well into the winter doldrums, the streets already dismally wet and the first real storm of the season predicted to arrive that evening, I walked my customary three miles to the office. There was a note from the city editor stuck on the edge of my computer screen. It said that she and the managing editor wanted me to come up with some suggestions for another Christmas special. In the wake of recent gloom-and-doom events filling the pages of the paper, she added: "P.S. Something on the hopeful side would be a great help!" It was in essence an offer no journalist with a yen for adventure and an inquiring mind could ever refuse. As long as there was a story to be told, it was a ground rule that expense was not an issue; I could travel wherever necessary to track it down.

With the phone and other interruptions I couldn't think straight, so I put my parka back on and walked down by the harbour for an hour or so. Then I went in, did some fact checking and typed up a memo for my editors with an outline for a Christmas series of four feature stories. It would be called *Signs of Hope, Christmas 1978*. For the first story I proposed going to visit Jean Vanier at L'Arche ("The Ark") in the French village of Trosly-Breuil, in the Forêt de Compiègne, close to the River Oise and the site of the historic railway carriage in which the armistice papers ending World War I were signed. From there I proposed going to a remarkable orphanage and school for needy children on the Bay of Naples, Casa Materna. It first came to prominence as a response to the large number of destitute children running in the streets of that teeming city at the end of World War II. Next I would take the readers to Krakow, Poland, the city where the newly elected Pope, John Paul II, had spent his youth and where he became the cardinal archbishop. Finally we would journey to one of the farthest boundaries of

Europe, the holy island of Iona in the Inner Hebrides, where new life had been breathed into a site that once was so crucial in the spread of Christianity in Ireland and beyond to Britain and even as far away as Russia.

I had never been to any of these places before, and so the sense of discovery would be the same for writer and reader alike. The response of management was a very enthusiastic "Go!" So, about a week and a half later, I set out once more, feeling like the most fortunate man alive. Looking back, I realize just how fortuitous it was that my days as a full-time working journalist at the *Star* came just when newspapers were still at the height of their powers, so to speak, and the current cost-cutting, survivalist mode had yet to arrive. It gave me on-the-ground insights into the contemporary religion scene that few writers could ever afford to have.

There are today more than 130 L'Arche communities for people with developmental disabilities all around the world. But in 1964, when Jean Vanier began his work, he little thought about numbers or the world fame he would one day garner. The son of the former Governor General of Canada, Georges Vanier, Jean had a brilliant career ahead of him as a professor at St. Michael's College, University of Toronto, having earned his doctorate at the Institut Catholique in Paris. Returning to France, however, he found himself deeply moved by and concerned about the plight of intellectually challenged persons, who were for the most part shut away in institutions. He accordingly welcomed two men from such an institution to come and live with him in the tiny village cited above. His unique "ministry" is now so widely recognized and well known that there is little need to enlarge upon it here. The message he has distilled, however, and the theme he has so eloquently articulated in his many books, TV interviews and lectures has always resonated powerfully in my own life and thinking. Vanier has found that these often despised and neglected men and women have a message for every one of us. In living with them, he found he was being taught much more than he had tried to give to them. While most of us spend much time and energy trying to pretend that we are strong, successful and free from any kind of weakness, the disabled cannot hide behind any pretence. Their weakness is out there for all the world to see, and so they often have an unusual honesty, an ability to see through posturing and sham of any kind. When we see their courage and their ability to persevere in spite of often dreadful incapacities, they bring a challenge and a spark of hope to us in our lesser struggles. The spiritual impact can be profound. That's why young people on every continent have responded so enthusiastically to Vanier's message through the years. It is why so many international honours have been and continue to be showered upon him. It's why he is such a sign of hope himself. I considered it a great privilege to be able to spend time with him at L'Arche, to observe him interacting with the larger community there and to sit in on a couple of "sharing" sessions with the men. Those who can handle tools have a variety of productive tasks to accomplish. There is a lot of laughter and a quiet joy running through it all.

Casa Materna ("a mother's house"), situated in Portici, a small suburb of Naples on the Corso Giuseppe Garibaldi, had come to my attention through some neighbours in Toronto who were longtime, enthusiastic supporters of its cause. The large, rambling villa and school, with the Mediterranean lapping on the shore and the Isle of Capri off in the dazzling distance of the bay, was first founded in 1905 by an Italian Methodist minister, Rev. Riccardo Santi. He had a vision of providing home and a "mother" for homeless street urchins whose parents were either missing or so poverty-stricken they were unable to care properly for their youngsters. Santi at first used his own home as a centre, but eventually, with generous help from the U.S. navy stationed in Naples and a growing network of charitable donors in the U.S. and Canada, the Portici property was purchased, and classrooms, workshops and a large, productive garden were added to the original building.

When I visited Casa Materna, I found once again the indelible signs on every side of what even one person's apparently impossible dream can accomplish when the central message of every world religion—active, practical, oftentimes heroic compassion—is lived out in the crucible of human suffering. In the children's faces, hope and its companion, unquenchable joy, beamed forth whether they were in the classroom or at play. Thinking of the hardships both adults and students alike had faced there through the years—the two world wars with their resulting desolation, the lean times when the leadership of the country necessarily changed, the prejudices of an overwhelmingly Catholic majority of Neapolitans against this rare Protestant enclave—made one realize again that next to compassion, endurance is an essential element of any attempt at fulfilling the will of God.

The Kingdom of God, or however one expresses that spiritual reality in her or his own tradition, comes about not by words but by courageous, patient doing. Today some of the children who were themselves nurtured and educated as a result of Santi's dream have taken over a new program for the needy children of Naples. Called Imparare Giocando, "learning through playing," it is part of a larger successor to Casa Materna, now known as the Italian Children's Mission. Significantly, the U.S. navy remains involved and deeply committed in its support.

Flying from sunny southern Italy to Krakow in December was a metaphor for leaving a democratic country for one still very much under the heel of Communism. There was, in spite of the enormous sense of pride and vindication felt by ordinary people in the street over the election of their fellow countryman as Pope, a pall of what one can only call glumness as palpable as the fog at the airport on our arrival. It reminded me of the atmosphere in Cuba when I had first visited there, a year or so earlier.

The churches were packed on Sundays and at other times—a far cry from the situation today, not only in Poland but increasingly throughout Europe—and there seemed to be considerable quality of life in the devotion of parents to their families, the way people seemed to enjoy walking together in the public gardens, or the clusters of elderly men watching chess matches near the historic city walls. But overall, the mood was heavy. The Solidarity movement among the workers was still almost two years away. Freedom of speech was severely restricted. There were plenty of fresh vegetables in the large open-stalled marketplace in the city centre, but if the fare at the hotel was anything to judge by, the joy had gone out of cooking some time ago.

I had to remember why I was there. It was important to get and to communicate a feel for the background of the new leader of the world's largest Christian denomination, and to inform the readers of the newspaper that as all the great spiritual wisdoms of the world have taught, heaviness endures for a season, but "joy cometh in the morning." In all the great mythologies it is at the moment of greatest darkness that the first light breaks through. As history went on to prove, Wojtyla's confrontation with the Communist darkness through his support for Solidarity played an important part in the eventual dawning of a new day of liberation. In Krakow too I found the seeds of hope.

One of the places I had always dreamed of travelling to was Iona, a tiny, windswept island three miles long by about a mile wide, set in the Inner Hebrides off the west coast of Scotland. As Dr. Samuel Johnson said, "A man is little to be envied whose piety would not grow warmer among the ruins of Iona." My feelings for that ancient, mystical centre of Celtic Christianity began very early in my life. My father's heart was never far from the British Isles, and he loved to read to us about St. Patrick and the other missionary saints of old, particularly the Irishman St. Columba. He had filled my head with stories of their exploits and adventures. Columba was the Christian son of an Irish nobleman, and through his founding of a monastery on Iona in 563 he helped keep the flame of faith alive when it was flickering and in danger of going out in England, Ireland, Scotland and parts of northern Europe. One of my best memories of being with my father was just after my graduation from Oxford. He and my mother, together with my younger sister, had flown over for the ceremony. Afterwards, during a visit with relatives in Ulster, we took the opportunity and drove to Glencolmcille in Donegal on the rugged northwest coast. The Gaelic name means "the glen of Columba" and it is one of the wildest spots on earth, with the North Atlantic breakers crashing relentlessly upon the rocky shore. Seeing it, I was held spellbound because it was from this dangerous cove in 563 that St. Columba (a saint in both the Church of Ireland and that of Scotland) had set out with twelve companions to travel to the already sacred island of Iona. Knowing something myself of travelling in rough waters by canoe, it was nevertheless hard to conjure up the huge challenge of shipping out into such waters in a frail craft, a coracle, a round boat made of skins tightly stretched over a frame of willow poles.

I was reminded of that day and of so much more when, following the few days in Poland, a hired photographer and I drove from Glasgow up through the Scottish Highlands to Oban, from there by car ferry to the island of Mull, and then in a very much smaller, open boat across the turbulent seas to Iona itself. The weather was gloomy and cold and the crossing was very rough indeed. As the locals (the tiny village has about ninety people in and around it, mostly fishermen and shepherds) are fond of saying: "The weather can be pretty bad, but it's often in places like this that people can come face to face with themselves."

This was my chance to witness and reflect upon the Celtic Christianity that St. Columba and his monks brought to Iona. It was so different in many ways from that officially being promulgated then by Rome. What's more, it radiated outwards far and wide and today brings over 200,000 pilgrims annually from around the world into its embrace. Celtic Christianity, instead of stressing human sinfulness and a need for personal salvation, boldly affirms the glory of the natural world, the connectedness of everything and everyone to God, and the centrality of justice and peace in human relations. That's why, in 1938, a maverick Scottish clergyman, later to become a peer as Lord George MacLeod of Fuinary, came to Iona with a handful of students, some unemployed workers from the Glasgow shipyards and a couple of other ministers and began work on restoring the ancient abbey and rebuilding part of the ruins of the monastery. He went on to found the Iona Community, which today has members scattered across the globe.

MacLeod, who was awarded the Military Cross and the French Croix de Guerre for his heroism both at Ypres and at Passchendaele in World War I, had worked in the slums of Glasgow and had served at one point as Moderator of the Church of Scotland. But he had become increasingly disenchanted with formal "Churchianity" and had become a champion of "a connected Christianity"—a Celtic-type spirituality that stressed that work and worship, humans and their environment, matter and spirit must always be understood as deeply interwoven in one fabric of life. MacLeod was also aware that in Columba's spreading communities long ago women had an equal voice; an abbess could tell a bishop what to do, and priests could marry. I remember avidly reading MacLeod's books over the years and realize now that I finally was able to express his kind of "incarnational theology" in my own writing, especially *The Pagan Christ* and *Water into Wine*. One phrase of his in particular has always stayed with me. He said that Christianity is not so much about "Glory to God in the highest" but about "glory to God in the High St." There is only the letter *e* missing, but a world of difference all the same.

We were only on Iona for three days, but I left there with a full heart and a lighter step. I could see why MacLeod had once described it as "a thin place." By that he meant that the "other side," the spiritual dimension of life, seems so much closer there. Any mental "tissue of separation" is so thin it virtually disappears. In other words, there is an end to erroneous dualistic thinking and all of life is one again. I needed to be reminded of that. We all do. It is a message of hope.

8

THE FORK
IN THE TRAIL

THE YEAR 1979 marked my fiftieth birthday, and a time when two critical personal matters came to a head and had to be resolved. The first had to do with my role as an ordained priest of the Anglican Church yet deeply involved in what was obviously a very secular profession as a working journalist.

For the first few years after joining the *Star* I had assisted at several parishes and then took a more or less regular posting as honorary assistant at the historic Little Trinity Church in the heart of downtown. The rector, Rev. Harry Robinson, had invited me to alternate with him in delivering either the morning or the evening Sunday sermon. The church used to be packed for both services as Robinson, a very popular minister, was a leading evangelical preacher. Also a graduate of Wycliffe College, he had preceded me as the Senior Student there in 1955. Readers of my book *Water into Wine* will know that we didn't always agree. In truth, my own steadily increasing discomfort on intellectual grounds with evangelical thinking had been quickly making the arrangement less and less satisfactory. By "evangelical," of course, I'm referring to that theological position which relies almost wholly on sacred scripture for its source of authority (in the Protestant Reformation the rallying cry was *sola scriptura*—only the Bible) and calls upon the individual to "accept Christ as his or her personal saviour." I eventually resigned from Little Trinity in 1976. Robinson and I parted on the most cordial of terms, but our paths separated from that point on and once he had left Little Trinity we never really saw one another again.

Meanwhile, I had continued what I had begun when I first went to the *Star* in 1971, that is, my role as unofficial chaplain to anyone in the media who felt a need for one. Although many reporters are not ardent churchgoers, there were nonetheless babies to be baptized, couples to be married and funerals to be performed. While it made things hectic at times, it was an important ministry and one that I had enjoyed. However, since I no longer had an institutional base and since Anglican canons or rules of discipline require that every functioning priest be officially licensed by the bishop to a specific church, chaplaincy or other post, I began to hear some distant rumblings from diocesan headquarters on Adelaide Street. I soon realized there was a good chance of my being summoned to the bishop's office, required to sign afresh my oath of obedience to him "in all godly admonitions" and asked to name some parish or post to which I could be assigned in an assistant capacity, however limited. Some called it a matter of discipline; others thought of it as a control mechanism.

By a synchronicity, at the very time I was feeling pressure to conform, an acrimonious controversy erupted at a prominent east end Anglican church. In the larger scale of things, like many church conflicts, it wasn't about very much—something about parishioners demanding their rector be fired because of his refusal to conduct the baptism of the children of certain "influential" members. A couple of brief stories appeared in Toronto media and as the fracas seemed to be escalating I decided to do a full feature on it. Naturally, I wanted to give Bishop Lewis S. Garnsworthy a full opportunity to air his official take on the matter. So, as I was in the habit of doing, I called his secretary and requested an interview. A short while afterwards Garnsworthy came on the line and exploded in my ear. "Tom," he thundered, "you're not helping me on this." When he calmed down a little, I pointed out that it wasn't my job to help him if by that he meant my not undertaking a perfectly valid investigation of a series of events of interest not just to Anglicans but to the wider community as well. I reminded him of his words to me at lunch in the Royal York Hotel early in 1971 when I first told him I had decided to become a religion journalist. Garnsworthy had given me his full approval and had said explicitly, "Tom, I want you to be the best reporter you can be." That reminder cooled his anger somewhat, but there could be no doubt on my part. I went ahead with the story, but the ambiguous nature of my situation had been made very evident. The more I reflected on it, the clearer it all became.

For some time in any case I had felt uncomfortable with the role of "professional holy man." I seldom if ever wore the Roman collar, the long black cassock or the white linen surplice of an Anglican priest, even when on official duties. Whenever I thought of the latter there rang in my ears the words of a young urchin of the streets who was hanging around the door outside Little Trinity one Sunday morning after the service. Robinson and I in full regalia were standing on the pavement by the door waiting to shake hands with the congregation as they filed out. The little girl with a soiled face tugged at my surplice and blurted out, "Whatcha got that there dress on for, mister?" I wondered what she would have said if she had ever attended a High Mass at the Vatican!

I knew there was a further tightening of the canons governing priestly conduct and teaching in process at Church headquarters on Adelaide Street, and that opposition to this had been turned down at a recent diocesan synod session. But beyond that, I was now deeply aware that I had a real conflict of interest, which I had never been made to feel before—between an oath of obedience to a bishop of one denomination and my desire to bring objective, unhindered coverage of every religion to the Canadian public and the rest of the world. In addition, while I remained totally committed to what I understood and knew about the reality of God, I had serious problems with much of the rest of Anglican orthodoxy.

Reflecting on this, I discussed it with a friend and reached my decision. I decided it was time for me to leave the priesthood chosen for me by my parents long ago. I invited Bishop Garnsworthy to lunch at the Royal York and told him of my intent. He took it all much better than I had thought he would. Perhaps he was secretly rather relieved. He even ordered a second Scotch as he gave his consent and wished me well. We continued on the very best of terms throughout his term as bishop and mine as religion editor for the *Toronto Star*.

When a notice of my decision to "leave the active use of holy orders," as it was described in official Church language, appeared in the monthly Anglican publication *The Journal*, two or three Toronto clergy called to chat about it. (Anglican doctrine, as in the Roman Catholic and Eastern Orthodox traditions, holds that "once a priest, forever a priest." The reasoning behind this is that ordination by a bishop in the Apostolic Succession confers upon the recipient an indelible character, *character indebilis*, which remains. Thus my action was described as giving up the use of holy orders, not the reality itself.) Their major concern was that I would feel a great sense of loss, particularly since I would no longer be officiating at the Eucharist, or Holy Communion. I assured them that I truly felt a new sense of freedom. I told them this was especially important to me because I hoped soon to write a book, together with a regular opinion column in which I would most likely be compelled by new insights and convictions to take positions that would at times conflict directly with official Anglican dogma and practice. As I was convinced that the Eucharist (for Roman Catholics, the Mass) was one of the most poorly worded and misunderstood parts of the ritual or liturgy, I shocked them a little by saying I didn't think I would miss celebrating it very much at all. The honest truth is, I never have. Over the years that followed, my understanding of "the ministry," like so many other things, broadened and deepened enormously as I came to see that through my writing and work in mass media it was possible to reach and in effect minister to a far larger parish than would ever have been reachable had I remained in a much more traditional role.

All columnists have critics and enemies. Some of these tried to circulate a rumour that I had been "unfrocked" by Garnsworthy. Nothing could have been more untrue.

Significantly, the one person I hadn't discussed this whole matter with was my then wife. When I finally told her, she became quite upset. We had sadly by this point reached that stage in the marriage where almost anything of major importance became a battleground.

Nobody was really surprised when the news came from Rome in the late spring of 1979 that Most Reverend G. Emmett Carter, the Roman Catholic Archbishop of Toronto, had been named a cardinal by the new Pope. The *Star* immediately hired a small plane to take a photographer to London, Ontario, the new cardinal's old stompin' ground, where it had been learned he would be playing tennis all that day with a staff member of St. Peter's Seminary. I wrote a story and it appeared with a large photo of His Eminence in full tennis garb in action on the court. I learned later that there had been a last-minute panic at the photo desk when the editor noticed that the fly on Carter's shorts was definitely not zipped up. Judicious touch-ups were required.

A few days following the announcement of his promotion, the Chancery Office sent out a press release outlining the date in June set for the induction in Rome of several new cardinals into the Church's highest office next to that of the papacy itself. The release also stated that a commercial jet was being chartered to take the archbishop, some aides, a couple of score of Canadian Catholic dignitaries, plus a full press corps from Toronto to Rome for the ceremony. The managing editor came to my office to give me the word that I would be going and that proper accreditation was being sent by courier that afternoon. Ron Bull, a *Star* photographer and a friend of long standing with whom I had often worked on previous stories at home and abroad, was to be part of our team as well.

The trip to Rome in June 1979 produced little hard news, but I did get to know Cardinal Carter a lot better, particularly during a lengthy interview on the plane going over. We were just over an hour out from the ETA at Rome's Leonardo da Vinci–Fiumicino Airport when the Chancery Office press secretary, Father Brad Massman, came back to where I was sitting and whispered in my ear that the cardinal-elect was inviting me to come forward and join him in the front row. Carter greeted me warmly and said he thought my readers might be interested in an interview on the eve of his being elevated as a prince of the Church. I was, of course, only too happy to seize the opportunity. It was obvious that in Rome, once he was caught up in the preparations and in the event itself, there would be little if any chance for a truly one-on-one conversation.

Before going any further, I should note for anyone not already aware that the College of Cardinals is unique in many ways but most notably in the function it has of electing his successor upon the death of a Pope. The word *cardinal* itself comes from the Latin word *cardo*, "a hinge." The members of the College of Cardinals are the critical hinge upon which the institution itself depends when the crisis of a vacancy in the succession occurs.

When I joined him, Carter was in a very expansive mood and went on at considerable length about his new role and about how he would have much greater influence than ever before on the Canadian scene. He made it clear he now saw himself as about to become one of the prominent movers and shakers of Canadian society. The message was that he was going to be given genuine power and that he fully intended to wield it for the benefit of his Church as well as for the wider common good. I had always liked Carter in the past, even though he often seemed more like a chairman of some large corporation than a leading spiritual figure. But in this interview the impression was of a very large ego about to become much larger, with a dash of potentially manipulative scheming thrown in.

As the outskirts of the city of Rome itself appeared beneath us and word came to prepare for landing, I fired off a quick question about the issue of religion in the schools. Now that Ontario premier Bill Davis had given full financial support to the separate schools in Ontario, did Carter not feel it was only just for the Catholic bishops to go to bat with the Ontario government to seek extension of funding to all religious schools—Jewish, Anglican and the rest? He said he agreed with that position and that he and the bishops would do that sometime in the near future. Of course, that never happened, and when the Progressive Conservative leader of the day, John Tory, made it a central plank of his platform in the Ontario election of 2007, he and his party were soundly defeated at the polls.

I thanked Archbishop Carter warmly and went back to my seat for landing.

The weather was glorious, with Rome at its very best. The pomp and ceremony was colourful and stirring—even moving at times. There is a reason that Italy has produced such great operas and opera stars: Italians have a natural gift for drama and music, and the Vatican, with its history, its setting and its resources, knows how to put on a show. Very few assignments were as wholly enjoyable and as soft to cover as that one turned out to be, and I was glad to have had the privilege. Spiritually speaking, however, I had to wonder seriously what all the pomp and show seen up close had to do with the Gospels or a true religion of the heart.

I heard indirectly in due time that the cardinal was pleased overall with my reporting on his receiving the cardinal's hat. However,

our relationship took a sharp downturn over my critique of John
Paul II later in the same year and culminated in a showdown of
sorts a few months afterwards. I received a note from press secretary Massman saying the cardinal wanted me to call his office and
offer a date on which we could meet for a chat. It sounded a little
ominous, but I was naturally keen to keep the door to communication open and so went along with the idea. When the day arrived, I
was shown into his large outer office (where he conducted most of
his business affairs) and told to wait. Carter soon afterwards opened
the door to his inner sanctum, a smaller, more private yet elegant
setting reserved for confidential consultations, discussions and
decision making. I recall seeing a marble bust of Pope John Paul II
on top of the bookcase as I entered. It was inscribed as a gift from
Premier Bill Davis.

The cardinal seemed sterner than I remembered ever seeing
him before, and he grew sterner still as the encounter went on. He
told me he thought I had been slanting my writing against Roman
Catholicism in general and the Vatican in particular in recent
months. He said this was most noticeable whenever I added a personal column to the religion page but that he felt its presence elsewhere as well. There was more, but that was the gist of the matter.

Apart from the minor tension once with Anglican Archbishop
Garnsworthy, I had never been fully leaned on by any religious
leader before, but as our session developed it was abundantly clear
that he was applying pressure on me to back off. I kept from showing my rising sense of indignation, but I admit it was a struggle. I
said it would be helpful if he could be a little more specific and cite
columns, news stories or features with my byline where the alleged
"slanting" had occurred. He replied that he didn't want to—or
couldn't—come up with exact examples at that time. I told him
he could get a secretary to look them up and send me copies, but
he didn't seem to think much of that idea either. I then took some

pains to make certain he understood the difference between an opinion column and stories reporting news.

Not surprisingly, perhaps, he got fairly hot under the collar at about that point and for a moment I thought he was going to end our conversation. In any case I made it plain that I was going to continue writing about all faiths with as much objectivity as possible and that I definitely had no animus against him, his archdiocese, his leader or his Church. (I might have added that I had paid to send two of my daughters to a separate school.) However, at the same time, I told him that Pope John Paul II in my view had been receiving a free ride from the media from the day of his election. I said it was my intention to ensure that the *Star* reported on all aspects of the papal persona and message regardless of what he or other members of the hierarchy thought or felt. We finally shook hands, but I knew that any friendship that had existed, however fragile, was now a matter of history.

The entire encounter with the cardinal left an unpleasant taste in its wake. It reminded me forcefully of something I was learning as a journalist—that, generally speaking, Church leaders and leaders of other faiths viewed the media with a mixture of guile and ignorance. Basically, they saw the media as there to be manipulated or used for their own ends. They had little knowledge of how the media really worked or of how best to approach them. Certainly their theology had no place for mass media, and it still lacks any depth of understanding, in my view. I remain of the opinion that my own denominational matrix, the Anglican Church in particular, is woefully backward where mass media are concerned. I felt so strongly about this when I finally resigned from my position as religion editor in 1984 that I shortly afterwards accepted a part-time lecturing post at the Toronto School of Theology. The course I taught for three or four years was called the Theology and Praxis of Mass Media.

The summer of 1979 was fairly quiet for a while. I was asked to be a speaker/panel member at the annual think tank at Lake Couchiching called the Geneva Conference. It dealt with the theme of religion and global social justice issues. The only memory remaining of it is that theologian Gregory Baum was also part of the proceedings and that I got into a heated argument at one point with a woman delegate who was upset by a recent column I had written somewhat critical of Ivan Illich. I was in a rather sour mood anyway, because my rocky marriage had grown even more so over the past year.

After Couchiching we went to Manitoulin Island on what was scheduled as a two-week camping trip. In brief, the holiday was an unfortunate domestic disaster. Both of us were in the wrong, as so often happens, but in spite of an attempt at marriage counselling, we realized that we were in an impossible relationship. Fortunately, the children were by then of an age and maturity to handle the breakup in as healthy a manner as possible. At the time, I saw the ending of twenty-three years of marriage as a sad though inescapable failure. In the eyes of my parents and those of the circles they moved in when I was growing up, divorce was looked upon with a kind of holy horror. I felt it could never happen to me. However, in retrospect and in truth, it heralded the beginning of a most creative and fulfilling second half of my life.

Before the end of the camping holiday, I called the *Star* one day from Little Current, the main town on the island, to check in and was relieved to receive a message from the managing editor about an upcoming assignment. On my return to Toronto, I was to be sent to Ireland and then the United States to cover Pope John Paul II's second trip abroad. The message said that the plan was to send me over to Northern Ireland a week or so ahead of the Pope's arrival in Dublin to do a special feature on the effects of the sectarian violence upon the children of Belfast. It was slated for the *Star*'s prestigious Insight section. I left for Belfast on the evening of September 15.

Belfast was vastly changed from when I had been there as a child of nine and then several times as a student at Oxford. Since at that time my grandparents were still living and nearly all my relatives were there, I was able to receive a greatly reduced fare that the airlines offered for students "going home" for school vacations. I usually visited family briefly in Belfast and then went down as soon as possible to Tullyhogue, the tiny, historic village where my father was born. His brother, my uncle Bob, was my favourite among all the kinfolk. He loved fishing, hunting and other outdoor pursuits as much as I did. We had many wonderful hours fishing for sea trout or salmon up on the moors. It mattered little to either of us whether we were soaked to the skin by the seemingly ever-present rain or not. I vividly recall on one such occasion how we sought temporary shelter in an isolated cottage up on the moor near Loch Fee in a sudden thunderstorm. It was a simple whitewashed stone farmhouse up above the small loch, or lake. The farmer's wife took instant pity on our bedraggled state and welcomed us in. Soon our coats and other apparel were steaming in front of a glowing peat fire in an open fireplace. The scent of the peat reminded me of the times when I was on the trail through the bush with Rev. Leslie Garrett and our guide, Henry Cutfeet, at Big Trout Lake many years before. Our impromptu hostess soon had two mugs of hot tea and some absolutely delicious buttered scones set before us. It was better than a feast.

In 1979, Belfast had British soldiers in full body armour and carrying assorted weaponry on every downtown street. It was a formidable experience walking past them because they were usually in groups of four, two with their automatic weapons aiming ahead and to the side while two comrades walked backwards behind them guarding against snipers from rooftops or windows. Armoured cars patrolled the major streets and the various districts known for their IRA presence. The Europa Hotel, in the city's core, had been bombed a number of times. That's where the *Star* staffer handling my travel arrangements had decided to put me. "All the journalists stay there," she said. The place looked badly beaten up and there were various barriers outside to prevent cars with explosives from ramming the entrances. Getting in and out through the security was a regular hassle. But the rest of the city bore the signs of the ongoing unrest and violence on all sides as well. I spent several days visiting schools, talking to parents, educators and doctors, and meeting with representative clergy. The Reverend Ian Paisley refused to talk to me. He was still furious over a column I had done once in which I had said bluntly that Toronto needed a congregation of his Free Presbyterian Church like the proverbial hole in the head. I lost no sleep over his unwillingness to talk.

The city was so bitterly divided that even getting a taxi involved knowing whether you wanted to go to a Roman Catholic area of dominance or a Protestant one. I remember going into what I was told was a storefront where I could order a cab. When you went in, you were immediately faced by a wall that cut the room in half. High up on it was a grille. A voice carried on a PA system said: "Where do you want to go?" There was no sign of anyone anywhere. I gave my destination in a loud reply and was then asked to give the purpose of my trip and the party I would be seeing there. Only when that was cleared out of the way was I told to go outside and wait for my ride.

When I finally left Belfast and headed down to the country for a very brief visit with the Harpurs in Tullyhogue, I felt so thankful that my parents had made the decision long ago to leave all the religious bitterness and fighting behind them and make a new life in Canada.

Fred Ross, a colleague and photographer from the *Star*, then met me in Dublin, and I was about to have some of my most hectic days as a journalist. The Pope's schedule called for a week in southern Ireland and then his first visit to the U.S.A. It was a non-stop ride from first to last. It began with a rally one million strong in

Dublin's Phoenix Park. An utterly incredible roar met his opening words. He raised his hand for silence and in the great hush that followed he shouted: "Ireland, *semper fidelis*!" And the crowd roared its approval once more. His words "Always faithful" have a sad irony about them today. Little did anyone know then the sorry fall from grace that lay ahead for the Irish hierarchy in general and certain of its bishops in particular. Ongoing revelations of abuse of hundreds of children by priests and lay brothers, including a massive cover-up by those in the highest positions of authority, have shocked and shaken the Irish laity to the core. Also a rampant secularism has eroded what was once a monolithic Irish commitment to institutional religion, Protestant and Catholic alike. Faithful Ireland is no more.*

The five or six days the Pope spent in Ireland in 1979 were a mad whirl for him and an even more hectic one for the international press corps trying to keep up. As happened in Mexico and was to be the hallmark of all the many tours of his pontificate, the trip was a non-stop succession of speeches, masses and visits to sacred sites. He had the advantage of a helicopter when needed to avoid the endless traffic jams caused by the vast throngs of people and the extreme narrowness of most of the rural roads off the main motorways. For example, after the youth mass celebrated in the open at Galway Bay, the buses carrying the journalists were stuck in car-choked country lanes for hours afterwards.

I realized more harshly than ever before that, as I had experienced with missionary work up north, a lot of journalism consists of "hurry up, then wait and wait." But eventually the stories got filed. Then it was time to catch a few hours' sleep before getting up

---

* It is relevant to note that on February 10, 2010, Pope Benedict was forced to hold special sessions with the Irish bishops to discuss the huge sex abuse scandal there. At the moment of writing, the Vatican and even the Pope himself are being dogged by emerging stories of cover-up in the highest echelons of the Church.

and tearing off in the papal wake again. When the Irish trip finished, the *Star*'s photographer and I were chosen in the draw for a seat on the Air Italia 747 that was to carry the Pope across the Atlantic to Boston for the American lap. Overall that was a big disappointment. We had been told he would be coming down from first class to meet with us during the flight. I was certain that, after so many addresses, so much talk in Ireland, he would do what any other world figure would do and at some point hold a press conference. Mid-Atlantic seemed as good a time and place as any. I felt we would have an opportunity at least for a few questions.

It was not to be. When it was announced over the plane's PA system that he was on his way to our encounter, there was a frantic rush of cameramen and reporters towards the front of the aircraft. There was a lot of shoving and pushing to be in the front ranks. I somehow managed to be struck on the back of the head by the tripod of an over-eager Italian TV correspondent in the process. Suddenly the Pope's white-robed figure appeared. He took one shocked look at the horde let loose upon him, turned abruptly around and fled the scene.

A few moments later, his voice came over the PA speakers: "This is the Pope speaking. My blessings be upon you and your families. If you have any object with you you'd like to have blessed, now is the time to hold it up. In the name of the Father, the Son, and the Holy Ghost, Amen." And that was it. It seemed preposterous to me then and still does today. Here was a genuine chance to engage people committed to carrying his message to the world, to get their feedback, to listen to their concerns, and if necessary to hear their critiques. But, as I knew already and as the world was slowly to learn throughout the whole of his pontificate, this was not a man who was prepared to do any listening even to his own clergy and his most devoted laity. He was highly courageous and single-minded, but at times at fault for his closed ears to everything but what he himself wished to hear, especially the sound of his own voice.

The American tour took in five cities—Boston, New York, Chicago, Philadelphia and Washington—plus a visit to rural Iowa. My most vivid memory—apart from the incident of the solitary nun who dared to speak out and question the Pope's stand of opposition to women priests during his speech to hundreds of women in religious orders at the cathedral in Washington—is of an outdoor mass in the great Mall in that city's centre. As was his wont, John Paul II had waxed eloquently, at times even stridently, on his already familiar themes of the sins of birth control and abortion and of how priestly celibacy can never be abandoned by the Church. He was of course aware of pressure from the liberal wing of American Catholicism on all these issues.

As he ended the sermon and moved ahead with the Mass, I noticed several young, smartly dressed and sophisticated-looking women in their mid-thirties who had been moved to tears. They joined vigorously in the loud applause when the event was coming to its close. So I took the opportunity to briefly interview several of them as they waited to disperse. All were unanimous in their joy and in their admiration for the man. "What about his message?" I asked. They didn't hesitate for a minute. One by one they said they really hadn't paid much attention to it. Asked about the various issues raised, they laughed and said, "We don't believe any of that at all." One of them, who happened to be wearing a wedding band, actually opened her purse and showed me her birth control pills. Of course, repeated polls in North America and elsewhere reveal that nowadays the majority of Roman Catholics no longer follow the Vatican's dictates on birth control or any other of the "hormone issues" either, if they ever did.

There was a certain thrill to some of the events—for example, being part of the papal motorcade with full motorcycle police escort for the press buses, with sirens screaming on every side as we rushed through New York on the way to a youth mass at Madison Square Garden. There they treated JP II as if he were a rock star, and he played the role of global celebrity to the hilt. Again, however, the young people loved the way he looked and sounded, but appeared to be paying little or no attention to what he was actually saying. There was, to my mind, an *appearance* of connecting but very little substance once the thrill of seeing a major world personality before them had faded away. I found myself wishing it were otherwise.

I returned home exhausted. Thankfully, it would be a couple of months before I set out on an unforgettable trip to India and Nepal, among other things to spend a week with Mother Teresa in Calcutta. She had just been awarded the Nobel Peace Prize.

My editors at the *Star* were immediately supportive when I proposed the concept of "Christmas in Asia" for four consecutive front-page features to run on the days leading up to Christmas 1979. The first and probably most important piece would be about Mother Teresa and her work in Calcutta. But I was also aware of two other people who were less well known but whose calling had taken them to Calcutta on the one hand and to a remote mountain village in Nepal on the other. Because of the unique forms their ministries had taken, I felt they deserved as much attention as the Nobel Prize winner. So photographer Bob Olsen and I were given the assignment. It was the most exciting journey of my career, and it changed my thinking about a lot of things. I had the opportunity to encounter Hinduism and Buddhism actually being lived instead of just hearing about them from lectures and books. Both religions, of course, have a much longer history than Christianity and, contrary to many predictions by missionaries and others, are reawakening and spreading in our time, rather than fading away. I found the things we had in common to be far greater than the differences. In *Water into Wine* I discuss the many wide-ranging parallels between Vedic or Hindu scriptures and the Christian Gospels.

This was the first visit to Calcutta for both Bob and me, and nothing we had read ahead of time had prepared us for the culture shock of suddenly landing in one of the most densely populated cities in the world. It is also one of the cities where the extremes of wealth and grinding poverty are most evident. Because of the sheer number of motorized vehicles of every size, shape and vintage— few if any of them with proper exhaust systems intact—and since the tens of thousands who have the streets as their only home use dried cow dung for cooking and washing, the air was constantly filled with smoke and fumes. The din was a constant, all-embracing cacophony. But a strange thing happened as you got used to all of that and looked behind and beyond to the people themselves. Calcutta's streets teem with humanity in all its glories and shames. It's hard to describe, but you somehow felt your appreciation of the full range of human emotions and inner depths gradually expanding. Even the poverty-stricken beggars had about them a dignity and a sturdy cheerfulness. There was a lot of joy on the faces and in the smiles of children and adults alike. At night, from the window of our hotel, you could see long rows of huddled figures sleeping on the pavement. Each with a shawl or a sack of some kind wrapped about his or her head, they looked like mummies.

Mother Teresa's amazing efforts to help "the poorest of the poor" by feeding the hungry, caring for the orphans and comforting the dying are so well known they need no cataloguing here. She was very gracious with us. She agreed to be interviewed and photographed and personally escorted us through her orphanage in the heart of the great city. She went with us also to the House of the Dying in the precincts of a temple of the Hindu goddess Kali, and encouraged us there to join in helping to feed some of the dying patients. I was standing there feeling rather at a loss in the face of so many sick and dying people when she suddenly picked up a tin plate with a few chunks of bread on it and said, "Feed that man on the pallet there." Coming from our germ-conscious culture, I felt at first a reluctance even to touch or come that close to one so dirty and so obviously in pain. But I did what she said and almost instantly knew it was not only right but something that I needed to do for my own sake as well as his. I had a small epiphany and learned through this experience that it was true: the other is oneself. It is in giving that we truly receive and recognize our deep unity with "all sorts and conditions of men," as the Anglican Book of Common Prayer so aptly says.

In September 2007, Mother Teresa's little book of personal correspondence, *Come Be My Light*, was published and shocked the world by revealing that for most of her life, certainly since the early 1950s, she had been weighed down by a terrible sense of depression and of the absence of God. "There is such terrible darkness within me, as if everything was dead," she wrote in 1953. "It has been like this more or less from the time I started the work." Then, in 1959, "If there be no God, there can be no soul—if there is no soul, then Jesus—you also are not true." Like most who try to lead a holy life, at times she found it very hard to pray. Her "darkness" plagued her right up to her death at age eighty-seven in 1997. Upon reading excerpts in *Time* magazine, I was saddened by her suffering. But I was amazed too at her courage and the grace she showed to us. Many saintly souls down the ages have been troubled by despondency and doubts. Her achievements, in my eyes and in the minds of countless millions, are all the greater in that light. In her presence you felt the power of purpose emanating from such a tiny, elderly woman. She made you feel that all things are indeed possible.

For the second feature I wanted to focus on a Canadian-born, American-based Pentecostal minister, Mark Buntain. Like Mother Teresa, Buntain has since "gone to his reward" as they say in some Christian circles, but what a remarkable story of dedication and of service he had. He had come to my attention sometime previously in a short news story in a Pentecostal magazine headed ST. MARK OF

CALCUTTA. I had never heard of him before and I was certain most of our readers hadn't either. Buntain and his wife had been in Calcutta for over thirty years. The salary was very low; they were rationed to one bucket of water each per day for all their needs; but I have never met a happier couple. Buntain's record was phenomenal. He had a motor mechanics school for young boys living on the streets. They were given a uniform each morning when they showed up at the school's entrance and left it behind when they went out to go back to the street each evening. Many had no family. In the school they were taught among other things how to build school buses for his program of schooling and feeding children who lived near the garbage dumps outside the city and scratched out a pittance there. Not only had he established a school for training nurses to meet the needs and hopes of homeless girls, but he had built a modern hospital as well. In fact it was Buntain's hospital that cared for Mother Teresa on more than one occasion in her later years.

I didn't share Buntain's theology any more than I did Mother Teresa's. But there was everything that truly mattered in common between us. He was so clearly doing the true work not just of a Christian but of any truly spiritual person, whatever their profession of faith. In fact, immersed as I was for the first time in a country where the prevailing, dominant religion was Hinduism, and seeing how in the case of both Mark Buntain and Mother Teresa it was human need that was the determining factor and not denomination or religious faith, it was brought home to me as never before that all our religions are really metaphors for the same Divine Mystery. At their core there is only the one imperative or commandment—to treat one another with true compassion, especially those who need it most. This was the spiritual message that fermented in me from all my various travels as a religion editor.

The same truth shone through when we met the third and final person featured in our Asian odyssey, Dr. Helen Huston, a medical missionary with the United Church of Canada. Here again my interest had been caught by a small news story, this one in the *United Church Observer* and headlined DOCTOR ON THE ROOF OF THE WORLD. That phrase haunted me from the first time I saw it. The article described how Dr. Huston was running a small front-line medical clinic in the foothills of the Himalayas in Nepal. Accordingly, when we left Calcutta we took a flight up to Kathmandu. There we hired a car to take us along a very dangerous single-lane road built by the Chinese into the remote interior of the country. It was a long, hair-raising journey of 140 kilometres made more so by our meeting the occasional large truck and having to stop suddenly and back up incredible distances in order to find a spot in which to pull aside and let it pass. There were no guardrails and the gorges on either side were at times totally precipitous. When we reached a tiny village called Dumre we asked the driver to meet us at the same spot in four days' time. We then arranged for a porter/guide to go with us. He shouldered our packs, including Bob's heavy camera equipment, and headed towards the snowy peaks in the distance. The name of the remote village that was our destination was Amp Pipal.

In the far distance we could see Annapurna gleaming in the early afternoon sunshine as we made our way across rice paddies, forded cold, snowmelt-filled streams and kept steadily climbing towards our destination. At one point a troop of monkeys scampered ahead of us across the sodden fields. It was very late in the day as we headed into the steep climb up Lig Lig Mountain to the nursing station. The path wound around as it rose until we were deep in the shadow of the mountain itself. It was then that a near disaster struck. I had taken the lead and suddenly, where the solid ground of the path should have been, there was only empty air. Grass growing out of the side of the opening had concealed it in the shadows. All at once I was falling, sliding into what seemed like an abyss. Within seconds, flat on my back and clawing at the steep wall of the gorge, the aluminum frame of my pack caught on a root. I held my breath and gave a yell. Just then I heard Bob Olsen shout and then a thud above me. He too had stepped into the hole in the path and had tumbled. Luckily, his camera strap had looped over a branch above and held him. Suddenly I felt the Sherpa reach down, and with a grip that was utterly surprising in a man so slimly built, he extracted me from my predicament. He did the same with Bob. We were both very shaken by the experience. When we returned to the spot a couple of days later on our descent, we looked over and could see the small huts of a settlement near the valley bottom. It was a dizzying height and it had been a very close call indeed.

The clinic or nursing station was the only such facility within over a hundred kilometres and had in its care a whole series of small villages tucked into folds in the mountains. There were no roads in most of the area, so the "ambulance" was a pole with a hammock slung under it that could be carried on the shoulders of two men. They walked single file along the narrow paths and across the swinging rope bridges over chasms where white water often churned below. When a person was ill, the family accompanied him or her to the hospital and stayed in a rough inn in order to be available to cook and do other necessary chores for the patient. In the short time we were there, Dr. Huston tended to the widest possible range of illnesses, including a man with a very badly infected eye. He had slashed it while working in a patch of sugar cane and, on the advice of some would-be helper, had rubbed rat dung in it as an alleged cure! There were cases of leprosy as well as a host of other ills. You could see from the faces of these finely featured people just how much Helen Huston meant to them and their families. It seemed to me to be the only kind of missionary work that made any sense. These folk had their own millennia-old Hindu faith. I knew from my familiarity with the Vedic scriptures, and especially the Bhagavad-Gita, that when the outer trappings were stripped away, the core doctrine was actually very close to what I believed myself. It looks outwardly like a religion of many gods and goddesses. However, there is only one ultimate source of divinity, or "Godness," and the various deities are manifestations of that. Each of us is a bearer of the divine light, or Atman, within.

When we finally got back to Kathmandu and caught a flight to Calcutta prior to returning home, the pilot came on the intercom not long after takeoff. He said that Mount Everest's peak was usually covered in clouds or mist but that at the moment it was perfectly clear there. So he announced he was going to do a favour to everyone aboard and fly as close as safety permitted. It was a truly glorious sight and a fitting close to our adventure on the other side of the globe. We felt a profound sense of gratitude. We had had the rare privilege of meeting with three "saints," had been preserved from serious harm by a deceptively slight Sherpa, and had seen the highest mountain in the world in all its breathtaking glory. It made what was probably the best Christmas series of any. In the fourth and final article I had the opportunity of summing it all up and of saying how Christmas could no longer be for me the story of the one life of one baby born so long ago. It had become the story of all humanity's quest for a restored unity and of the need for the birth of compassion in the heart.

9

LIVING MY
OWN DREAM

WHAT HAS BEEN most remarkable about my particular journey to this moment is that the second half of my life has been much more productive and creative, more fulfilling in so many different ways, than the beginning. What came before certainly contained many wonderful moments and was a time of great activity also, but from this vantage point it all seems to have been preparation and prologue for what was to come. Central to this is the fact that somebody new came into my life. Susan, now my wife of thirty years, was working at the *Star* when in 1971 we had first met very fleetingly while I was submitting travelling expense reports from a trip. We remained polite, distant acquaintances until quite suddenly at the beginning of 1980 we were thrown together once more by circumstance and fell deeply in love. Some things are too profound and personal to be the subject of pedestrian description. But, like Robert Frost's traveller in the woods who took "the road less travelled by," I can truly say that knowing and being with Susan "has made all the difference" in my life. My life has been infinitely blessed by her love and companionship.

On Valentine's Day 1981, Susan called to tell me she had just made an offer for us on a small cottage on Lake Wilcox, a kettle lake that was part of a chain of such waters sparkling in the midst of the suburban sprawl surrounding Richmond Hill, a town about twenty-five kilometres north of downtown Toronto. We were both very excited when we heard that the small lot was actually a waterfront property. We would be able to swim, canoe and fish in summer and then skate on it in winter. In fact in winter, once the snow came and the lake was frozen, I could actually ski at times from our front door, alongside a frozen creek bed, out to the highway to the post office for mail. It was like living in a cabin up north.

Wilcox Lake itself had a somewhat dubious reputation because of an earlier period when it was known for wild partying by motorcycle gangs and all the other disreputable activities generally associated with the poorly policed, more remote regions of any vast and growing modern city. Rumour had it that the infamous Boyd gang of bank robbers had once dumped a collection of revolvers and other guns out in the middle of the lake. Somebody from the ".old days" later told me that the reason there was so little policing then was that "the cops were afraid to go in there." But that was more or less apocryphal. The price was right, and with about nine hundred square feet of room, it was all we needed. It would remain our home for the next eighteen years. We could reach the Star building on Toronto's waterfront at the foot of Yonge Street ("the longest street in the world") either by car fairly quickly or, later, by GO train from the station in Richmond Hill.

We soon grew to love it by the lake. We could work in the city by day and then return to what was really a cottage retreat at night. There were rolling fields, woodlands and parks on every side of the community and always the presence of the changing waters. Wildlife of all sorts made it seem at times as though the city was many miles away instead of gradually reaching up to our front door. There were plenty of muskrats, the occasional beaver, great blue herons and many other species of waterfowl, especially during the migration seasons of spring and fall. You could sit at times on a bench by the lake and watch an osprey hover, dive and then emerge shaking the water from its wings as it took off with a fish in its talons. On our many walks there often were deer and coyotes in full view. The house was simplicity itself even after we eventually enlarged it somewhat, making a spacious study where I could write overlooking the view to the east, with its beach and conservation area. Over the years from 1981 to 1999 it was to be the place where several of my books were written. It gave one a real sense of perspective to know that this lake and others nearby had been here for over ten thousand years. They dated to the end of the last ice age, before any holy scriptures of any kind were written down. As the geologian the late Thomas Berry was fond of saying, "The very first holy book is the creation and the cosmos itself." He also said he thought the Church should put the Bible on a shelf for a few years and read the "Book of Nature" for a while instead.

Having lived in the very heart of the city for so many years, I found it literally a breath of fresh air to be in the country. As soon as I did not have to travel to the *Star* every day, my normal working day began with a seven-kilometre walk, usually on country roads or trails in the "mink and manure" belt in King Township. I was sometimes asked if I found it boring, but I knew what a privilege it was. Most of my best ideas for both columns and books over this highly productive time were born of these walks; on most days I could scarcely wait to get home and start writing. I found the setting helped keep me connected with the deeper rhythms of life. Cows in the meadows stared at me as though I were the first human they'd ever seen; horses nickered softly as they grazed; everything was redolent of earthy, growing things. Yet in the very far distance I could at times see clearly the CN Tower, near to the Star building. On more than one occasion there were deer grazing in the immediate foreground with the tower as a distant, almost surreal backdrop.

As Easter 1981 approached, my editors began putting some pressure on me to come up with a special feature of some kind as I had

done a few times before, including a visit to a Canadian-run project for orphans in Costa Rica. By coincidence, I had mentioned
this in passing to my very good friend Father Tom McKillop, who
was the director of youth work for the Roman Catholic Archdiocese of Toronto. He was an important contact and had become a
firm friend. It was because of him that I was able to meet and interview, among others, Victor Frankel, who wrote *Man's Search for
Meaning*, a book of great significance in my own life and the lives
of so many hundreds of thousands of people around the world. You
knew in meeting Frankel that his message of our deep need to find
meaning even through suffering was one he had authenticated in
his own life.

A few days later McKillop called me and invited me to meet him
for coffee to discuss an idea. When we met, he told me that in his
regular visits to Catholic high schools over the past several months
he had been struck by the amount of apprehension and concern
there was among the students over the dangers and possibility of
nuclear war. "There is a terrible weight of worry and fear out there
just now because of some recent news stories and the general
geopolitical tensions currently in the headlines," he said. He went
on, "Have you ever thought of going to Japan and writing about
Hiroshima, Nagasaki and the bomb? Maybe there's something
really important there."

I pondered his suggestion all afternoon. Later that night I
decided to put the concept to the managing editor the next day. It
turned out that Martin Goodman was away, and so I went to the
next in command, Ray Timson, a long-time colleague and friend,
and suggested that I go to Hiroshima and write a major feature on
the 1945 dropping of the bomb, its horrors, its overall meaning for
humanity and all the options still confronting us today in the wake
of that awesome event. Timson, in his typical fashion, greeted the
idea with real enthusiasm and told me to go ahead. He added that he
would alert the publicity department and give the story major play.

So, on the Monday before Easter, I caught a plane to Vancouver, where there was an hour stopover before a non-stop flight to Tokyo. Because of my height, and because *Star* staff—except for upper management—always flew in economy class, I was stiff and sore after the four or five hours from Toronto to Vancouver. However, that was as nothing beside the nine- or ten-hour lap over the rim of the Pacific to Narita Airport. After what seemed a near eternity, including an almost hour-long taxi ride to my hotel in downtown Tokyo, I finally arrived, exhausted but also ravenously hungry. It was the Tokyo Hilton Hotel and I'm sure the meal was terrific, with a view out over the lovely gardens and pool, but it was wasted; I was just too tired. Once in my room, I fell into the luxurious bed and was almost instantly asleep.

Unfortunately, it was not to last. It seemed only minutes later, although it was in fact a couple of hours, when the phone beside the bed began ringing. I struggled to drag myself awake only to find a voice on the other end of the line saying he was the *Star*'s public relations manager and that they'd like to cut a commercial spot for radio to promo the weekend feature. He was calling from a studio in Yorkville, in the centre of Toronto, saying, "Whenever you're ready, we'll cue you up. Just say where you are, what you're doing and why it all matters. You've got forty-five seconds." I hardly knew where I was myself never mind being prepared to talk about a place I had yet to visit. I explained the situation, that I wouldn't reach Hiroshima until the following day. He told me to take a few moments to "put myself into the scene" and then he'd roll tape. "This is the only opportunity we have," he said. "Just ad lib." I still feel some embarrassment over this incident even after all these years. My only excuse is that I couldn't think of a quick alternative and I knew it was going to be the kind of story that merited the widest possible readership simply because of the issues involved. I took a few deep breaths, thought for a few moments and then did the best job I could. "That was great," he said when I finished the terse message.

"You really put a lot into that. It's a go. You can go back to sleep."
When I said I didn't feel very good about faking being in a place
before I had set foot there, he said not to worry. "By the time this
goes to air here in Toronto, you'll have been all over Hiroshima and
well on your way back home." One thing I do remember about all
of that was resolving it would never occur again.

There was one benefit to the way it all happened. Many people
told me later that they really felt the deep emotion and even trauma
the Hiroshima visit had brought to me—they could hear it in my
voice. I didn't want to tell them that perhaps what they were sens-
ing was simply surprise and exhaustion. The truth is that after taking the bullet train to Hiroshima the next day, standing at ground
zero, and visiting the hospital that still housed survivors who had
been terribly burned in the August 6, 1945, holocaust, I was indeed
profoundly moved. I will never forget getting up very early on the
day following my arrival there and walking under cherry blossoms in the Peace Park, its skeletal dome the only vestige of buildings that had once stood there but which were all burned up in the
Armageddon-like conflagration. There was a kind of simple shrine
with an altar on one side of the park, and in the silence I noticed
that early morning joggers would stop before it and, hands clasped
in front in an attitude of prayer, stand for a period of meditation
before continuing their run. Cherry blossoms fell softly in the glory
of the morning sunshine and carpeted the ground. For a moment it
seemed that the earth itself stood still to remember the awful cata-
clysm long ago in which the city was all but obliterated and 140,000
people perished. I visited the Atomic Bomb Museum, dedicated to
making certain the world can never forget what happened there
or the apocalyptic demons then unleashed and henceforth forever
threatening to bring a final judgment on our planet and ourselves. I
spoke to doctors and to clergy of various faiths.

Since I had already done some interviews with two or three key
thinkers, including of course McKillop, in Toronto (at the *Star* you

always had to keep in mind the maxim "What does it mean to Toronto?"), I had all the material I needed for the story as I retraced my steps. During the long hours of flight over the Pacific and then across Canada I wrote and then rewrote the story until it met my hopes and original intentions. When I saw the weekend edition on Easter Day, I was absolutely stunned. The largest headline I had ever seen in a Toronto paper since the famous editions announcing the end of the war with Japan stood out in huge type across the front page. It said CHOOSE LIFE! and had a photo of the Hiroshima dome in the Peace Park taken by the award-winning photographer Boris Spremo. The shot was even more powerful because the only person in it was a little girl in a pretty dress caught running below the ruin. Some editors I know were unhappy with the sheer in-your-face nature of the play given to the story, but it was widely discussed not just in journalism classes at various colleges but in schools, churches and many, many other venues across Metropolitan Toronto and far beyond. Gary Lautens, the former humour columnist who was then managing editor, sent me a special note of congratulation. It was to be my last major trip as a staff writer for the *Star*.

The issue of the bomb has faded somewhat from public consciousness just now, replaced by looming environmental and economic problems. However, in the light of present geopolitical tensions, I view the risks of either a terrorist act involving the bomb or a nuclear attack by a rogue state as of the most urgent concern. Nuclear disarmament must be at the top of the agenda for all nations.

In the spring of 1982, Richard Teleky, a Canadian novelist who was then the senior editor at Oxford University Press Canada, phoned me at the *Star*. He introduced himself and said he thought it would be a good idea for us to meet for lunch as soon as possible to discuss the possibility of a book. We met at a bistro in Don Mills and over a glass of Japanese beer he said it seemed obvious to him that I should be writing in a more permanent and extended form than the *Star*'s

religion page and columns permitted. We discussed several possi-
bilities and finally agreed on a book based largely upon my take
on where the churches were at that time and the major problems
they faced, together with a truly forthright airing of strong, controversial opinions I held on everything from the hormone issues of
premarital sex and abortion to situation ethics (the so-called New
Morality) in general. He said that since it would be about ultimate
concerns, it should be titled *Harpur's Heaven and Hell*. As with the
radio show, the name only had to be heard once to stick permanently in the public mind, he assured me.

To the surprise both of Oxford University Press and of other
Canadian publishing houses, the book—issued simultaneously in
hardcover and paperback—took off immediately and was very
soon a Canadian bestseller. I did what every successful author was
expected to do at that time: I went on a gruelling cross-country tour,
the first of well over a dozen I was to undertake down the years.
The reception from radio hosts and interviewers as well as from
those on television and in churches from coast to coast was little
short of amazing. CBC's Peter Gzowski did five sessions with me
on *Morningside* dealing with a different topic each day. In the following week we did another show on responses he had received in
the mail. I particularly remember speaking during the tour to a
packed Christ Church Cathedral (Anglican) in the heart of downtown Vancouver. The crowd was mainly composed of young people, several of whom came up and hugged me afterwards. I also
remember a slightly over-refreshed woman in the front row who
approached to say she was my cousin from Ireland. It sounds like
the beginning of a bad joke, but I later discovered she really was a
relative on my father's side. She had married a prospector who
spent all his time in northern B.C. Unfortunately, he never found
the fortune he had in mind.

At about this time, I was invited to attend a showing of Ingmar
Bergman's haunting classic film *The Seventh Seal* at University Col-

lege, my old alma mater at the University of Toronto. The event
was being sponsored by the Varsity Student Christian Movement
(SCM). A lecturer from the philosophy department who was an
agnostic had been asked to join me in leading a discussion when
the screening was over. A good crowd turned out and things went
well for a time. But somehow, in the midst of the toing and froing
between the agnostic, the students and myself, I began listening to
myself as I had never done before.

It was a chilling experience. It wasn't that I wasn't holding my
own, but quite suddenly some of my words and arguments began
coming back to me with a strangely hollow sound and feel. It happened while I was setting forth my reasons for being a Christian,
and particularly when it came to defending the claim that Jesus was
the unique Son of God. What I was proclaiming was what I had
thought I thought for many years—ever since childhood, in fact.
It was what I had signed on to at my ordination. It had been at the
heart of many of my sermons as a parish priest. Even when looked
at from a much more historical-critical point of view, as a professor
of New Testament, it was what I had taught during my years of lecturing at the Toronto School of Theology. Ever since my Oxford
days and membership in the Socratic Club chaired by C.S. Lewis, I
had accepted his oft-repeated dictum that Jesus Christ was "either
mad, bad, or God." But after the SCM meeting dispersed and the
hall emptied, I left the building feeling quite disturbed, with a hundred questions whirling in my head. I walked for a couple of hours
around the soccer fields between University College and Convoca-
tion Hall, struggling to clarify what was troubling me and what
I truly believed. My belief and trust in God were rock-solid. I saw
agnosticism as a form of "polite atheism." My real difficulty focused
upon Jesus.

The total inadequacy of Lewis's glib formulation suddenly leaped
out at me. What if none of his alternatives was correct? Why should
there be only three of them? Once I looked at it in this light, it was

obvious immediately that Jesus could have been mad, bad, the Son of God, or else completely misunderstood! What evidence was there that he ever actually claimed in any absolute sense to be divine? Didn't he once tell the rich young ruler that "there is none good, only God"? How could we be certain that the New Testament texts themselves were truly reliable documents? I had long been aware of the many contradictions within the Gospels. Why did it take Church councils almost five centuries to formulate a satisfactory (to the theologians of the day) definition of the Trinity and of Jesus's coequal status in it? How could the sacrificial death or martyrdom of one person, however exalted and holy, wipe out the "sins of the whole world"? And so on and so on.

Finally, I got in my car and drove home. As I did, the questions only multiplied. This had been nagging at me for some time now and it seemed I was facing another crisis. But before long, once the furor over *Harpur's Heaven and Hell* had quieted down, I realized that one way of dealing with this serious problem would be to research and write a book on the subject. Obviously my dilemma was far from unique to me, and this is what all my previous experience and training was really about: communicating a faith that makes sense to modern men and women. It was time for further exploration.

So, with Teleky's keen support, I plunged eagerly into the task and began preparing for what was eventually to be the slim paperback *For Christ's Sake*, published in the spring of 1986, again by Oxford University Press. I set out to examine the Gospels carefully to see for myself what they actually said rather than what the Church has traditionally claimed they convey. The book was met with a storm of controversy right from the start. Some former mentors wrote to tell of their dismay at my describing the virgin birth as a sacred myth and my doubts over the doctrine of the Atonement—salvation through the "blood" of Christ—and much, much more besides. Pastors denounced the book from their pulpits and in some cases even took out ads in local papers announcing upcoming sermons exposing *For Christ's Sake*'s "heresies." Ironically, some of these same critics were to reappear later, in 2004, quoting parts of this book in an attempt to refute claims made in *The Pagan Christ*! The central position reached in *For Christ's Sake* was that Jesus may have been the greatest person ever to have lived on planet earth but "he is also the most misunderstood." Using the New Testament itself as the key witness, I was convinced I had shown how the Church had mistakenly taken Jesus the messenger—or in McLuhan's terms, Jesus the medium of the message—for the message itself.

What is most surprising to me today, as I glance through *For Christ's Sake* once more, is how much further, on the one hand, my thinking has developed and matured since that turbulent time and, on the other, how clearly the themes to be explored and elaborated almost twenty years later in *The Pagan Christ* were already there. For example, in the final chapter titled "Jesus From Now On," I quote the verse from the Prologue of John's Gospel that speaks of the Logos as being "the true light which lighteth every person who comes into the world." This is followed by: "What is being so sublimely stated is that all of us . . . have within us a spark or seed (to use the Stoic concept) of divine light that is none other than God . . . Our true humanity lies, paradoxically, in our divinity." That's really what *The Pagan Christ* and its sequel, *Water into Wine*, are all about. Nothing could have been much further from the fundamentalist beliefs of my youth. But the final revelation was not the result of some sudden change of consciousness, but the product of a process begun long ago and simmering within for many years.

Writing and promoting *Harpur's Heaven and Hell* had given me for the first time a truly liberating opportunity to express freely in a more permanent form my own opinions, research and analysis of religious/spiritual matters. It made me realize that the time had come to free myself entirely from the responsibility of only reporting what other theologians, religious leaders and experts in the field had to say. I decided to launch out into the deep, so to speak, as a freelance writer and broadcaster. The job of working for the *Toronto Star* had been quite remarkable. It was an adventure that took me many places I would perhaps never have seen and into close company with scores of leading personalities in religion whom I would otherwise possibly never have met. But a different challenge now was calling. In the fall of 1983, with some genuine feeling of regret, I handed in my resignation as religion editor. A few months later, early in 1984, publisher Beland Honderich wrote to suggest that I consider returning as a regular freelance columnist for the Sunday paper. I was more than happy to get the invitation. As it happened, I was to continue the column "Always on Sunday"—to use the title of a later collection—for over twenty years.

Now I was able finally to distill the lessons and experience of all the preceding years and to concentrate on the kinds of issues that truly interested me and on which I believed the churches' message had been woefully unconvincing and garbled at best. There was much talk on all sides in Christian circles about "the Gospel" and the "Good News" supposedly available on Sundays from the pulpit and in the bosom of the "assembly of faith"—as indeed there always had been. But just what this alleged Good News was and how it was either "good" or "news" for modern men and women was anything but clear.

Already in the 1980s there was a falling away of those once assumed to have been stalwart in their commitment to church membership and attendance. In the 1990s and the following decade, the trickle running from the churches was to become a flood. Not surprisingly, the beginning of the third millennium of the Christian era has been accompanied by dire warnings of the likely total disappearance of some of the former major denominations in the Western world before this first century is over. Anglicanism, even though it may continue growing in the Third World, chiefly Africa, is the most obvious case in point. In Canada, for example, church poll-sters have varied in their suggested timings, but all are agreed that unless current trends are reversed, the "last Anglican" will close the door and turn out the lights some Sunday well before 2100. Some experts predict it will come about much sooner.

Accordingly, it seemed important to focus on some of the key areas where "the faith once delivered to the saints" had formerly imparted a timely, relevant message. In the process of investigating and attempting to put the results in a communicable form, I had a further, perhaps even ulterior motivation as well: I wanted to clar-ify for myself what I actually still believed about each question. The journey of my writing from the very beginning has been an extremely personal affair. It became an unwritten principle: "Don't try to take people where one has never been oneself." That's why even before the furor created by *For Christ's Sake* had begun to set-tle down I had already conducted interviews in England (at Oxford) and elsewhere on the central question of "eternal life" or, as the resulting 1991 book was titled, *Life After Death*.

No subject is more basic to the Christian faith. It was part of the apostolic *kerygma*, or preaching, from the very beginning, and was one of the many reasons for the rapid growth of the Christian movement from the start. In its negative aspect, the development of the teaching that the Church alone held the keys to a pleasant afterlife, as well as the power to condemn one to everlasting fires of hell for heresy and a whole range of other lesser offences, gave this religion as it quickly expanded an incredibly potent hold on the human souls within its vast reach. Millions of people today are still in great mental and spiritual bondage to guilt and dread because of this unseemly grab for power and control. The major theme of the many hundreds of grateful letters received in response to *The Pagan Christ* has been the great sense of liberation from fear and guilt on the part of former fundamentalists, including pastors.

It is not my intention to expatiate further here upon the message of the earlier book, *Life After Death*; it speaks for itself. (A highly revised edition in light of the latest thinking on the subject and of changes in my own views entitled *There Is Life After Death* is being published simultaneously with this book.) But it is, I think, relevant to say that my exploration confirmed for me beyond a shadow of a doubt that not only the Church's interpretation of what its original documents set forth but its further explication of them in its preaching and teaching down the centuries are at times virtual caricatures of what was meant to be communicated at the outset. Just one small example will suffice. It shouldn't be surprising that the concept of eternal life has little or no appeal once you take the trouble to really think about it. It's actually a frightening thought: life going on forever, and ever, and ever . . . But in the Greek words of the New Testament that are regularly translated as "eternal life," a quite different meaning is contained. *Zoe aionios*, the Greek says. That means "the life of the age to come." In other words, eternal life is not about a never-ending, virtually inconceivable length of time. It's not a temporal matter at all. It's a qualitative idea. What is being announced is a life that is qualitatively different, a kind only possible in another dimension of being altogether, where time itself is no more. This is much closer to the Eastern concept of nirvana than to the phrase "eternal life."

The book *Life After Death* concludes, therefore, among many other things, that the Church has failed miserably to speak meaningfully today to its followers and outsiders alike about what is believed to happen when we die. No question could be more urgent, more universally relevant, more existential than this. Yet preachers and priests continue to mumble ancient shibboleths at funerals and elsewhere. Where, for example, has the Church made plain its response to or understanding of the now universally known near-death experience? The NDE is today familiar to everyone. Scientists debate its significance. TV programs herald its pros and cons. But from religion itself comes a deafening silence. The result is that a leading opportunity to speak to people where they are in terms they can understand is still being wholly missed. I would like to be wrong on this, but my suspicion is that churchly authorities realize that if the NDE is a real glimpse of a life beyond the grave, then there goes all that centuries-long power to say who goes where and when at the last call. Think of it: a future life may be infinitely more democratic than we supposed.

Life After Death was made into a twelve-part documentary for VisionTV and was later adapted for the Learning Channel in the U.S.A. Overall the book met with such success that the editors at McClelland & Stewart were quite keen to follow it with another similar exploration. I at once proposed a volume exploring the theme of spiritual healing in particular and alternative medicine in general. While continuing to write weekly columns (McClelland & Stewart published a collection of them under the title *God Help Us* in 1992) I travelled to Britain and the U.S. as well as other major centres in Canada to interview researchers and healers of all kinds and practices. I was committed to the belief that if religion has any part to play in contemporary life, it must become what it was originally intended to be—a source of healing of the whole person and of society itself. The language of healing was there—*salvation* means "being made whole"—but the reality too often was not. It was a fascinating task for the nearly three years it took to investigate and then write. The result was *The Uncommon Touch: An Investigation of Spiritual Healing* (1994). It too became a ten-part VisionTV series of the same name. Interestingly, in the same week of 2010 that this last sentence was written, the *Toronto Star* ran a review of a new book by an American sociologist, William Bengston, Ph.D., called *Chasing the Cure*. The book describes Bengston's own career as a hands-on healer. His many lab experiments with mice, the results of which were published in peer-reviewed journals, together with documentation of positive results with human ailments ranging from several forms of cancer to diabetes, are cited as reasons to undertake wider scientific studies to examine the whole phenomenon of "energy healing." Therapeutic Touch is now widely practised as an adjunct to regular medicine.

Other books followed quickly, as somehow the creative juices were truly flowing. There was *Would You Believe? Finding God Without Losing Your Mind* (1996), which aimed to set forth a reasonable framework for believing in God in an often chaotic world. Then came *Prayer: The Hidden Fire* in 1998, in which I explored among other things my own scary encounter with heart disease and the amazing self-healing powers of the body in creating a non-surgical bypass for a totally blocked main coronary artery. Thankfully, with appropriate medical care, the "miracle" has been fully sustained.

In 1998, having become keenly aware that the city was increasingly invading our semi-rural retreat at Wilcox Lake, we decided to make a move to the "real" country. Before long we had moved to a stone cottage–type farmhouse overlooking the sparkling waters of Georgian Bay. I continued writing the column, keeping up with major trends in religion and working on another book with Susan's help— she has excellent editorial skills and an amazing ability to organize, which I never possessed—while together we gardened our vegetables and roses, gently updated our home and settled into a slightly quieter style of living. Bluebirds make their home around our apple trees and split-rail fencing, and the wrens in the birdhouses near our windows sing their morning matins and evening vespers. John Muir, the famous American environmentalist, once spent a year in the region near our forty-odd acres, and in a letter now in the Meaford museum he pronounced it one of the loveliest parts of North America he had visited during a lifetime of travel. We loved the peace and the feeling of freedom flowing from the wide vistas on every side. This tranquility contributed a great deal to my 2000 book, *Finding the Still Point: A Spiritual Response to Stress*, but it was about to be disturbed suddenly and on a major scale.

The whole thing began with the arrival one day of a letter from a Toronto clergyman in which the Reverend Larry Marshall introduced himself as a faithful reader with something he felt an urgent need to share. He wrote that during a recent long, serious illness which involved a lengthy confinement he had been surfing the Internet when one day he stumbled across the extensive work of an American author and lecturer named Alvin Boyd Kuhn. He said that from following the development of my thinking through my books and columns over the years, he felt "led" to bring Kuhn's work to my attention. Would I mind very much, he inquired, if he were to forward copies of a few of Kuhn's monographs on a variety of themes to me for "a quick scan"? Since one thing is certain when you are writing regularly in a newspaper—that everybody with a question, a suggestion or a criticism on your topic of choice will one day or another write to you—I was naturally somewhat cautious. I sent a note saying I was inundated with similar requests weekly, if not daily. But he didn't let it go and so one day the inevitable brown envelope arrived with *Rev. L. Marshall* on the return address. It was thrown on top of a heap of mail of a similarly unwanted kind on a shelf in the study and lay there for some time.

One day, however, while tidying up, I took it down and began to glance at the contents. There were three or four papers by Alvin Boyd Kuhn, Ph.D., including one on ancient sun gods. The subject was new to me and I began to read the article with growing fascination. If what Kuhn was saying was true, the parallels and affinities between the Jesus Story and the accounts of the sun deities of the ancient Middle East and of the Vedic lore of India were not only numerous but extremely close as well. I was both surprised and intrigued. Marshall and I began an email correspondence and before long more monographs arrived. Meanwhile, Google provided some necessary background information.

Soon, apart from writing the weekly column and taking our daily walk over the fields or on a part of the Bruce Trail that winds near our home, all my time was given over to reading more and more of Kuhn. That was accompanied by reading his major sources as well. In particular, I was riveted by the writings of Gerald Massey (1828–1911), an English scholar who in his early life had become acknowledged as a poet of some note. He had then spent many years in arduous study of Christian origins, focusing particularly on ancient Egypt. Working closely with noted Assyriologists and Egyptologists at the British Museum in London, he taught himself to read Egyptian hieroglyphics. He then was able to read ancient Egyptian versions of the Book of the Dead, in which he found dozens of exact parallels between the Egyptian Son of God, Horus, and the Jesus of the Gospels. In other words, Horus, a Christ-like prototype, was in the Egyptian mythology millennia before the events recorded in the New Testament. Massey's books and Kuhn's four chief works, particularly *The Lost Light*, held me spellbound because in all my reading and training over many years I had never come across anything that was so shocking on the one hand or so uplifting and inspiring on the other.

As weeks turned into months, the more I read, the more I was convinced that what these men were saying had the ring of truth. What they had to say about the origins and nature of Christianity was not merely illuminating, it was radical to the point of explosive. Relying not only upon his own wide knowledge of Platonism, the Neoplatonists, other world religions and the Bible itself, but also on the earlier research and writings of Massey and others, Kuhn argued with passion that Christianity is indeed but a pale copy of an earlier narrative theme. The Jesus Story has been told before, most notably in the myths surrounding the Egyptian sun god Horus, the son of the god Osiris, and the goddess Isis (like Mary, called Queen of Heaven, and Theotokos, "Mother of God"). As I read on hour after hour, day after day, I was gradually transfixed by the dawning realization that if what was being said was indeed true, then my whole understanding of the faith in which I had been reared and to which I had dedicated my entire life was being called into question in a more radical way than ever before. At times it seemed as though the whole world was being turned upside down. I was semi-retired now, and so at first I would have liked to be able to deny the challenge, to refute the case being so credibly presented, to turn back the clock to before that first encounter with Kuhn's ideas. But a determined willingness to follow the truth wherever it led left no alternative but to press ahead.

I began to read more widely in this area, including, amongst many other writings, the work of the top contemporary Egyptologist Eric Hornung. Most of today's Egyptologists are chiefly concerned with archaeological discoveries and specific artifacts, but Hornung has made a study of the more esoteric, religious aspects of his field. For example, in *The Secret Lore of Egypt: Its Impact on the West*, he wrote: "Early Christianity was deeply indebted to ancient Egypt . . . There was a smooth transition from the image of the nursing Isis, Isis lactans, to that of Maria lactans. The miraculous birth of Jesus could be viewed as analogous to that of Horus . . ." I also discovered that the scholar Karl W. Luckert at the University of Chicago had written a book in 1991 about the huge debt that Christianity owes to Egyptian sources. It was called *Egyptian Light and Hebrew Fire*. One of many well-known authorities in the area of mythology, Joseph Campbell, said in his highly popular PBS TV series of interviews with Bill Moyers, "When you stand before the cathedral of Chartres, you will see over one of the portals of the western front an image of the Madonna as the throne upon which the child Jesus blesses the world as its Emperor. That is precisely the image [Isis and Horus] that has come down to us from most ancient Egypt. The early Fathers and the early artists took over these images intentionally." In similar fashion, I noted that in his classic book *Man and His Symbols*, Carl Jung, the renowned psychiatrist and expert on mythology, said, "The Christian era itself owes its name and significance to the antique mystery of the god-man, which has its roots in the archetypal Osiris–Horus myth."

The process of digesting all of this previously unknown material is given some space in chapter 1 of *The Pagan Christ*. I wrote there: "What if it is true? The implications were enormous. It meant . . . that much of the thinking of much of the civilized West has been based upon a 'history' that never occurred, and that the Christian Church had been founded on a set of miracles that were never performed literally . . . And that has made all the difference, a huge and immensely positive difference for my understanding of my faith and my own spiritual life. Simultaneously, it has transformed my view of the future of Christianity into one of hope." Many things came together in a synchronism of influences, ripening ideas and insights that together gave me the courage and conviction necessary to write *The Pagan Christ*, to promote it through the media, and then to defend it against what I correctly foresaw would be a very formidable storm of criticism.

Looking back at the 2004 publication of *The Pagan Christ*, followed in 2007 by its sequel, *Water into Wine*, I have a deep awareness now of how perfectly it flows from all that had gone before. One has only to look at the earlier books and columns to see how the realization was already there that the only way forward for any rationally based religion of the future was that of a cosmic-oriented faith. The realization that the old creeds were now defunct and that they presented rigid, irrelevant obstacles rather than means to wider understanding was there almost from the very beginning. So too was the birth (for me) of the perception that the Jesus Story was not only a very old story but an archetypal drama of the Self in every one of us. In fact, chapter 14 in *Life After Death* (which offended some theologians at the time) was actually titled "The Christ Myth as the Ultimate Myth of the Self." It was written in 1990, fourteen years before *The Pagan Christ*.

The part of *The Pagan Christ* that was the most striking and that stood the most apart from anything that had come before—also the part that I laboured over the hardest and that the media naturally exploited—was the chapter called "Was There a Jesus of History?" Other scholars as early as a hundred years ago had questioned the historicity of Jesus—and definitely the number of those doing so is growing today—but nobody mentioned them in divinity schools and certainly never from the pulpit. Indeed, if Christianity has been marked by any one single development beyond others in the past 150 years, it has been a paradoxical trend in North America particularly: on the one hand, an ever greater idolizing of a literal Jesus, who has usurped the place of God; and on the other hand, the work of critical scholars who have been busy removing the credibility of almost everything the historical Jesus is alleged to have said and done. The California-based Jesus Seminar's twofold research projects—one into the words of Jesus, the other into his "acts"—eventually resulted in two books which between them said that less than 20 percent of either category had any claim to authenticity. Had the scores of participating scholars been less tightly connected with various Christian denominational schools and seminaries, there is no doubt in my mind that this figure would have been much smaller still.

The truth is that when my research for *The Pagan Christ* first began, the last thing on my mind was the possibility that it would lead where eventually it did on this issue. Once I realized that it might, I redoubled my efforts to get at the truth at all costs. Using all that I had learned at the feet of Professor Peter Brunt, my old tutor in Greek and Roman history, I checked and rechecked the very few lines of testimony that come to us from the second century CE. There is no secular evidence whatsoever for Jesus from the first century unless one ignores the fact that what Josephus, a Jewish historian who lived and wrote at that time, seems to say has been judged from earliest times to have been an egregious forgery. As pointed out in *The Pagan Christ*, the Jesus Story itself has a history.

Indeed, it is woven into the very fabric of Western culture, its art, music and literature. It has been repeated and read literally so many myriads of times that it is the supreme meme of all time. The virtually total absence of any truly reliable hard historical evidence for the story has seldom been noticed because that's the very essence of a meme; it is simply a unit of information repeated and repeated over and over again without question, indeed without the beginning of any thought of a question. While I don't agree with the position of atheist Richard Dawkins, he is certainly right about this phenomenon in our culture, as outlined in his 1976 book *The Selfish Gene*. One of the most interesting aspects of the response to *The Pagan Christ* (which is continuing as I write) is that to date none of the critics who unanimously affirm Jesus's historicity has come up with a single bit of solid evidence to support their position. Yet clearly theirs is the burden of proof. It rests upon their shoulders to establish their case. They have not done so.

What is truly significant, considering the important ramifications of this vital question, is that in the United States, in the fall of 2009, it was announced by the Scientific Committee for the Examination of Religion that the Jesus Project has been established. Noting that previous inquiries—most recently the Jesus Seminar—had not directly addressed the central issue of the historicity of Jesus and also that such undertakings in the past have always been largely directed by those with some professional ties to churches and various hierarchies, the founders of the project stated that they planned to bring together some fifty scholars from different but closely related fields over a five-year period. They have promised that the research will be done with no a priori assumptions one way or another. The total commitment is to objectivity and truth. The prevailing standards for all peer-reviewed historical investigation will be scrupulously followed and upheld. The simple question will be: "Did Jesus exist?"

While obviously it is too early to guess what the project's findings will be, the fact that, after nearly two thousand years, such an endeavour is deemed by a scholarly body to be reasonable, academically legitimate and of some urgency says a very great deal. Clearly the matter is anything but the firm, settled and obvious "gospel truth" that a popular majority would have it believed to be.

To tell the full story of the response to *The Pagan Christ* would take a book of its own. There has been an incredible outpouring of letters to this day witnessing to the joy and sense of relief experienced by people from Canada and around the world, from priests and nuns to evangelical pastors, lifelong fundamentalists, writers and artists, students, agnostics and a host of others. At the same time, it must be said, an immediate torrent of negative criticism also was unleashed in the spring of 2004. It came chiefly from conservative Roman Catholics and ultra-conservative Protestant evangelicals, but there were some loud liberal voices as well. Some of the hostile email was abusive and insulting; some of it was simply vindictive; a few letters threatened reprisal, but mostly in terms that were too vague to be actionable. As expected, there were attacks upon my scholarship, attacks upon my major sources, especially upon Kuhn and Massey, attacks upon the Egyptian origins thesis, and general scorn for my even daring to suggest that the historical foundations of the Christian Story were scanty to the point of total absence. Kuhn was born in 1880 and died in 1963. The latter date is important because it is the same year in which C.S. Lewis and J.F. Kennedy died. It's interesting that neither of these two men is dismissed on the grounds that he is from another era, but critics, desperate to find any point from which to attack Kuhn's radical message, would try to suggest that because his work was done in that same era, it was of no importance. In the United States there was a concerted effort by some fundamentalists to savage the book and prevent its being picked up by major media. Some of them still feel so threatened that they continue to snipe away in blogs and other forms of networking.

After a long career of writing and broadcasting on the highly controversial themes of religion and ethics, I have learned that it is futile to attempt a rational debate on every issue raised by fundamentalists from any camp. But a small number of matters deserve a brief discussion here. Contrary to what one or two leading critics have maintained, the major thesis that Christianity is in large measure dependent upon ancient Egypt for its message and content—a Hebraized version of ancient Egyptian myth—is by no means an isolated or idiosyncratic view of a couple of scholarly oddities from another era. Several top scholars, including the orientalist Jacob Alexander in his recent book *Atman*, have acknowledged the central importance of this clear dependency of the one narrative upon earlier myths of antiquity.

Nor is the scholarship of Massey and Kuhn in any legitimate doubt. Gerald Massey, according to the *Encyclopaedia Britannica*, was chiefly known for his work as an "Egyptologist" at the time of his death. The truth is that he spent many, many years of study in the Egyptian and Assyrian wing of the British Museum at the very time that the Temple of Horus at Edfu was being excavated. He worked closely with several successive curators of this department of the museum, including Dr. Samuel Birch, the most famous Egyptologist of that day. Massey checked his facts with Birch whenever in doubt. Some commentators have even tried to undermine his authority on the ancient texts by arguing that he was an "autodidact"; in other words, he was self-taught. But this has been true of many of the world's greatest thinkers and investigators. It certainly was true of most of the authors of the books of the Bible itself. Socrates held no university degrees; he was an autodidact. Take John Muir, the famous environmentalist already cited. He taught himself geology by hiking and investigating almost inch by inch the terrain of the Sierras and many of the sites in the United States destined to become national parks. He once had a spirited and ongoing debate with the chief geologist of the State of California over the origins of the large bowl-shaped valley that fronts the most salient rocks and cliffs of Yosemite National Park. The geologist Josiah J. Whitney, who had a doctoral degree from Harvard in his field, maintained that the apparently sunken expanse was the result of past seismic activity. Whitney ridiculed Muir as an "ignorant sheepherder." Muir argued that it was the product of millennia of glacial and other forms of water erosion. Having traced the courses of ancient streams and rivers on foot over many years, he had learned how to tell the true history of the place. In any case, subsequent follow-up investigations by today's geologists have proven Muir to have been right. Every scientist in this field now accepts his explanation as correct.* Frank Lloyd Wright, the leading American architect in the modern era, who died in 1959, author of twenty books, never completed a university degree of any kind either.

When you realize not only that Massey had the courage to confront the powerful Christian establishment of his day with the wholly mythical nature of their religion's "founder" but that he dared to challenge the vaunted superiority of the white race—and most particularly that of its ruling elite in the British Empire, the English themselves—with the thesis that their religion was based upon an African original, you appreciate the amazing courage of the man. It is small wonder that only a few hundred copies of each of his important books were ever published or that there was such a strong effort made to suppress those that were. But we do well to recall that there were fewer than two thousand copies in the first printing of Charles Darwin's epochal book *On the Origin of Species*.

When critics of *The Pagan Christ* found that I had made substantial use of the books of Alvin Boyd Kuhn, they could not accuse him

---

* *The Wilderness World of John Muir* by Edwin Teale, Houghton Mifflin, Boston, 1976, p. xix.

of being an autodidact since he had earned his doctorate at Columbia University. Accordingly, they tried to build a case upon the fact
that he had never been a professor at a university and that his thesis
subject had been theosophy. In fact, Kuhn was the first scholar to
examine this key subject in a fully objective, academic way. They
neglected the fact that in his career as a visiting freelance lecturer
on philosophy and the earliest origins of Christianity he had given
over two thousand lectures to packed halls in the U.S.A. and Canada
and had written six books and scores of learned monographs. While
he had once been an active member of the Theosophical Society, so
too had many leading thinkers of the late nineteenth and early
twentieth centuries. Theosophy (literally, wisdom about or of God)
helped many Western thinkers to understand for the first time the
religions of the East, especially the ancient writings of the Vedic
tradition in India. In the broadest sense theosophy includes all systems of intuitive knowledge of the Divine. Kuhn differed at times
with its leading figures on several issues, including the importance of the natural world in any "canon of knowledge," and upon
the centrality of philosophy and mythology in all attempts to come
to grips with the wisdom of the past. The point is that Kuhn was an
extraordinarily well-educated man as a result both of a top-notch
formal education and of his own diligent years of private study and
research. He was a most able teacher in the field of comparative
religion, and his late-life book *A Rebirth for Christianity* remains as
relevant as ever. At this point I can say I found reading him to be
one of the most intellectually bracing and enlightening experiences
of my own lengthy career. The truth has to be squarely faced: his
critics dislike him and try to savage him because they dislike what
he has to say. Its truth or untruth ultimately seems the least of their
concerns.

What I find of special interest is that at the very time when the
towering scholar Northrop Frye was telling his students that if
there was any history in the Bible, it was there by accident—history

is not what the Bible is about—Kuhn was writing his brilliant monograph *Science and Religion*. In it he wrote: "The only hope of lifting religion out from under the pall of hypnotic superstition is to effect the disenchantment of the Western mind of its obsession that the Old Testament is Hebrew history . . . As history it is next to valueless; as allegory and drama of the interplay of God and man's linked potencies in the human organism, it holds immeasurable enlightenment for all humanity." Both men were struggling to end the world's obsession with religious literalism knowing that, as St. Paul said, the letter kills, while it is the Spirit that gives life.

Elsewhere I have written that whether or not the Jesus Story is historical is not in the end of the greatest importance. After all, one can never prove a negative, and so even though no evidence may be found, it will never be possible to prove conclusively that Jesus never existed. And that has certainly never been a goal of my studies. My sole aim and hope is to have shown that it is the Story itself that bears the meaning and significance of this "Hero's tale." However, I wish to return here to a most important strand in the overall narrative for which none of the critics whom I have read or met appears to have an answer or a solution. I am thinking specifically of the quite astounding silence of the earliest witness in the New Testament, indeed of the one who is responsible himself for a large portion of that entire document, namely St. Paul. I raised this crucial issue in the chapter of *The Pagan Christ* entitled "Was There a Jesus of History?" but it merits further expansion here because in so many ways Paul is the real founder of Christianity. Without him it would have remained a small and soon-expiring Jewish sect.

It must be kept in mind that all of the authentic letters of Paul belong to the period from about 55 to 60 CE. His opus does not include several of the letters attributed to him in the King James Version of the Bible, for example, the Epistle to the Hebrews, II Thessalonians and the pastoral epistles—I and II Timothy and Titus. This finding is based upon significant differences of language, style and theological point of view. In addition, most critical scholars today regard the authorship of Colossians and Ephesians (traditionally also attributed to Paul) as highly debatable as well. They are most probably best described as deutero-Pauline, that is to say, highly influenced by Pauline motifs but plainly later in date.

The problem is not that Paul never mentions Jesus Christ. He does so frequently, although curiously enough he never once speaks of him as "Jesus of Nazareth." Nazareth makes no appearance whatever. What is puzzling is that Paul makes no firm biographical references to Jesus. The bulk of what is said about Jesus in the four Gospels has to do with two categories of activity: his miracles and his teachings. But with a silence that scholars such as G. Bornkamm have described as "astonishing," Paul makes no direct references to either of these. Miracles were widely regarded in the Judaism of that time as expected accompaniments of any would-be valid claim to Messianic authenticity. Jesus purportedly performed dozens of them, but Paul says not a word in this regard. The silence over Jesus's teachings is perhaps even more surprising since Paul's letters are filled with moral admonitions, often upon subjects where Jesus reportedly had much to say himself. Surely Paul's arguments would have been enormously strengthened if he had been able to quote from the Master. But, quite surprisingly, he does not.

One instance of this discrepancy has always leaped out at me as particularly glaring, and I have yet to read a persuasive conservative response to the dilemma it poses. What I have in mind is a very moving passage in Paul's Epistle to the Romans. It is in chapter 8, one of my favourite chapters in this, his most famous letter. Speaking of prayer, the Apostle makes the quite startling statement in verse 26: "For we know not what we should pray for as we ought . . ." Here, if anywhere, if it really was an accepted tradition based on historical fact and he knew about it, is the place one would expect him to quote or in some way refer to the Lord's Prayer. After all, remember that in the Gospels Jesus is said in Matthew 6:9 to have introduced the prayer with the words: "Pray then like this . . ." He is responding to a direct request from his disciples: "Lord, teach us how to pray." But Paul nowhere cites this prayer in whole or in part! This is little short of astounding.

The British scholar George A. Wells, who has written seven books on the mythical nature of the New Testament's portrayal of Jesus, sifts the relevant Pauline materials extremely finely. He finds it particularly revealing that when it comes to the Crucifixion—which is so basic to Paul's thinking about Jesus—there is no mention of significant historical details of any kind. In *Did Jesus Exist?* Wells states: "Even when he [Paul] writes of Jesus's death in I Corinthians 2:8 he says nothing of Pilate, or of Jerusalem, but declares Jesus was crucified at the instigation of wicked angels—'the rulers of this age.'" The truth is that when it comes to when Jesus is supposed to have died on the Cross, or indeed when he was supposed to have entered upon his human phase of existence in the first place, Paul is incredibly vague to the point of hopelessness. The distinguished New Testament scholar Ernst Kasemann finds that this scantiness of witness concerning concrete circumstances of the Crucifixion, where Paul's theology "is so deeply engaged, is positively shocking." Of course, like Horus of Egypt and all the other man-gods of antiquity, Jesus is said to have been "born of a woman." Because he was allegedly fulfilling Jewish prophecies, Paul also can say he was "born of the seed of David" and "born under the law," but this is not historical evidence at all. There were many centuries between David's time and Jesus's, but Paul tells us nothing that indicates in which one of them Jesus's life was believed to have taken place. What is more, Paul never mentions the virgin birth or empty tomb! In short, Paul's Christ was a spiritual or mystical Christ, not a man of flesh and blood at all.

There is so much that could be added, but that would take yet another volume. Let me conclude by saying that for me the most powerful argument of all against the view that Jesus was a historical person—and not what literary critic Harold Bloom has named "a theological God" specifically constructed by the early Church—is this: the amazingly varied theologies (Christologies) of Jesus Christ in the pages of the New Testament itself. There are at least six or seven opposing pictures of who he was assumed to be. To quote Kasemann once more, if he had truly lived, early Christian literature would not "show nearly everywhere churchly and theological conflicts and fierce quarrels between opponents" who disagreed "radically" as to "what kind of person he was."

Having read the attempted explanations of the critics, I want to stress two things:

1. The position on the non-historicity of Jesus taken in *The Pagan Christ* and now held by an increasing number of scholars has never been given credible rebuttal; and

2. It is impossible to convince those who have already decided never to alter their opinions come what may. With the great majority of rank-and-file Christians, as well as most of their clergy, this seems to be the case. Some of the latter, including those who really should know better, have told me frankly that they have not read *The Pagan Christ* for fear of "upsetting my beliefs." So much for the promise that the Holy Spirit will guide us "into all truth."

10

CAN CHRISTIANITY BE BORN AGAIN?

I N HIS BOOK *Modern Man in Search of a Soul*, Carl Jung emphasized that one should never simply dismiss divergent views and opinions, however unpleasant or wrong-headed they may seem. Neither does it matter if these differ radically from the more widely accepted ideas or traditions of majority communities or groups. "Such opinions could never arise—much less secure a following—if they did not correspond to some special disposition, some fundamental psychic experience that is more or less prevalent," Jung wrote. Such flat rejection, he argued, means one is directly doing "violence" to the data that alone hold the key to what is happening around us in our time. It means turning one's back on part of the only material from which we must work to make sense of our own lives and the lives of those around us.

The depth and power of this insight really hits home when you look at a contemporary development that has shocked and shaken persons of all religious backgrounds in our time. A militant atheism has emerged as a major opponent of religious belief and faith in every part of the Western world. While books trumpeting atheistic positions have taken over the bestseller lists and their authors preach their positions in the media, the campaign is having an effect and is as deep as it is widespread today in our culture. The numbers of those telling pollsters and census takers that they are themselves either agnostic/atheistic or "of no religion" are a fast-burgeoning statistic in every developed country in the world, even in the still highly religious United States. This reality has been and continues to be well documented by others, so it's not necessary to go into further detail here.

But since the growth of atheism and of general unbelief in matters of religion is an empirical fact, the challenging question, of course, is why is it happening? There are many sources for every river, but one usually takes precedence over all the rest. That is true here. The major reason for the growth and spread of a flood of atheism at this hour is that much of the God-talk we hear can't be believed in by growing numbers of people because it has become utterly unbelievable. Human reason and common sense have their limits, and they have now been strained to the breaking point for millions who once owed loyalty to a denomination or Church or other religious affiliation. The message is loud and clear for spiritual leaders: those who are joining the ranks of non-believers do so because the tenets, creeds and language of religion today too often defy comprehension. They are not accepted and believed because they are for the most part unacceptable and unbelievable. They belong to another time, another place. As Harvey Cox, Dean of Divinity Emeritus at Harvard, argues in his 2009 bestseller *The Future of Faith*, the age of creedal allegiances is over.

I want to be very clear here: none of this means that the atheists are right. In actual fact, upon closer examination their position is seen to be based upon non-rational, fallacious presuppositions every bit as fundamentalist in nature as those espoused by extremist religionists. But at the same time, they carry a message: our thinking and language about God must change. Thich Nhat Hahn reminds us eloquently that old concepts of God must die to be replaced by new thinking and understanding. In *Living Buddha, Living Christ* he writes: "Simple and primitive images may have been the object of our faith in God in the beginning, but as we advance, He becomes present without any image, beyond any satisfactory mental representation. We come to a point where any notion we can have can no longer represent God."

As described earlier, ever since I was a very young child, sitting in church for hours, not just on Sundays but at other times as well, I have often thought that there is something wrong with the traditional interpretation of the Biblical narrative. It has been badly skewed by an overemphasis upon sin and misunderstandings of "salvation." My deepest intuition from earliest days, since then corroborated by years of study and reflection, is that we, each of us, come from divinity and are destined to return to God again. Certainly this is by no means a unique or original experience or idea. The fact that it has always felt so deeply a part of oneself is, I believe, a testimony to its belonging to a very wide base indeed. In fact, it belongs to what Carl Jung called the collective unconscious of humanity. It is really the basic monomyth or underlying story that lies at the core of every one of the major religions today. It is often obscured by rituals and almost buried by dogmas, but it is there all the same. It needs to be rediscovered and reaffirmed for the common good. Here are some Biblical pointers that for me are foundational to such a view.

The Genesis mythos of the creation of Adam and Eve makes it abundantly clear that we are "made in the image of God"—the *Imago Dei*. The text says further that God breathed into Adam and "he became a living soul." The words in Hebrew and Greek for "spirit" are virtually the same, and both words also mean wind or breath. Accordingly, we are made in the likeness of God and it is God's breath or life force that forms our essence or being. There is a profound and spiritually rich wisdom in that.

But there is more. Psalm 82:6, in the heart of the Hebrew Bible and thus at the centre of both Jewish and Christian worship, states quite boldly: "Have I not said you are gods and children of the Most High?" Those being addressed are the people of Israel, but also through them the whole of humanity. It is a very significant assertion of who we are.

When we come to the Gospels, there is a passage in John's account that one seldom if ever hears mentioned. While arguing with the officials of Judaism over allegations that he was making himself out to be the Son of God—which they said was "blasphemy"—Jesus is given this response: "Is it not written in your law 'I said you are gods'?" He goes on to point out that if those to whom the word of God had been given were called gods, then why do they say that he is blaspheming "because I said I am the son of God"? His opponents are unable to answer him. Quite plainly, then, according to the Jesus of the Gospels, we are all "gods" and sons or daughters of God, as he knew himself to be. The blunt truth is that Jesus nowhere makes claims to be God or the son of God in any absolute sense that does not apply equally to everyone who had "ears to hear." Hence his sharp rebuke to the rich young man in Mark's account who calls him "good master." Jesus retorts, "There is none good except God himself."

I want to return just for a moment to that wonderful account in the Acts of the Apostles of Paul's experience while preaching in Athens. He tells the crowd that he is most impressed by all the signs about him of Athenian devotion to various deities. He notes there is an altar to "the Unknown God" and tells them that this is the God he has come to make known to them. This God, he says, made all nations to inhabit the whole earth, and he allotted the times of their existence and the boundaries of the places where they would live, so that they would search for God and perhaps grope for him and find him—"though indeed he is not far from each one of us." Then comes the crucial passage beginning: "For in Him we live and move and have our being; as even some of your own poets have said, '*for we too are his offspring*'" (italics mine).* The fact that the author/ editors inserted such an admission—that early Christian and Pagan thinking were in agreement on our divine origins, the divine "spark" in every person—is of profound importance. It's crucial for under- standing the core of the message in both camps. And it's of critical importance now if we are to find a truly universal ground on which all religions can meet and offer a global view of human evolution and destiny.

Agreement on this is not by any means a step towards having one lowest-common-denominator-type world religion to replace the great religions of the earth. God must love diversity since the whole story of Creation from the beginning has been of an overflowing, abundant, proliferating splendour of differentiation throughout the whole phenomenon of life. Science witnesses to this daily in the new species discovered, often in the most unlikely places, such as in hot springs in the ocean's floor or in the deepest, darkest caves. The differences will remain. But what an incredibly unifying and pacifying reverberation would spread throughout the whole inhabited planet if every believer of every faith, from Islam to the smallest sect, held that every single one of us, those inside and those outside this or that faith or specific denomination, are truly "God's offspring" bearing the spirit and image of the one source of all that is. That's my lifelong vision and my hope.

One thing I have remained deeply certain of, even back in the days of my discussions and debates with my atheist tutor at Oriel, Richard Robinson: atheists and agnostics too have a deep intuitive awareness of an emptiness within that only God or something they cannot name can fill. Their hunger for transcendence is too often quelled or wholly deterred by bad religion, by thinking and behav- iour that give the lie to claims made on behalf of an unbelievable,

---

* *Tou gar kai to genos esmen* in the Greek original.

highly anthropomorphic deity. The noted literary critic Harold Bloom in his 2005 book *Jesus and Yahweh: The Names Divine* speaks eloquently of this deeply human longing for transcendence, "the saving remnant of divine light" without which "we stumble about in the void, beggars with amputated feet"—that profound yearning in the human heart without which we remain "mere vessels of entropy" bound for extinction. I believe that is why I get so many more letters from skeptics and agnostics than anyone would suppose.

Before he retired, the old archdeacon under whom I had served my curacy in 1955/6 paid me a visit in my West Hill parish, at the end of which he said, "Let me give you a piece of wisdom. If you can survive as many years as I have in the ecclesiastical industry [the institutional church], you have to still believe in miracles." I spent enough time in and around "the industry" to know it intimately myself. He certainly spoke the truth. I want to claim that miracle here. While my understanding of religion in particular has been utterly transformed, reaching out to every living being on the planet and to the farthest reaches of the cosmos, I find my belief in the dimension of being that most of us call God is stronger than ever before. I have witnessed the shadow side of religion both in its bitter, warring past and in the various religions today. When doing investigative journalism on religion, I learned "where the bodies are buried"—and have critics and even enemies because of that. But I have also seen and known first-hand its glories, its great achievements for good, its help for the needy and championship of the oppressed. There is deep within me a confidence that not only Christianity but the other world religions can be born again.

But there is a secret to this. It cannot happen simply out of enthusiasm for something fresh or fear of failure. The secret has two fundamental aspects. In the first place, all faiths need to recover the central meaning and transforming power of myth. The greatest potential for evil done in the name of God flows from a failure to comprehend this. All religions begin with mythology because mere history and dead literalism cannot convey eternal truths. However, the huge error of taking myth as history has wreaked untold havoc, from the earliest book burnings and slaughter of "heretics" by overzealous Christians to the horrors perpetrated today by Islamic terrorists in the Middle East and around the world. Ultra-extremist Jews in Israel are victims of the same phenomenon. I repeat: the "letter kills" as Paul says, but the Spirit gives life.

The second insight that is essential to a rebirth for not just the Church but the other faiths as well is equally potent and indispensable. It is this: all language about God and the activity of God's Spirit is first and foremost that of symbol, of metaphor, of verbal imagery, poetry, music and art. As Nhat Hahn says in the passage quoted earlier, no notion or idea we can formulate can represent or verbally communicate that ultimate presence. The ultimate dimension of reality (which is as close as words can come) cannot be precisely conceived of, cannot be contained in creeds or formulae. He-She can only be known by a deep, intuitive knowing of the heart and mind together. That is why the Psalmist of old said, "Taste and see that the Lord is good." It is an invitation, under a metaphor, to experiment and to trust that ultimate presence for oneself. You can know God's reality both with intuition and rationally. This is true gnosis, a knowing that nothing can shake.

World religions can never experience what it means to be born again without a clear awareness of their true purpose and raison d'être. It is to constantly remind their followers of who they really are, from whence they came and whither they eventually are bound. The authentic spiritual journey the religions came into being to foster and nurture is that of personal transformation for the believer. There is an illustration from the lore of classical Greece which for me illuminates this process. The famous sculptor Pheidias (*c.* 480–*c.* 430 BCE) spoke of his art not as imposing his own form on the blocks of marble upon which he worked. Instead, he said he saw his task as that of liberating from the inert stone the lovely shape or being that was already there within. Each cut or blow of his chisel was aimed at revealing the beauty of the image that was already present beneath the rough exterior, as it were, struggling to be free. So too with the spiritual dynamics of transformation or metamorphosis from within ourselves. With our inner eye fixed steadfastly upon the model of wholeness (holiness) afforded by the teachings of all the great world faiths, we are daily being changed and set ever freer to be what we are meant to become. The Spirit is the master sculptor behind it all. As St. Paul says, "We all . . . beholding as in a mirror the glory of the Lord, are being changed into the same image from glory unto glory, as by the spirit of the Lord" (2 Corinthians 3:18). The Greek word for "changed" in the text means "metamorphosized."

Although my eightieth birthday is behind me, I feel so much younger now in spirit because of a lively, reasonable hope engendered by a fresh understanding of life itself. Because, in the end, there is the assurance that while here we have no "continuing city," ultimately "we seek one which is to come." If we daily practise sitting still and "waiting upon God," as the Psalmist says (what the Buddhists and those who use their meditative approach call "mindfulness"), we find the Spirit of God working always within us. I believe that while the natural body steadily grows older, our inner self (the true self) is being renewed by the energy of the Spirit within. To be very direct—I don't mean that I hear some voice speaking to me, or see some mystical visions of another realm, or feel some strange otherworldly emotions within, although I am aware that some do. In a lifetime of prayer and of trying to be faithful to such truth as has been made plain to me, I have never once had what I would describe as a supernatural encounter of any kind. Yes, there have been great heights and some inevitable lows. But I do try to spend some time in meditation—or directing my thoughts and heart to the God within me and without—every day. In Christian terms, this is the Christ within. This often happens when I am alone in my study in the morning. But if not there, then while walking the dog or enjoying nature in our daily strolls. At times the awareness of the divine presence is very vivid, at others not so much. However, one's trust in God doesn't depend on what you feel; it depends on an act of will and of total commitment.

Readers of my work over the years and of what I have set out in these pages are naturally aware that I am critical of the evangelical faith in which I was reared and which for many years I served. It would be an error, however, to suppose that I am unaware of great debts owed by me to that community of believers or to think that I make the mistake of lumping all of them together under the label "the religious right." Evangelicals today are far from being a homogeneous group and significant changes are presently taking place within their ranks. Top American evangelist Tony Campolo, who in the 1990s made headlines when he agreed to be a spiritual counsellor to President Bill Clinton, in his 2004 book *Speaking My Mind* said that evangelical Christianity "has been highjacked by the religious right." He hammers those in the movement who have given the world the impression that to be evangelical is to be anti-feminist, anti-gay, pro-war and pro-gun, pro–capital punishment, negative towards other faiths and oblivious of the world's poor. Campolo is on the liberal side on all these issues. He notes in particular the deep need for respect of Islam: "We don't want to call its prophet evil. We believe we have got to learn to live in the same world with our Islamic brothers and sisters and we want to be friends. We do not want to be in some kind of holy war." Campolo has been severely criticized by extremists, of course. But it is a fact that he represents a fast-growing group of evangelicals in the United States and Canada who are breaking through the typical media stereotypes. These folks are anything but anti-intellectual or dumb. They are grounds for hope.

My real conflict with even the most liberal of them, however, is over the distorted view they have of Jesus Christ. Contrary to the plain sense of the very Bible that they profess to revere and live by, they have made him into the greatest American Idol of them all. The hard truth is that in North American culture today, the one who is presented in the Gospels as carefully avoiding doing or saying anything that conflicts with the absolute majesty and "otherness" of the "Father"—Jesus—has been exalted into the grossest example of idolatry (taking the place of God) the world has ever seen. The Bible says he pointed away from himself to God. But in conservative evangelical preaching, worship and thinking generally (and elsewhere as well) Jesus usurps the place of the Almighty entirely. The prayers and hymns confuse the two completely. Faced by Christian apparent double-speak on the issue of the unity or oneness of the ultimate mystery, God, it is not surprising that Orthodox Jews and Muslims say little but are greatly—and rightly—offended. There may be three "People of the Book," but Christianity, it must be said, has succumbed to idolatry. A much more spiritual and at the same time ecumenical faith would result from taking a mystical/mythical view of Jesus and restoring the ultimate dimension of reality to His/Her rightful place. The Jesus Story has profound importance, but it must not take the place of God.

By a strange coincidence, I was writing this chapter in early June 2010 when I stopped briefly for a coffee and a glance at the morning's paper. A small news story in a bottom corner caught my eye. The headline said LIGHTNING STRIKE SETS ON FIRE "TOUCHDOWN JESUS" IN OHIO. I immediately read the short clip because "Touchdown Jesus" was one of the best-known landmarks in southwestern Ohio. Every winter for the past twenty years, Susan and I, like thousands of Canadians, have driven down Interstate 75 to spend a few weeks on the Gulf coast at Destin, Florida. En route, at Monroe, just north of Cincinnati, we would regularly pass the evangelical Solid Rock Church on the east side of the freeway. In 2004, just after sending the finished manuscript of *The Pagan Christ* to the publisher, we were surprised to see that there was a large new feature added to the building. There was a reflection pool in front and rising up out of it was an enormous statue of Jesus Christ—six storeys, or roughly thirty metres, in height. We later learned its official title was *King of Kings*. Appearing to be carved from stone, the sculpture was a conventionally conceived Jesus likeness standing waist deep in the pond and with both arms raised in the air like a referee signalling a touchdown in football—hence the soon-famous nickname. To us it stood as a metaphor for, as well as an example of, the idolatry I'm describing. As fate was to reveal, the statue was not built of solid rock at all but of steel framing and some kind of foam. The brief newspaper account said it had been struck by lightning during the night and had been reduced to a blackened "steel skeleton" and burnt bits of fibre. Its final moment has an almost Biblical ring to it.

I take some solace from the fact that ultimately the steady advance of critical scholarship on the "life" of Jesus will continue to erode any Bible-based foundations for the current Jesuolatry. For example, in a letter to Jesus in his book *The Great Deception*, Gerd Ludemann, one of the world's leading authorities on Christian origins, writes about how strange he now finds it to address Jesus at all. Current studies now show, he says, "you aren't at all the one depicted by the Bible and church tradition. You weren't without sin and you weren't God's son . . ." Ludemann's views are now much more widely shared by scholars than people in the pews have as yet realized.*

What is of importance to remember at this point, however, is the core message of the Jesus tradition or teaching (the Sanskrit, Buddhist word *dharma* expresses best what is intended here). Whether Jesus was historical or not, the body of teaching focused upon his name—the ethic of social justice, self-sacrificing compassion and non-violence—remains as bedrock to any Christianity of

---

* SCM Press, 1998. See www.Y-Jesus.com/historicalJesus.

the future. The shame of the past has been the failure to honour these values even while often at the same time loudly trumpeting strict adherence to orthodox beliefs. The Jesus teaching, divorced from dogma, affords the common ground upon which a unity of all religions can be firmly based.

There are two burning questions one must ask oneself somewhere along the journey of life. The best time for this is always now. They are: Where have I come from? and Where am I ultimately going? Is the answer "from oblivion into oblivion"? That is what the materialists have always said. Or perhaps this ancient wisdom from the Gospel of Thomas is the rock on which to build your life: "If they ask you from whence you come, say: 'We are come from the light, from the place where the Light came into being by itself.'"*

In the second century CE, an Egyptian intellectual, Valentinus, who was baptized and raised as a Christian, found the faith as it was being presented in its increasingly literalistic mode unable to meet the criteria set by his philosophical and highly rational bent of mind. He became a Gnostic and eventually gathered a school of his own, the Valentinians. Valentinus said, "This is Liberation: to know from whence you come and into what you have been cast; to know what is birth and what is rebirth" (or, in other words, being spiritually "born again" with the dawning of the recognition of who you really are). It is a fact that many of the Church's earliest thinkers, including St. Paul, were Gnostics without necessarily calling themselves that. In the end, from long experience, I have found these ancient words to be the truth I was seeking all my life. What a changed world there could be if all six billion–plus of us could come to know that for ourselves. What is more, you cannot know true Buddha consciousness or genuine Christ consciousness without possessing that pearl of great price, a truly compassionate heart. In the final summation of any life, that is what really matters.

---

* Saying 50, about 50 CE.

I believe that Christianity can be born again to give spiritual hope to those members still hanging on and looking for signs of its coming. It must do so for the millions who have dropped away or have always been outside looking in. True rebirth, however, will not come from the top down. Many of today's leaders show little indication of even realizing how great a disaster awaits them if they blunder on in the same old way. They are still committed to yesterday's thinking and refuse to come either awake or fully alive. So it really depends on you, the laity, the vast body of ordinary people around the world, catching a new vision and moving ahead until the "leaders" get pulled forward in your wake. They must be challenged from below. The early Church got along for several centuries without an official Bible, without seminary-trained professional clergy, even without creeds and precise dogmas. Anything is possible now with a fresh start.

My humble prayer is that this present narrative will help spread and strengthen that impulse. A new day is dawning for humanity, I believe. May *Born Again* and all who read it be a part of that new story.

EPILOGUE

THE READER may be pardoned for thinking that my major preoccupation these days is looking backwards at the past. But what truly fascinates me is what lies ahead, both from a personal point of view and from the vastly more important perspective of our future as a very small, some might say insignificant, part of the cosmos. Like many millions down the ages, the big passion of my life since earliest childhood has been for the wonders of the natural world. Intuition has revealed the truth already quoted from Thomas Berry, that nature or the "Creation" is the world's primary and most comprehensive holy book or Bible. There is far more to learn of the mystery we call God from the world around us than from all the holy books and preachers put together. That is why—though I can't always even pretend to understand everything they're saying—it is today's physicists whose writings most appeal to me as I grow older. As their name expresses clearly, they have nature, the physical world, as their focus for meditation. But what an extraordinary world of absolute wonderment and amazing surprises they have begun to reveal!

People once scoffed when it was claimed that God had created everything *ex nihilo*—out of nothing. If anyone a hundred years ago had said there was such a thing as "immaterial matter," they too would have been ridiculed by philosophers and plumbers alike. But modern physicists now constantly expatiate about "dark matter" and "dark energy," which are precisely that—immaterial, virtually ineffable realities making up the larger portion of the known universe. Today it is not the navel-gazing theologians who are speaking powerfully about that which is unseen and indescribable except in symbols but the leading-edge scientists themselves. And when it comes to miracles, none ever recorded can begin to compare with the incredible, unimaginable miracle of the Big Bang. As scientist and philosopher Nick Brykczynski has written in his paper *The Theological Origins of Science*: "The Big Bang—the notion of the entire universe—and parallel universes besides—exploding in an instant from a single almost invisible point is impossible to fathom rationally and can only be perceived on an intuitive level . . . it is a 'singularity' in which the laws of physics have no application." He says "this state is not so much unknown as unknowable."

The old paradigms that were the very foundations of traditional Newtonian physics have literally melted away. The very basis of the materialistic, mechanistic thinking that is at the root of most skepticism and agnosticism has been rendered obsolete. The physical world has now become an indissoluble unity—a field of dancing energy winking in and out of measurable being. That, together with the discoveries by the astrophysicists of billions of galaxies made up of countless billions of stars surrounding our tiny planetary "pale blue dot," have led to an unexpected interest in mysticism on the part of leading physicists everywhere.

As Ken Wilber has pointed out in his highly important work *Quantum Questions: Mystical Writings of the World's Greatest Physicists*, no less a figure than Einstein himself believed that "there is a central order to the cosmos, an order that can be directly apprehended by the soul in mystical union." That indeed is why elsewhere the great pioneer of quantum thought was moved to say: "I maintain that the cosmic religious feeling is the strongest and noblest motive for scientific research." From the moment I first read this there was an immediate resonance with what I had learned from the thinking of Pythagoras and Plato, encountered at Oxford so many years before. A circle was closing. Both of those great Greek thinkers were mystics. Both believed that the outward physical world is deeply significant but nonetheless a mere shadow compared with the invisible realities at its heart. With St. Paul they believed there is a physical body and a spiritual body and that at death "this mortality puts on immortality." I believe the day is coming when each of us will experience a sense of "cosmic religious feeling" as further mysteries and wonders unfold.

The human experiment is very far from finished. The Christ Principle, the Divine Spirit within, is striving to achieve full divinization or "Christhood" in each of us. All of Creation eagerly awaits that day.

> Some dream of brave epitaphs
> emblazoned in gold
> or cut in marble pillars
> for the world to see . . .
> But, let them write this for us
> in all simplicity:
> *"To Be Continued"*
>
> – Tom Harpur

Acknowledgements

Ancient wisdom has it that a simple prayer of gratitude to God sums up the whole burden and essence of all other prayers. Certainly an overwhelming sense of gratitude floods my mind and heart as this narrative comes to its close. One's own praying, of course, belongs elsewhere. Here I want to express the enormous appreciation I feel, first of all for my parents—for the deep trust in God they tried to live by and for the grounding in faith and sacred teachings they instilled in us. Then, looking back over the years, there has been a vast company of those who sometimes perhaps even unknown to themselves were a source of great encouragement, of assistance, of comfort, of challenge, and of generous example and guidance. I owe so much to so many—teachers, tutors and professors, clerical friends, editors, producers, readers, and a larger host of others too numerous to name. I give thanks for them every one.

Finally, my warmest gratitude for the wonderful folk at Thomas Allen Publishing and in particular for the privilege of once again partnering with publisher and editor Patrick Crean in shaping a book. Patrick first suggested the concept of "more than a memoir" many months ago. His wisdom, unparalleled editorial skills, and his steady encouragement have been of invaluable assistance throughout. There's a reason he's the best.

Tom Harpur
Eastertide, 2011

Index

- written by someone
willing to study, think,
learn & be willing to
change his thinking.
Would that more people
do this. CD.

wonderful book! cm